CHICANA/O STRUGGLES FOR EDUCATION

NUMBER SEVEN

University of Houston Series in Mexican American Studies
Sponsored by the Center for Mexican American Studies

Tatcho Mindiola
DIRECTOR AND GENERAL EDITOR

A complete list of other titles in this series appears at the back of the book.

Chicana/o Struggles for Education

Activism in the Community

GUADALUPE SAN MIGUEL JR.

Texas A&M University Press • College Station

Copyright© 2013 by University of Houston–Center
for Mexican American Studies
Manufactured in the United States of America
All rights reserved
First edition

This paper meets the requirements of ANSI/NISO
Z39.48-1992.
(Permanence of Paper)
Binding materials have been chosen for durability.
∞ ♻

Library of Congress Cataloging-in-Publication Data
San Miguel, Guadalupe, 1950–
    Chicana/o struggles for education : activism in the
community / Guadalupe San Miguel Jr. — 1st ed.
        p. cm. — (University of Houston series in Mexican
American studies ; no. 7)
    Includes bibliographical references and index.
ISBN 978-1-60344-937-3 (cloth : alk. paper)—
ISBN 1-60344-937-x (cloth : alk. paper)—
ISBN 978-1-60344-996-0 (e-book)—
ISBN 1-60344-996-5 (e-book)
    1. Mexican Americans—Education—History—20th
century. 2. Mexican Americans—Social conditions—
20th century. 3. Chicano movement—United States—
History. 4. Mexican American teachers—United
States—Political activity—20th century. 5. Educational
equalization—United States—History—20th century.
6. Discrimination in education—United States—
History—20th century. 7. Education, Bilingual—
United States—History—20th Century. I. Title.
    LC2683.S35 2013
    371.829'68073—dc23
                                    2012044173

This book is dedicated to all those activists who continue to fight on behalf of the community. It is especially dedicated to Elizabeth "Betita" Martinez and Rudy Acuña for their courage, passion, and commitment to social justice and human rights.

*[Educational change] is not for the faint-hearted, it is not for the undaring;
it is for those who are willing to dare, to try, to stumble, and perhaps fall.*

—Armando M. Rodriguez, 1971

Contents

Acknowledgments

I would like to thank the University of Houston history department, the Center for Mexican American Studies, and the University of Houston administration for giving me both the necessary funds to conduct the much-needed research for this project and for providing me with the opportunity to write up the results. Thanks also to all the graduate students who influenced my thinking on many of the issues dealt with in the book. Of particular importance are Felipe Hinojosa, Juan Galvan, Alberto Rodriguez, and Carlos Cantú. A special thanks to my colleague Rubén Donato for the many conversations we have had over the years discussing the plight and struggles of Mexican American education.

I want to thank my sweet-natured teenage son, Gabriel, and my precious daughter, Aimeé-Anali, for putting up with my shifting moods during these past few years. Finally, special thanks go to my wonderful and caring significant other, Lorena Lopez, for appearing at a very critical period in my life. She not only inspired me to finish this project, but more importantly she gave me a reason to live life to its fullest. She believed in me and in all that could be done. She loved me and gave me hope when I most needed it. She also gave me another child and significantly enriched my life. Gracias a ti y a todos los demas.

CHICANA/O STRUGGLES FOR EDUCATION

Introduction

For over a hundred years, Mexican Americans have contested the limited and inferior educational opportunities public school officials have offered them.[1] For most of the twentieth century, however, history books have failed to document these efforts. Not until the 1970s did historians begin to seriously record the community's struggles for educational equality. The process of discovering and documenting Mexican American activism in education was part of a larger revisionist trend in US social and ethnic history that began a decade earlier. The initial studies appeared in state or regional historical journals.[2] Their numbers gradually increased during the next four decades.[3] The first monograph on the quest for educational equality appeared in 1987.[4] Since then several additional book-length studies have been published.[5]

This small but important scholarship on community activism and educational reform exemplifies the tendency of viewing Mexican American education history primarily through the lens of discrimination.[6] The vast majority of these studies, for instance, document the many ways in which community groups challenged a variety of exclusionary and discriminatory school policies and practices in the United States during the twentieth century. The struggle against school segregation has attracted the most attention by scholars because of its importance to the community and because Mexican Americans have spent a significant amount of time, energy, and effort contesting it.[7] Scholars also note how prior to 1960 Mexican American activists at the local, state, or regional level occasionally contested unequal school facilities, standardized testing, and English-only laws.[8] These studies, Richard Valencia notes, indicate that "Mexican Americans have demonstrated an indefatigable commitment in their struggle for a more equitable education."[9]

While documenting the long and arduous campaign to achieve educational equality is important, it provides an incomplete picture of community activism in education. It suggests that community and parent activists only engaged in contesting public school policies and practices. The existing literature on Mexican origin educational history prior to the 1960s, however, suggests that community activists engaged in at least two additional reform strategies: advocacy and private schooling.

ADVOCACY

Advocacy involved promoting reforms that met the community's cultural, academic, and political needs and interests. The historical literature on education indicates that one of the many reforms Mexican American activists promoted during the first half of the twentieth century was curricular and instructional pluralism. During World War II, for instance, activist groups advocated the teaching of Spanish in the schools and the inclusion of Mexican heritage in the textbooks.[10]

Additionally, community and parent activists supported the development of either specific or comprehensive school reforms aimed at improving their children's academic achievement. An example of the latter occurred during the 1930s and 1940s in several northern New Mexican communities. In this period, New Mexican Hispanos, the term of preference for Mexican Americans in this state, supported the comprehensive school reform efforts of Lloyd S. Tireman, a nationally known educator. With their support as well as with state financial assistance, Tireman modified the curriculum, introduced innovative teaching methods, and increased parental involvement in four distinct communities—San Jose (in Bernalillo County), Nambe (in Santa Fe County), Cedro (in Bernalillo County), and Taos (in Taos County). His ultimate purpose was to ensure that the schools related to the community in more positive ways. And for a number of years, they became more responsive to the Hispano community, more reflective of its linguistic and cultural heritage, and more successful in educating Spanish-speaking children. However, for a variety of reasons, including the loss of community support, these schools soon closed their doors.[11] Despite their closure, these experiments indicated that Hispano parents were willing to support comprehensive reforms that improved their children's educational opportunities.

In the first half of the twentieth century, Mexican Americans additionally supported instructional and curricular reforms aimed at improving their children's academic achievement. Reading reforms in the 1920s, project-based teaching in the 1940s, and preschool English language instruction in the 1950s were some of the specific changes they favored during these decades.[12]

Another reform for which Mexican American activists, parents, and students advocated was increased access to different levels of public education.

Carl Allsup briefly noted in his study of the American GI Forum (AGIF) that the organization not only challenged discrimination in the schools but it also played a key role in promoting school enrollment during the 1950s. He discussed how the AGIF engaged in back-to-school rallies at midcentury and how it went about encouraging parents to send their children to school once it opened. These back-to-school rallies were part of a larger strategy to ensure that Mexican origin access to K-12 education increased at a rate comparable to Anglo student enrollment.

Mexican Americans, on occasion, also advocated and supported a variety of reforms aimed at promoting student access to higher education. Carlos Muñoz, for instance, traced the participation of student activists as they sought and encouraged higher educational opportunities for Mexican Americans in the 1930s and 1940s. He argued that during these decades they took advantage of the higher educational opportunities American society offered. College-educated youth formed an organization—the Mexican American movement—and a newspaper—*The Mexican Voice*—to encourage others to be proud of their Mexican and American heritage, to excel in school, and to attend college. The theme of their publication was "progress for Mexican American youth through the attainment of a higher education." One nineteen-year-old junior college student best illustrated the aspirations of Mexican origin youth during this period:

> Education is the only tool which will raise our influence, command the respect of the rich class, and enable us to mingle in their social, political, and religious life . . . [A] college education is absolutely necessary for us to succeed in the professional world.[13]

PRIVATE EDUCATION

The existing research points to at least one other strategy Mexican American educational activists pursued prior to 1960—that of private education. Most people assume that Mexican American parents, community activists, and organizations only sought educational opportunities from public schools, but this is historically incorrect. They also sought increased learning opportunities from private elementary, secondary, and postsecondary schools.

Most private schools were church sponsored, but others were nonsectarian in character and established by Mexican Americans. A few were established by Anglos but supported by ethnic Mexicans. Private schools offered Mexican American parents an opportunity to send children to an institution of their own choice and for their own particular reasons—to maintain religious and cultural values, to undermine discriminatory or exclusionary policies, to challenge Americanization, and to seek excellence in education.

The historical literature indicates that since the Spanish colonial period Mexican Americans have enrolled in Catholic schools. This tradition expanded during the nineteenth and early twentieth century. In both rural and urban communities of the Southwest and wherever else significant numbers of Mexican children were found, they attended Catholic boarding schools, academies, or parochial schools and colleges.[14]

Mexican children also enrolled in Protestant parochial schools. This tradition began in the 1850s in Texas and soon expanded to other parts of the Southwest. The greatest number of schools were established in New Mexico because of the lack of public and Catholic school facilities, the vast distances between villages, and the strong desire by Protestants to convert Mexican children. Between 1881 and 1885, Mexican children attended over twenty-three mission or "plaza" schools. Some of these schools lasted from one to ten years; others lasted for many years largely because of devoted teachers and strong community support. By 1886, 1,131 Mexican children were attending more than thirty-three missionary schools established by various Protestant denominations.[15]

An example of strong community support for Protestant schools occurred in Albuquerque, New Mexico. From the late 1890s to the 1950s, the Mexican community in this city supported the Presbyterian Menaul School for boys despite the church leaders' negative views of the character, culture, and religious beliefs of the local community. Although a few students converted to Protestantism, the majority did not. Despite remaining Catholic, those who attended benefited greatly from this school and acquired a new identity and a new status. High school graduates became successful leaders in the community. Graduates defined success not in terms of wealth but service to the church and the community.[16]

Those attending this school, especially the ones that converted, likewise did not abandon their heritage. They utilized the knowledge and skills learned at Menaul to fight against stereotypes and discrimination in the church. More specifically, Menaul students challenged a subtractive form of Americanization in the school, a form of education that sought to stamp out or "subtract" their language and culture, and forged a distinct Hispano identity within the Protestant faith. These individuals used their Protestantism to reshape mission attitudes toward Catholicism and Mexicans. As a result anti-Catholicism was muted and racism was confronted.[17]

Finally, Mexican American activists established or supported the establishment of community-based schools.[18] These institutions were quite diverse with respect to whom they served, how long they lasted, what they taught, and how they were governed. It included not only private schools aimed at teaching the basic skills but also nationalist ones aimed at contesting Americanization and segregation and at promoting Spanish language instruction and Mexican cultural knowledge.[19]

The existing, albeit limited, historical literature on education then indicates that Mexican Americans did more than simply contest discrimination. During the first half of the twentieth century they also advocated for reforms that met their varied academic needs and sought private educational opportunities.

What about after the 1960s? How did the quest for education change as a result of the new social, economic, and political context? Who became involved in promoting education, for what reasons, and with what impact? What strategies did activists pursue to attain their goals and how did this differ from the past? Was it a break from the past or a continuation of actions? What impact did the Chicano movement of the 1960s and 1970s and the looming conservative political climate of later decades have on this quest?

This book provides a history of the multiple and complex strategies Mexican origin individuals used to improve and enrich their educational opportunities in the United States from the 1960s to 2010. I argue that those involved in these efforts both extended and intensified the historic struggle for education that earlier activists had initiated. As in earlier decades, activists contested discrimination, advocated for specific public school reforms, and sought private schooling, but in ways that were different from those developed in the first half of the twentieth century. By activists I make reference to all those individuals and organizations involved in seeking better educational opportunities for Mexican origin children. This includes parents, students, community activists, civil rights leaders, educators, scholars, and a host of others who dared to speak up on behalf of improved schooling.

The book is divided into several chapters. The first one provides a sketch of the changes and continuities in the historic patterns of ethnic Mexican education in the United States since the 1960s and the forces impacting them over time. The following four chapters emphasize the specific strategies Mexican American activists used to promote equality, excellence, and pluralism in American education. Chapter 2 describes the variety of ways in which activists contested discriminatory school policies and practices in the contemporary period. Chapter 3 describes the reforms they advocated in order to make the schools more reflective of their heritage and more responsive to their needs and desires. The following chapter examines the struggle for bilingual education in greater detail. This program became the dominant means for educating not only Mexican Americans after 1970 but also all of those children who had a language other than English. The final chapter provides a sketch of the community's continued support for religious and private forms of education during the post-1960 years.

ONE

Changing Patterns of Mexican American Education

Between 1900 and 1960, school officials provided Mexican Americans with limited, substandard, and inferior public educational opportunities because of their subordinate status in the society and their cultural and linguistic characteristics.

Those in power made sure that the adult members of the Mexican American community were structurally excluded from influential positions in public education and denied or discouraged from participating in the shaping of public school systems and their content. The pattern of education that developed in the first half of the twentieth century, with a few minor exceptions, then was that of community exclusion.[1]

Mexican origin students also were unwanted in the schools. Local and state school officials as well as political leaders, Anglo parents, and the general public viewed them as racially inferior, culturally backward, and socially undesirable. These negative views in combination with intense pressures from political and economic interests opposed to their education soon led to the development of substandard and inferior forms of schooling. Students were denied equitable access to the schools, given separate and unequal facilities, institutionally mistreated in the schools, and provided with an imbalanced and subtractive curriculum. The imbalanced curriculum focused more on vocational training than academic instruction. The subtractive curriculum sought to divest the children of their Spanish language and their cultural heritage. The result of these actions was the emergence of a pattern of poor school performance.[2]

During the latter part of the twentieth and early twenty-first century, these historic patterns of education changed as a result of new social, economic, and political factors. The following provides a sketch of these changes and continuities since the 1960s and the forces impacting them over the decades.

DISCONTINUITIES IN PATTERNS

During this period, two distinct patterns were significantly changed—the structural exclusion of the Mexican community and the linguistically subtractive curriculum. Prior to 1960, as noted above, Mexican Americans were excluded from important positions of influence in the public schools. Officials also demeaned, devalued, and suppressed the children's language. Both of these patterns were significantly modified in the post-1960 years.

From Structural Exclusion to Differentiated Inclusion

The pattern of structural exclusion was disrupted and replaced with one of inclusion after the 1960s. During the latter part of the twentieth and early twenty-first century, Mexican origin individuals gained increased access to important positions in all areas of public education. They were elected to state, county, and local boards of education, appointed to state and private university boards of regents, and hired in increasing numbers as superintendents, principals, teachers, counselors, and faculty members. A new development in this period was their appointment or election to federal policy-making positions in Congress and in the Department of Education.[3]

Notwithstanding this increased access, they continued to be underrepresented in all of these positions. Their inclusion, in other words, was not significant but limited and uneven in nature. Generally speaking, two patterns emerged—one of differentiation and one of tokenism and exclusion. The former pertained to positions within institutions that served the elementary and secondary grades in the public schools, the latter to those in higher education.

The pattern of differentiated access to power can be observed in local and state board representation. Representation in these institutions ranged from moderate to significant. In major urban areas where Mexican Americans comprised a significant proportion of the school-age population, access to local school boards was relatively moderate. In 1960, for example, there were no ethnic Mexican school board members in three of the top five largest school districts in the country, although the percentage of Latina/o students in these cities was either growing or already appreciable. The school districts with significant numbers of ethnic Mexican children and no school board representation were Houston, Los Angeles, and Chicago. This situation changed by 2009. In this year, their representation in these local school

TABLE 1.1. SCHOOL BOARD MEMBERS OF SELECT CITIES WITH LARGE LATINA/O
STUDENT POPULATIONS, 2009

City	total members	total Latino	%	% of school age pop
Houston	9	2	22%	61%
LA	7	2	28%	73%
Chicago	7	2	28%	39%

Source: HoustonISD.org; LAusd.k2.ca.us/laud/board/secretary; cps.edu/About_CPS/the
_Board_of_Education/BoardBios/Pages/Boardbios.aspx (accessed March 30, 2009).

boards increased, but only moderately. It ranged from 22 percent in Houston
to 28 percent in Los Angeles.[4]

Despite their increased representation, it failed to keep pace with the overall percentage of Latina/o students in the school-age population.[5] Their proportion of the total school-age population for each of these cities in 2009 was:
Houston—61 percent, Los Angeles—73 percent, and Chicago—39 percent.
Mexican Americans thus continued to be underrepresented on these local
boards.

The process of gaining board representation was an extremely gradual,
uneven, and contested one. Progress, in other words, occurred at a glacial
pace. The example of Houston shows how this pattern originated and developed over time.

In this city Mexican-origin individuals were absent from the local school
board up until 1971. In this year one was elected to the board. This officially broke the twentieth-century pattern of Mexican American exclusion
from policy-making positions. The number of Mexican Americans increased
from one in 1971 to two in 2003. This meant that their percentage increased
from 11 percent in 1971 to 22 percent thirty odd years later.[6] The percentage of Latina/o students in the Houston Independent School District, however, also increased from 13 percent in the former year to over 55 percent in
the latter.[7]

While local school board representation in major urban areas was moderate, it increased rapidly and significantly in many small, rural school districts.
Several examples from South Texas illustrate this important trend. In Lar-
edo, Mission, McAllen, and Edinburg, for instance, school board representation jumped from less than 10 percent in 1960 to over 75 percent in 2007 (see
table 1.2). The large percentage of Mexican American voters in these small

TABLE 1.2. MEXICAN AMERICAN AND NON—MEXICAN AMERICAN SCHOOL BOARD
MEMBERS IN SELECT TEXAS CITIES, 2007

City	Total	Mex Ams	%
McAllen	8	6	75
Laredo	7	6	86
Mission	7	6	86
Edinburg	7	7	100

Source: mcallen.isd.tenet.edu/board; laredoisd.org/board/members.htm; missions-cons.k12.
tx.us; ecisd.us/users/ecisd/index.htm (accessed December 10, 2007).

urban and rural communities and their desire for power among the population probably accounted for the significant increase.

At the state level, a less diverse pattern of ethnic Mexican representation
in school board positions can be found. State boards of education play crucial
roles in determining the content and instruction of public education in each
state. In three of the states where the vast majority of Mexican Americans
were concentrated, only Texas had more than one person serving in the state
board of education. The other two states had a token Mexican American on
its board (see table 1.3).

At the postsecondary level, ethnic Mexicans, as mentioned above, gained
some access to important positions of power in university governance, administration, and teaching. But it was mostly one of tokenism. In major university boards of regents, they were lucky to have one of their own appointed
to this position. A selective review of a few major universities located in
states with significant numbers of Latina/o students illustrates this point. As
the table shows, ethnic Mexicans only have token positions in the boards
of regents of four major university systems in the country (see table 1.4).

The presence of Mexican Americans in top administrative positions, especially in major research universities, is rare indeed. Several scholars have
commented on how few if any of them are hired in important leadership
positions in higher education.[8] Out of all the major universities throughout
the country, only one—the University of Texas at Austin—had appointed a
Mexican American to head the campus. And this only happened recently, in
2009. Other major institutions, such as the University of California, University of New Mexico, and the University of Illinois, have yet to appoint any
to head their flagship institutions.[9] A similar pattern of severe underrepre-

TABLE 1.3. MEXICAN AMERICAN REPRESENTATION IN SELECT STATE BOARDS OF
EDUCATION, 2009

State	Total Bd Members	Total Mex Ams	%
Texas	15	3	20
California	9	1	11
Illinois	9	1	11

Source: http://ritter.tea.state.tx.us/sboe/members.html; www.cde.ca.gov/be/ms/mm/; www
.isbe.state.il.us/board/default.htm (accessed April 1, 2009).

sentation of Mexican Americans in the senior ranks of the faculties in these
universities, that is, of tokenism, can be found as we reach the second decade
of the twenty-first century.[10]

From Linguistically Subtractive to Linguistically Additive

Another pattern that underwent significant modification was the linguistically subtractive curriculum. Prior to the 1960s, Spanish and other non-
English languages were excluded from the public school curriculum and con-
stantly devalued through English-only laws or repressed, suppressed, and
discouraged through no-Spanish-speaking rules. This changed after the passage of the federal Bilingual Education Act of 1968. This bill led to several
important developments, including the elimination of no-Spanish-speaking
rules at the local school level, the repeal of English-only laws throughout
the country, and the passage of state policies that sanctioned, encouraged,
or mandated the use of non-English languages in the schools. These policies were usually referred to as bilingual education policies. Between 1968
and 1978 more than thirty-four states repealed their English-only laws and
enacted bilingual education policies.[11]

The successful repeal of English-only laws, repressive no-Spanish-speaking
rules, and the continued growth of bilingualism in the society, among other
factors, led to a backlash in the 1980s and 1990s. In this period, both prescrip-
tive and repressive language legislation resurfaced and became increasingly
widespread. This was reflected in policies aimed at formulating and enacting English-only laws or at undermining, dismantling, or repealing those
sanctioning the use of non-English languages in the schools. In states such
as California, Arizona, and Massachusetts it became illegal to use Spanish

TABLE 1.4. A SELECT LIST OF MEXICAN AMERICAN REPRESENTATION IN UNIVERSITY
GOVERNANCE, 2009

Name of institution	Number of Regents	Mex Am regents	%
University of Illinois	13	0	0
California State University	25	3	12
University of Texas	10	1	10
University of New Mexico	7	2	28

Source: www.utsystem.edu/BOR/currentRegents.htm; www.uillinois.edu/trustees/meet.cfm;
www.calstate.edu/bot/trustees.shtml; www.unm.edu/regents/members/ (accessed April 7, 2009).

and other non-English languages in the public school during the mid- and late 1990s.[12] Between 1984 and 2004, more than twenty-five states enacted English-only laws.[13] Bilingual education policies also came under attack in countless cities such as Houston, El Paso, Chicago, New York, and Miami. Educators responded in many cases by curtailing the use of these languages as mediums of instruction and implementing English-only classes.[14] Despite the reemergence of linguistic prescription and repression in the schools, the majority of states in the country and hundreds of cities throughout the nation maintained policies favoring the use of non-English languages in the classroom and on the school grounds.

MODIFICATION IN PATTERNS

Several patterns of Mexican American education were slightly modified but not significantly changed during the post-1960 years. The two patterns discussed in this section are those dealing with student access to education and the culturally subtractive curriculum. Prior to the 1960s, students were provided limited access to the preschool and postsecondary grades. Students also were provided with a curriculum that sought to subtract or divest them of their cultural heritage.[15] Both of these patterns underwent some minor modifications during the years after 1960.

Student Access to Education

By the 1960s, the vast majority of Mexican Americans had gained parity in access to the elementary and secondary grades, but they had not gained equitable access to the preschool grades or to postsecondary education. In the latter decades of the twentieth and early twenty-first century, these became the key areas of concern.

Access to the preschool grades increased gradually but inconsistently after 1960. By the early twenty-first century Chicana/o and Latina/o children were among those least likely to attend preschool. In 2001, for instance, approximately 36 percent of Latina/o preschool-aged children participated in a preschool program. In comparison, 64 percent of black and 46 percent of white children attended preschool that year.[16] Enrollment continued to increase, but at a slow pace, by the latter part of the decade.[17]

A similar development occurred in higher education. Prior to the 1960s less than 5 percent of Latinas/os were enrolled in institutions of higher education in the United States.[18] In the period after 1960, enrollments steadily increased but they continued to be underrepresented.

Latina/o undergraduate enrollments steadily increased from the 1970s to 2007. In 1976 it stood at 3.8 percent. This percentage rose during the next two decades as reflected in the following figures: 1980–4.2 percent, 1984–4.4 percent, 1991–6.5 percent, and 1997–8.6 percent.[19] Their percentage continued to increase in the early twenty-first century. In 2006 about 10 percent were enrolled in college. The following year it stood at 12 percent.[20]

It is important to note, however, that while their percentage steadily increased, most were enrolled in community colleges. In 1999–2000, for instance, 60 percent of those attending postsecondary institutions were enrolled in two-year colleges, the largest percentage of any other racial and ethnic group.[21] This was problematic, noted Patricia Gándara, because "no more than 5% of these students will actually go on to complete a B.A."[22] Indeed, the number of Latinas/os attending four-year colleges and universities out of high school was very small. A 1998 survey, for example, found that of all the first-full-time students attending public universities in the United States, 82.6 percent of freshman were white, 7.2 percent African American, and 1.4 percent Latina/o.[23] As Michal Kurlaender and Stella Flores noted, Latina/o students showed the lowest rate of entry into four-year institutions and had the highest participation rates at two-year colleges.[24] While community colleges have benefited many groups over time, critics noted that they "can actually exacerbate race and class inequalities in educational attainment."[25]

The Culturally Subtractive Curriculum

Another pattern that underwent some slight modification was the culturally subtractive curriculum. Prior to the 1960s, the curriculum schools offered to

Mexican American children sought to divest them of their cultural heritage by either omitting or else distorting, devaluing, and disparaging their cultural heritage in the textbooks and instructional methodologies, and in the operation of the school.[26] The subtractive curriculum changed in the latter part of the twentieth century. Unlike the pre-1960 years, it did not seek to divest them of their heritage. Instead, it sought to affirm this heritage by valuing and incorporating Mexican and Latino-origin cultures and histories in the schools. This pattern of incremental change is best reflected in the revision of textbooks for the public schools.

During the late 1960s and early 1970s, some of the most demeaning and distorted views of Mexican Americans in the history, social studies, and other textbooks were replaced with more positive ones. These efforts continued into the following decades. Despite these changes, problems remained in their portrayal, with many textbooks providing insufficient and inadequate treatment of their heritage and of their contributions to the history of individual states or the nation.

One can observe the gradual but positive changes over time in several major studies conducted between 1960 and 2000. In 1961 and 1970, Marcus Lloyd, on behalf of the Anti-Defamation League of B'nai B'rith, conducted two national studies of minority content in history and social studies textbooks. The first study indicated that Mexican Americans, for the most part, were ignored in these textbooks. In a few cases, however, some references were made to them, but these were largely stereotypical.[27]

The patterns of omission and of inadequate and inaccurate portrayals continued into 1970. Only eight of the forty-five textbooks Lloyd examined offered some references to this group, and most of these were social studies textbooks. American history texts, for the most part, "flagrantly" avoided references to Mexican Americans or Latinas/os. The few comments found in these books created or reinforced unfavorable stereotypes.[28]

The failure to include the contributions of Mexican origin individuals to American history or to provide positive comments continued into the 1970s. The historian Carlos Cortés, after an exhaustive evaluation of a dozen history textbooks published in the early part of the decade, concluded the following:

> Content analysis of a dozen popular US history textbooks revealed little in these texts which would specifically contribute to the pride of the young Chicano, but much that could assault his ego and reinforce a concept of Anglo superiority.[29]

Some progress was made in the next two decades, as Linda K. Salvucci's evaluations of textbooks indicate. In the mid-1980s, Salvucci analyzed ten history textbooks Texas adopted in 1985 and approved for use in the public schools between 1986 and 1992. Five of these were eighth grade pre-Civil War textbooks and five were ninth grade post-Civil War textbooks. She argued that these textbooks represented a distinct improvement over earlier ones although distorted images or, as she stated "inconsistent, idiosyncratic, incorrect or empty images," still prevailed.[30]

In her study, Salvucci noted that the history of Mexico before the 1820s was more extensive and more objective than that of subsequent periods. Still, there were glaring omissions and distortions. With the exception of the Aztecs, she stated, most indigenous peoples as well as the Spanish colonization were ignored. The histories suggested that "real" history began with the British presence in the New World.

Discussions of the Aztecs varied widely in quality and scope but most were incomplete. Only one textbook devoted a considerable amount of space to a description of Aztec society. Another textbook devoted several chapters to an extended discussion of several Native American cultures, including the Aztecs. This textbook, unlike the others, tried to demythologize the conquest of Mexico, taught students to construct multicausal explanations of historical events, and afforded dignity and historical significance to pre-Columbian peoples.[31]

With respect to the wars of independence, Texas independence, and the war with Mexico, historical treatment was uneven. In the case of the Texas war, most textbooks provided an accurate portrayal of Anglo settlers but a biased one of Mexicans. The latter were viewed as ruthless and bloodthirsty people bent on subduing the "brave," "inspired," and "outnumbered" Texans. Most of the accounts of the Texas rebellion also were one-sided and failed to include Mexican perspectives. With respect to the war with the United States, most of the accounts were more multidimensional, although they did not provide Mexican viewpoints. In these accounts, the United States was viewed as expansionist, but Mexico was viewed as eager for a fight.[32]

Most of the textbooks Salvucci reviewed painted a sketchy and undifferentiated picture of two other important events in Mexican history—the French intervention and the Mexican Revolution. With respect to the former, textbooks provided little information on the reasons for the origins and termination of the intervention. Most suggested that its end had to do more with the Monroe Doctrine than with the Mexican soldiers who drove out the invading army. These textbooks ignored the Porfiriato (Porfirio Díaz regime, 1877–1910) and only discussed the Mexican Revolution as it impacted American society. Only one revolutionary leader was mentioned and in a negative manner—Pancho Villa.[33]

Finally, Salvucci noted that Mexicans and Mexican Americans were mentioned more often in the twentieth century than in prior books, but their experiences were not integrated into the narrative and only inadequately covered. Mexicans and Mexican Americans were provided token mentions and usually lumped into a section on "minorities." Mexican immigration was discussed, but only the current situation was covered. The books also covered other topics including César Chávez and issues of poverty and housing. None of the books, however, provided positive views of Mexican and Mexican American contributions, although some discussed a few heroes without incorporating them effectively into the narrative. Modern Mexico was ignored in this period.

These ten textbooks then included more information on Mexico, Mexicans, and Mexican Americans, but they provided inconsistent images. Some textbooks dealt effectively with the pre-1821 period or Mexican immigration in the current period. Most, however, were weak in covering events and issues during the nineteenth and twentieth centuries. The most obvious shortcomings involved simple omission, closely followed by a lack of unity and consistency in coverage. Mexican and Mexican American perspectives were almost never presented, even for key events in the histories of both Mexico and the United States. Rather, things Mexican were implicitly and even explicitly characterized as problems for the United States.

Information about Mexico, Mexicans, and Mexican Americans increased by the early 1990s, but problems remained. This is the conclusion that Salvucci made after analyzing ten new history textbooks Texas adopted in January 1992 for use in the public schools from 1992 to 1998. Four of these were eighth grade pre-Civil War textbooks and six were ninth grade post–Civil War textbooks. These textbooks, she argued, represented a qualitative improvement over earlier ones. They were fresh, stimulating, and inclusive of Mexico, Mexicans, and Mexican Americans. Distorted images were missing and Mexican perspectives and Mexican American experiences were woven into the larger story of American history.[34] The history of modern Mexico and of Mexican Americans in the twentieth century, however, were either not provided or not discussed.

Despite the increased coverage of Mexicans and Latinas/os in American history textbooks, several scholars argued that by the late 1990s they were still absent from the national narrative or not fully incorporated into it. Joseph A. Rodríguez and Vicki L. Ruiz analyzed eight national surveys published in the second half of the 1990s. These textbooks, they noted, included more of the Latina/o heritage but they were "still too frequently reduced to numbers, faceless statistics who wander in and out of the text—nameless lost souls, seemingly at loose ends." "Individual stories remain untold in these baseline narratives, especially with regard to women's aspirations and attainments," they added.[35]

Thus important strides were made in the inclusion of Mexican Americans and Latinas/os in American history, but the degree of change was slow in coming. They continued to be "voiceless and nameless" in American history. The curriculum, however, was less subtractive than in the early part of the century and more inclusive of their history and culture. Unlike the past it did not seek to divest students of their cultural heritage. It sought to affirm this identity through the process of cultural inclusion in the curriculum.

CONTINUITY AND STRENGTHENING OF PATTERNS

Although most aspects of Mexican American education were modified or reformed, three patterns continued to be immune to change and actually strengthened during the post-1960s: segregation, unequal schools, and poor school performance.

Segregation

Despite federal court rulings, legislation, and community protests, Latina/o children continued to attend separate school facilities. Data suggest that their segregation increased significantly between 1968 and 1998. In the former year, more than half (54.8 percent) of these students attended predominantly minority schools across the nation. (Predominantly = a school with over 50 percent of Latina/o students.) Three decades later, three-fourths, or 75.6 percent, of them were enrolled in such schools. In this year, 70.2 percent of African American children were attending predominantly African American schools. Thus by 1998, Latinas/os were more segregated than even African American students.[36]

These children were not only segregated in their own schools, they also experienced resegregation in desegregated schools. This type of "academic"

segregation, noted Richard Valencia, was as invidious as segregation on racial grounds.[37]

Unequal Schools

The pattern of unequal education, similar to school segregation, continued
and strengthened during the post-1960 years. Mexican origin individuals not
only attended segregated schools, they also attended unequal ones. During
the past four decades, because of federal legislation and litigation additional
resources were provided for these schools. Despite the additional resources,
these schools continued to be unequal in many respects. Many of these
schools were understaffed, inadequately funded, overcrowded, and substandard.[38]

School Performance

The final pattern experiencing little change during the post-1960 years was
school performance. Prior to the 1960s, Mexican Americans had mostly
negative experiences in education, failed to complete high school in large
numbers, and rarely enrolled in postsecondary educational institutions. This
pattern of poor school performance continued in the latter part of the twentieth and early twenty-first century. As in prior decades, scholars provided
evidence of this pattern and a variety of explanations for its presence.[39]

a. Pattern of Underachievement

Through a variety of studies and reports, scholars documented the multifaceted
dimensions of the problem of poor school performance. Although complex,
many scholars showed that despite improvements, Latinas/os continued to
score lower than Anglos or Asians on standardized test scores, to be over aged,
to be retained in larger numbers in the same grade, to be disciplined for minor
infractions, to drop out in higher percentages, and to enroll in fewer numbers in
four-year institutions of higher learning or graduate and professional schools.[40]

   High school completion rates starkly illustrated one aspect of this pattern of poor school performance. Government data from 1972 to 2000, for
instance, suggested that the high school completion rates for Latinas/os was
much lower than for non-Latina/o whites and non-Latina/o blacks. While
the dropout rate for all other groups decreased over time, by 2000, approxi-

TABLE 1.5. HIGH SCHOOL COMPLETION RATES FOR EIGHTEEN- TO TWENTY-FOUR-
YEAR-OLDS BY RACE/ETHNICITY, 1972–2000

Year	1972	1980	1990	2000
Totals	82.8	83.9	85.6	96.5
White, non-Latino	86.0	87.5	89.6	91.8
Black, non-Latino	72.1	75.2	83.2	83.7
Latino	56.2	57.1	59.1	64.1

Source: US Department of Education, National Center for Education Statistics (NCES), *Dropout Rates in the United States: 2000*, based on US Department of Commerce, Bureau of the Census, October Current Population Surveys, various years. Cited in *From Risk to Opportunity: Fulfilling the Educational Needs of Hispanic Americans in the 21st Century* (Washington, DC: The President's Advisory Commission on Educational Excellence for Hispanic Americans, 2003), 2.

mately one of every three Latinas/os dropped out of high school. White and black rates were lower and stood at 9 percent and 16 percent, respectively.

A host of studies in the early twenty-first century also indicated that the problem of dropping out among Latinas/os in particular and of poor school performance in general was still significant. It did not improve appreciably over time.[41]

Scholarly explanations of poor school performance changed over time, but they tended to focus on the student, the school organization and its policies and practices, social and economic structures, or a combination of these.

The dominant interpretation during this period—the deficit model—focused on identifying the characteristics of students that helped explain the pattern of poor school performance. In most cases these characteristics were viewed as deficits or as deficiencies to be eliminated or corrected. Several deficiencies responsible for low academic achievement were identified over the decades—genetic, cultural, and linguistic. Genetic or biological interpretations of school failure, developed in the late nineteenth century, blamed inferior genes for poor school progress.[42] Cultural models emerged in the early twentieth century and looked at the values and beliefs students held. They argued that these values were contrary to school success. Linguistic interpretations focused on language, or in this case, the lack of linguistic skills in English, that is, language handicap, as the primary factor for low academic achievement.[43]

During the 1960s, the cultural deficit view and all its variants became the dominant model for explaining poor academic achievement and low test scores. The reason for this was ideological—it absolved American society from taking responsibility for this social problem and placed the burden on the victim. It shifted the blame of underachievement from the shoulders of "guilty" educational institutions unto the Chicana/o community.[44]

Another major interpretation of poor school performance focused on the school and factors within it that contributed to this pattern. Those who shared this perspective argued that exclusionary and discriminatory school policies and practices led to low academic achievement and high dropout rates. The schools and their institutional structures, policies, and practices, these activists argued, were to blame for the pattern of poor school performance, not the children.[45]

A third major interpretation pointed to larger environmental or social forces and structures as explanations for low academic achievement. Among the most controversial were the social caste and reproduction theories that held that the larger power relationships found in the society or the nature of the capitalist structure of American society led to differential rates of school success in general and to the poor performance of racial, ethnic, and working-class students in particular.[46]

A final approach to explaining low academic achievement, especially the dropout problem, focused on more complex interactionist models that considered multiple contributors to achievement.[47] According to these scholars, dropping out and poor school performance were due to the interaction of a variety of in-school, out-of school, and personality factors.[48]

b. Beyond Failure: An Emergent Trend

During the post-1960s years, as noted above, most scholars investigated, explained, and tried to improve the pattern of poor school performance in the Latina/o community. In the late 1980s and early 1990s, however, a few of them began to focus on school success as well and on the unexplored tradition of achievement in the community.

Educational anthropologists were instrumental in initiating the discussion on school success after the seminal publications of John Ogbu's works in the 1970s seeking to explain why "subordinate" minorities did poorly in school. Subordinate minorities were defined as those who came unwillingly to the United States, in this case, mainly African Americans, Mexican Americans, and Puerto Ricans. Ogbu argued that their caste-like status played a determining role in this school failure.[49]

During the 1980s some anthropologists challenged Ogbu's findings and began to show that not all minorities did poorly in school. Some of them succeeded. This was the case with nonsubordinate minorities, especially immigrants. Additional ethnographic and comparative works showed that even caste-like minorities under certain conditions succeeded as well. Two Mexican American anthropologists played prominent roles in challenging Ogbu's thesis in the 1980s and in showing that there was variability between caste-like (involuntary) and non-caste-like (voluntary) minorities and within caste-like minorities such as Latinas/os.[50]

The research on minorities in general and Latinas/os in particular among educational anthropology by the late 1980s then shifted from one based mostly on explaining school failure to one based on explaining academic performance more broadly. Some sought to document and explain in general terms the variability in school performance, that is, the patterns of both school failure and success among these students.[51] Others turned to investigating how individuals, especially minority students as well as teachers, parents, and community members, forged successful experiences within the schools.[52] These new studies documented and gave voice to the children and adults as they attempted to "radically alter the social structures and educational practices that affect[ed] their everyday lives."[53] In some cases, scholars focusing on minority achievement were more interested in pointing out how students became successful without losing their distinct ethnic identities than in resisting debilitating school policies and practices.[54] Finally, a few of them focused on the schools themselves and on how their organizational practices and cultural processes could be structured to encourage high academic achievement for all students, especially minority and working-class students.[55]

Sometime during the late 1980s and early 1990s scholars in other disciplines, including psychology and history, also began to focus on documenting and explaining both school failure and educational success in the Latina/o community.[56]

The increased concern with school success among educational anthropologists dovetailed and complemented the emerging "effective schools" movement initiated in the late 1970s and led by activist administrators throughout the country. This movement showed that schools could be transformed from low-performing to high-performing institutions and positively impact the academic achievement of all students, especially minority ones.[57]

The increasing number of studies aimed at investigating and explaining the minority tradition of Latina/o school success was initially focused on

elementary and secondary education. It soon expanded to the postsecondary grades. Beginning in the 1970s, a few studies focused on the small but
increasing percentage of Latinas/os who enrolled in institutions of higher
learning, obtained graduate or professional degrees, and joined the growing ranks of the middle class. Those focusing on higher education initially
viewed it in critical terms and usually within the context of colonialism.[58]
During the 1980s, however, many scholars began to conceptualize education as a pipeline that began with elementary schooling and ended with some
form of postsecondary education.[59] This conceptualization provided educators with a comprehensive look at the problems involved in educating La-
tinas/os at all levels of education and with ways to fix the "leaks" in the
educational pipeline.[60]

The scholarship on Latina/o higher education, while recent, is quite extensive and has several foci. Among the most common were: documenting
the status of Latinas/os in higher education;[61] exploring the contextual factors—social, demographic, political, economic, and historic—that shape
their education;[62] identifying issues affecting student access to higher education in general and to undergraduate, graduate, and professional schools
in particular;[63] resolving the transfer dilemma from community college to a
four-year institution;[64] predicting and explaining academic achievement in
postsecondary schools;[65] and documenting a host of other concerns dealing
with gender,[66] curricular reform,[67] and access to leadership positions.[68]

Much of the literature on the academic performance of Latina/o students
in higher education focuses on the contextual and institutional factors that impede access to and successful completion of a college education.[69] An emerging literature, however, has begun to look at the factors that contribute to,
rather than impede, academic achievement. This literature tends to fall into
two broad categories—those that focus on institutional practices and those
that underscore the role that student characteristics play in school success.

Educators, for the most part, have tended to view successful students as
exceptions to the general rule. School achievement has been interpreted as
due to personal, nonacademic qualities such as self-esteem, leadership ability, persistence, and community involvement, and strong emotional support,
especially from mothers.[70]

Other studies point to institutional practices that impact the achievement
of these students. Placement in a rigorous secondary program, for instance,
has been viewed as an important institutional practice leading to the attaining of a bachelor's degree. A rigorous secondary program of study provides

the requisite knowledge and skills for college curriculum and communicates high expectations and high regard for a student's capacity to learn. It offers students an opportunity to develop a positive self-concept and gain leadership experience, both of which are correlated with good grade point averages during the first years of higher education.[71] These studies also suggest that culturally sensitive sources of institutional support, for example, culturally sensitive counseling and student services, sufficient financial assistance, opportunities to build relationships with faculty, and a useful and relevant curriculum, need to be in place in order for academic success to occur.[72]

CONCLUSION

The patterns of Mexican American education since the 1960s then have evolved in various ways as a result of new social, economic, and political factors. Some of them changed significantly, while others did so only moderately. A few of them continued or strengthened over the years despite the changing context swirling around them.

What role did Mexican Americans play in the evolution of these historic patterns? More specifically, what type of strategies did parents, community activists, students, and educators seek to oppose the discriminatory and subtractive school structures, policies, and practices they encountered and to ensure that they received an equitable, excellent, and culturally responsive education? The following chapters document the many ways in which individuals and organizations resisted, adapted, or negotiated the conformist and marginalizing intentions of public schools from the 1960s to the present. They also document and explain the diverse strategies they developed to support or create schools that validated their cultural values and interests and that encouraged the development of pluralism in American society.

TWO

Contestation

D uring the post-1960 years, ethnic Mexican responses to educational inequality intensified and diversified. In the first half of the twentieth century, activists engaged in a variety of actions aimed at contesting the exclusionary, discriminatory, and subtractive character of American public school systems. These actions challenged the many ways in which school systems excluded Mexican origin individuals from positions of power, mistreated them on the basis of race and ethnicity, and sought to stamp out or "subtract" their cultural identity.[1] These expanded in the post-1960 era.

As in earlier decades, activists and educators pursued several major strategies. The most well known was that of contestation. Ethnic Mexicans contested or actively challenged those policies and practices perceived as detrimental to their cultural, academic, or political interests. They used a variety of methods to achieve their goals. The most dramatic were the political actions parents, students, and grassroots individuals took. The most enduring were the legal ones initiated by community-based organizations. The following provides an overview of the multiple ways in which these activists contested the various forms of discrimination in the schools during the post-1960 era.

PROTESTS, PICKETS, AND WALKOUTS

In the late 1960s and early 1970s, Chicana/o student, parent, and grassroots activists used a variety of direct action tactics to protest an array of exclusionary and discriminatory school practices at the local level.

High school students protested inadequate and inferior conditions by walking out of the schools. The first and largest walkout took place in Los Angeles in 1968. In March thousands of Mexican American students walked out of the public schools in East Los Angeles to challenge their second-class treatment by educators. The boycotts dramatized some of the most blatant forms of discrimination against students. Among the key policies and practices they challenged were prejudicial and insensitive teachers, the existence of no-Spanish-speaking rules, the exclusion of Mexican culture from the curriculum, the failure to hire Mexican American teachers, counselors, and other professional staff, and lack of student rights.[2]

The walkouts, or "blowouts" as they were called, were inspired by Sal Castro, a charismatic history teacher at Lincoln High School. He encouraged students to challenge authorities and to take a risk in improving their schools.[3] These actions, as Carlos Muñoz noted in the early 1970s, had a profound impact on the politics of the Mexican American community and ignited the urban aspect of the Chicana/o movement. The blowouts also significantly impacted students. Those who participated in them acquired a renewed sense of empowerment and of faith in their abilities to promote social and educational change.[4]

School walkouts soon spread to other parts of the country, such as to Denver, Colorado, and Chicago, Illinois.[5] The majority of them took place in Texas. From 1968 to 1972, for instance, high school students conducted over thirty-nine walkouts in that state.[6]

The walkouts took place for several reasons. Among the most important were underlying patterns of racial discrimination, inferior school conditions, and exclusionary school policies and practices. Active mobilization by community political organizations, as several authors have noted, also played an important part in encouraging students to walk out of the public schools.[7]

Although aimed at bringing about important changes, not all of them were successful in accomplishing their goals. Those in Kingsville, Texas, for instance, did not lead to any significant reform of the schools.[8] Those in Los Angeles, California, had mixed results. The student protests in this city served to publicize the plight of Chicana/o schooling and to momentarily encourage community militancy and political mobilization, but they failed to produce significant structural change in education. After the walkouts Mexican Americans continued to be powerless and the schools continued to be inferior. The walkouts in Los Angeles then led to short-term significant changes in the Mexican American community but not in the public schools.[9] Finally, those in Cucamonga, California, as well as Crystal City, Houston,

1. Hector P. Garcia, founder of AGIF, arrested at school board sit-in, Corpus Christi, August 14, 1972. Garcia and seventeen Chicanos refused to follow a police order to vacate the building. Courtesy Hector P. Garcia, Special Collections, Bell Library, Texas A&M University, Corpus Christi, Texas.

2. Students Nora Juarez and Patty Flores making a point at a rally in front of the courthouse in 1975. Courtesy José Angel Gutiérrez Papers, Nettie Lee Benson Latin American Collection, University of Texas Libraries, the University of Texas at Austin. (Kelly Kerbow Hudson, Archival Processing)

3. MAYO members being arrested at school board sit-in, Corpus Christi, August 14, 1972. Courtesy Hector P. Garcia, Special Collections, Bell Library, Texas A&M University, Corpus Christi, Texas.

4. Two female MAYO members being arrested at a school board sit-in, Corpus Christi, August 14, 1972. Courtesy Hector P. Garcia, Special Collections, Bell Library, Texas A&M University, Corpus Christi, Texas.

Uvalde, and Elsa, Texas, did lead to significant changes in the schools and in the social and political environment.[10]

Despite the mixed results of student actions, the walkouts of the 1960s and 1970s served to inspire thousands of young people to envision a world where their heritage was recognized, their academic needs met, and their dignity respected. Student walkouts might not have immediately changed the structure or conditions of schooling, but they definitely changed the po-

5.

7.

6.

5. *Hector P. Garcia being arrested at the Corpus Christi school board, with sister Clotilde in support, August 14, 1972. Courtesy Hector P. Garcia, Special Collections, Bell Library, Texas A&M University, Corpus Christi, Texas.*

6. *MAYO members and Hector P. Garcia confronting Superintendent Dana Williams, Corpus Christi, August 14, 1972. Courtesy Hector P. Garcia, Special Collections, Bell Library, Texas A&M University, Corpus Christi, Texas.*

7. *MAYO member Mike Carranco, with protest shirt, being arrested at school board sit-in, Corpus Christi, August 14, 1972. Courtesy Hector P. Garcia, Special Collections, Bell Library, Texas A&M University, Corpus Christi, Texas.*

litical dynamics of the Mexican origin community and the consciousness of those who participated in them. These actions empowered them. The actions increased their awareness of oppression, of who they were, and of their potential for initiating significant change through collective action.

Student walkouts declined significantly by the late 1970s. During the next several decades, high school students rarely walked out of the schools. The one major exception to this trend in the 1980s occurred in Houston, Texas. In 1989, high school students walked out of Austin High School to protest continuing inferior conditions. The effectiveness of the walkout, the tremendous support of the Mexican American community, and the school administration's tepid response led to the taping of a segment of the Geraldo Rivera show, a nationally syndicated series. Rivera showed the student's resolve to take matters into their hands in order to improve their education, the community's strong support of these actions, and the school district's lack of concern for the deplorable conditions of learning at that particular school. This incident showed that the schools continued to ignore the students' academic and cultural needs and provided them with an inferior education. It also showed that students were willing to protest these unjust conditions despite the consequences.[11]

High school students were not the only ones engaged in walkouts and protest activity during the 1960s and 1970s. Grassroots individuals and organizations also occasionally utilized these tactics to oppose specific instances of discrimination, such as school segregation or school closures.[12] One of the better-known examples of community-based walkouts occurred in Houston, Texas, in the early 1970s.[13]

In this city, local school officials in the fall of 1970 circumvented a court order for desegregation by classifying Mexican American children as "white" and integrating them with African American children. This plan did not include any Anglo children, although they comprised more than 85 percent of the total white school-age population. It left them in segregated schools.

Mexican American parents, grassroots activists, and student and youth groups opposed this action and demanded that the local school board members and administrators recognize Mexican Americans as a minority group for desegregation purposes. This was a highly unusual demand, because for many years activists in Houston and throughout the country had viewed themselves as part of the white or Caucasian race in order to obtain social justice and equal educational opportunity. Now that their "whiteness" was being used to circumvent desegregation, however, many of them rejected this racial identity and acquired a new one. They were "brown," not white. These activists wanted local school officials to recognize their new identity and to develop a just desegregation plan involving all three major groups in the schools—Mexican Americans, African Americans, and Anglos. They, however, refused to make any changes in their desegregation plans.

In response, activists organized a broad-based community organization, the Mexican American Education Council (MAEC), to call for and coordinate a series of protest actions, including boycotts of the public schools, mass demonstrations, street marches, and pickets of local schools. This struggle ended in September 1972, when both educational policy makers and the courts finally recognized Mexican Americans as an identifiable minority group for desegregation purposes. The struggle's ultimate success eventually forced local officials to include Mexican American interests in the formulation and implementation of school policies and in the development of educational programs.[14]

College students also protested. Unlike high school activists they did not engage in walkouts. They demonstrated, went on hunger strikes, marched, and protested on behalf of their concerns.

Prior to 1960, Chicana/o students, for the most part, did not attend institutions of higher learning in large numbers due to discrimination, inferior secondary schooling, and poverty. Antipoverty federal legislation, the black civil rights movement, and concerted efforts by Mexican Americans, among many factors, led to their increased enrollment in colleges and universities during the mid-1960s. Once in these institutions, the students began to form their own organizations. This type of mobilization was part of a broad youth mobilization in the United States and an even more general political mobilization within the Mexican American community.[15]

Mexican American student organizations tackled a variety of issues on campus and in the community.[16] The primary one rotated around discrimination in the universities. They contested university recruitment and curricular policies and demanded the establishment of Chicano Studies departments, the recruitment of Chicana/o students, and the development of student support programs. Students also supported community struggles for social justice and equality in American life. Among the most prominent during the 1960s were the farmworkers' struggle for economic justice César Chávez waged, the effort to regain the lost land grants of former Spanish settlers in New Mexico Reies Lopez Tijerina conducted, and the campaign against police brutality and for civil and cultural rights Gonzáles undertook in Denver, Colorado.[17]

Because of their small numbers in institutions of higher learning in the latter part of the 1960s, Chicana/o students engaged in two types of organizing. One of these involved forming alliances with African American, Asian, or Puerto Rican activists. These students engaged in protest activity on campus as part of a pan-Latino or "third world" alliance.

Multiracial protest activity took place in at least three universities in California between 1968 and 1972—San Francisco State University (SFSU), University of California at Berkeley (UCB), and University of California at San Diego (UCSD). In these campuses students engaged in multiethnic coalitions, affirmed nonwhite racial and gendered identities, and participated in protest politics to make the university more sensitive to them and their particular interests.[18] More particularly, they organized on each campus and proposed the establishment of third world colleges with one of them devoted to Chicanos.[19]

A second type of organizing emerged. This focused on independently tackling issues on university campuses that pertained mostly to Mexican American students. This was the dominant form of organizing among Chicana/o college students.

In early 1969, activists from several university campuses met in Santa Barbara, California, to develop a plan of action for the emerging Chicana/o student movement. The document they developed, known as El Plan de Santa Bárbara, served as a blueprint for waging relentless battles against intransigent university presidents, administrators, and policy makers. This plan provided a framework for contesting discrimination in institutions of higher learning and for institutionalizing Chicano Studies programs on any given campus. Additionally, it provided strategies for the development of comprehensive approaches to the recruitment, retention, and promotion of Chicana/o students, faculty, and staff and for the creation of student support services.

After 1969, students began to more systematically demand Chicano Studies programs and the recruitment of additional Mexican American students. Although the demands revealed a wide variety of perspectives on the purpose, scope, and structure of the proposed programs, they were infused with the nationalist ideology of El Plan de Santa Bárbara.

The majority of these programs were established in California.[20] Chicano Studies programs of some sort were established in community colleges located in areas with a substantial Mexican American community, in most of the state colleges, and in many of the University of California campuses. Several programs also were established in Texas (Houston in 1972, Austin and University of Texas at El Paso in 1970), New Mexico, Arizona, and Wisconsin (UW–Milwaukee, 1970s), to name a few.[21]

Although Chicana/o students were unable to sustain their militancy and political momentum or to realize all of their goals, they did make significant inroads in actualizing significant structural and cultural reform in higher education. In addition to mobilizing thousands of young people to act on behalf of the larger community, students helped create Chicana/o Studies departments and curricula throughout the nation, increased the enrollment of Chicanas/os into higher education, and contributed to the development of a generation of professionals and leaders infused, in the words of Marisol Moreno, "with an ethos of social justice and community service."[22]

Protest activities of all kinds decreased significantly in the 1970s due in large part to the decline of the Chicana/o movement, governmental repression, and a changing political climate less conducive to militant activism. The decrease of protest activity, however, was quite uneven. It was greatest among high school students and grassroots activists, but less so among college students. Although college student activism continued in select campuses, it changed over the decades and tended to emphasize community struggles. In earlier years much of this activity centered on issues directly related to individual college campuses, for example, student recruitment, the establishment of Chicano Studies programs, and such. The post-Chicano movement emphasis was on community concerns, that is, on protesting larger social and political issues such as proposed state budget cutbacks or legal challenges to affirmative action.

This new emphasis in student activism began in the mid-1970s. Let me cite one important example from this decade. In 1976, college students joined thousands of others to protest a state court ruling upholding a challenge to affirmative action in university admissions. This case was filed by Alan Bakke, a thirty-four-year-old white male engineer. During 1973 and 1974, Bakke applied to thirteen medical schools, but he did not get accepted into any of them largely because of his age. A white administrator at the University of California at Davis encouraged Bakke to sue. He was told that "less qualified minorities" had been admitted to the medical school. Bakke sued the university's special admission program. This program, initiated in 1970, set aside sixteen out of one hundred slots for disadvantaged students. The local court ruled on his behalf and found that Bakke had been denied admission to the medical school because of his race. This decision popularized the concept of "reverse racism" and struck a significant blow to the use of race in university admissions.

In 1976, thousands of individuals, including college students, protested in the streets to support a favorable ruling by the state supreme court. Despite these actions, the state supreme court ruled in favor of Bakke and against affirmative action. Although students failed to significantly impact the state supreme court decision, their participation in protest marches served to keep the legacy of awareness and resistance alive within the younger generation.[23]

College student protest activity on campuses and in the community picked up in the 1980s and 1990s. Much of this activism in the 1980s emerged over concerns such as apartheid in South Africa, US intervention in Central America, racism on campus, and defense of affirmative action but, as notes Carlos Muñoz, "those issues did not have the same level of impact on Chicano student activists as had the issues of the 1960s."[24] During the 1990s, college student protests were in response to continued conservative attacks on affirmative action, bilingual education, and other programs they supported. Most protest activity, despite its intensity, was limited to the Southwest, especially California and Texas.[25]

In the early twenty-first century, the level of student protest activity on college campuses gradually increased, as shown in table 2.1. In the years from 2000 to 2010, college students protested a variety of discriminatory actions on different campuses throughout the country: racist Mexican theme parties, the failure to hire or to tenure Latina/o faculty, the lack of support for or the dismantling of Chicano Studies programs, and the demonization of immigrants. In some cases, protesters were successful in halting specific discriminatory practices or actions. In others, they were not. Regardless of their impact on discrimination, student protest activity was and continues to be a primary means for increasing the political consciousness of young people and for inspiring others to join the collective struggle for social justice and equality in American life.

LEGAL CHALLENGES TO DISCRIMINATION

Notwithstanding the dramatic protests on behalf of better schools, the vast majority of activists in the post-1960s years did not attack multiple forms of discrimination at the same time nor did they use confrontational methods. They generally tackled specific forms of discrimination in education and used the federal and state courts to mount these challenges. Mexican American organizations and individuals throughout the country filed legal challenges to discrimination in school governance, hiring practices, access (undocumented), segregation, finance, school closures, testing, and exclusion from the curriculum. Because of a dearth of historical studies on all of these legal challenges, emphasis will be placed on six particular types of policies and practices legal activists targeted. Among the policies and practices challenged during the latter part of the twentieth century were school segregation, school finance, the uses and abuses of testing, exclusion from the curriculum, school access, and school closures.[26]

Struggles against Segregation

The Mexican American struggle against school segregation originated in the early twentieth century. The first phase lasted several decades and ended in the late 1950s. A decade later, activists renewed their efforts to eliminate the segregation of Mexican origin children in the schools. Various tactics were used to contest educational segregation in this most recent period. Activists took local school districts to court, applied pressure on federal agencies to investigate and eliminate segregation against Latinas/os in the public schools, and supported pieces of legislation encouraging integration or opposed those that undermined it. Of particular importance were the lawsuits against segregation because of their impact on public education and on the community.

The initial antisegregation cases, as mentioned above, were filed in the late 1920s and early 1930s. Legal challenges to segregation halted during the Depression and the war years of the early 1940s but they increased between 1946 and 1957. In this decade, a large number of lawsuits were filed against segregation in the southwestern states of Texas, California, and Arizona.[27]

Mexican American school segregation cases were different from those African American activists filed during the post-World War II years. The strategies, arguments, and results were different. African American actions against segregation were the result of a long-term legal strategy developed in the early twentieth century. They were based on constitutional arguments of equal protection and dealt both with de jure segregation and with notions of "coloredness." This long-term legal strategy started with the desegregation of graduate schools then shifted its efforts to the lower grades. On the other hand, Mexican American desegregation lawsuits were based on constitutional arguments of due process and dealt with de facto segregation. These lawsuits also were the result of pragmatic litigation decisions based on notions of "whiteness."[28]

The African American struggle against segregation reached its peak with the *Brown v. Board of Education of Topeka* ruling of 1954.[29] This ruling, which outlawed racial discrimination in the public schools, had no immediate impact on Mexican American desegregation efforts, but it did complicate the community's lengthy quest against segregation in the Southwest during the 1950s.

The first desegregation case after *Brown* was filed in California. In *Romero v. Weakley* Mexican Americans filed an action against officials of El Centro

School District. The case, however, became caught in technicalities after the US District Court, in response to the defendants' request, exercised its discretion to abstain.[30] Known as the abstention doctrine, it eventually served to doom the suit.[31]

Soon after *Romero*, Mexican American parents filed a lawsuit against local school officials in Driscoll, Texas, a small, rural community outside of Corpus Christi. *Hernandez v. Driscoll Independent School District* became the first desegregation case to be successfully litigated after *Brown*. Despite its importance, *Brown* had no impact on the legal strategy of Mexican American lawyers in this Texas case or on the merits of the case.[32]

The ethnic Mexican community won the Driscoll case, but because of its limited benefits (it only affected those residing in this one small town on the outskirts of Corpus Christi), and the high costs of litigation, activists decided to abandon litigation as a strategy of reform. There would be a hiatus in Mexican American desegregation litigation for a decade. In the meantime, activists turned their attention to electoral involvement and other forms of activism.[33]

The struggle against segregation intensified in the late 1960s because of favorable political circumstances, continuing belief in the power of integration to improve the schooling of Mexican origin children, and the growing impact of the emerging Brown Power or Chicana/o movements. Between 1967 and 1977, community activists filed over two-dozen court cases against school segregation. The initial lawsuits were filed against local school districts in Texas in the late 1960s.[34] Similar cases were also filed in other states such as California and Colorado.[35]

Unlike earlier decades, activists changed their strategy to reflect the new ideas about race and ethnicity, to take advantage of the desegregation litigation African Americans advanced, especially of the *Brown* ruling, and to use the federal government and all of its branches to dismantle segregation. The main strategy used in *Brown* (equal protection of the laws under the Fourteenth Amendment) specifically encouraged Mexican American civil rights lawyers to abandon the "other white" legal strategy that was used in prior years. To accomplish this shift in legal strategy and in order to gain legal protection under *Brown*, attorneys had to gain legal acceptance of Mexican Americans as an "identifiable ethnic minority group."

This struggle for legal protection under *Brown* began in US District Court in 1969 in Corpus Christi, Texas. In this case, *Cisneros v. Corpus Christi Independent School District*, district court judge Owen Cox found that on the basis of their physical characteristics, their Spanish language, their Catholic religion, their distinct culture, and their Spanish surnames, Mexican Americans were an identifiable ethnic minority group for desegregation purposes and that *Brown* applied to them. Judge Cox also ruled that Mexican Americans and blacks were unconstitutionally segregated "in all three levels of the school system," and that state action was responsible for this. He then ruled that an appropriate desegregation plan that included Anglos, Mexican Americans, and blacks be submitted to him as soon as possible.[36]

The Mexican American Legal Defense and Educational Fund (MALDEF), as well as other civil rights and community groups were elated with the *Cisneros* decision. This was the first case in which a court officially recognized Mexican Americans as an identifiable minority group in the public schools. More importantly the ruling introduced a new group into the national desegregation process. Federal courts now had to consider Mexican American students in determining whether a unitary school system was in operation.

Soon after this decision, however, the Fifth Circuit Court of Appeals in New Orleans handed down a decision in a Houston desegregation case that disregarded the district court's findings in *Cisneros*. In June 1970 the Fifth Circuit upheld a lower court decision in *Ross v. Eckels*, which stated that for purposes of desegregation Mexican Americans were white.[37] The appeals decision allowed the Houston school officials to pair blacks with Mexican Americans while leaving the all-Anglo schools intact. Judge Clark held the only dissenting opinion. "I say it is mock justice when we 'force' the numbers by pairing disadvantaged negro students into schools with numbers of this equally disadvantaged ethnic group," he noted.[38]

Mexican Americans in Houston and throughout the state also viewed this pairing plan in particular and the appellate court's decision as unfair. MALDEF immediately requested to intervene on behalf of Mexican American students in Houston. In August 1970 it filed a friend of the court brief with the Fifth Circuit. "We want to know where we stand," said Abraham Ramírez Jr., one of three lawyers representing MALDEF. Its brief disputed the court of appeal's findings on the legal and educational status of Mexican Americans. "It is the position in this brief that the Mexican American is a distinct, identifiable minority group; that he has suffered discrimination in schools throughout the Southwest; and that the conditions existing in other parts of Texas exist in the Houston Independent School District," the brief stated. It offered no special desegregation plan but asked that the present plan before the Fifth Circuit be remanded for "additional hearings."[39]

MALDEF also intervened in other cases in 1971 and in a statewide desegregation case against the Texas Education Agency in 1972. In all of these cases, most of which had been filed by the Department of Justice on behalf of blacks, MALDEF sought a clear determination of whether Mexican Americans were legally a distinct minority group.

In early August 1972, MALDEF received word that the Fifth Circuit had decided on two cases relating to Mexican Americans in the desegregation process. These decisions were based on appeals made by Corpus Christi and Austin city officials. In both cases the court declared that Mexican Americans were an identifiable minority group that had been denied their constitutional rights by local school officials. The court also held that these school districts had the duty to desegregate them.[40]

These decisions created further confusion at the appeals level, for now there were contrary decisions by the same court. In the earlier *Ross* case, the Fifth Circuit had held that Mexican Americans were not an identifiable minority group for desegregation purposes. Now the same court held the opposite in the Corpus Christi and Austin cases, stating that they were an identifiable minority group.

The US Supreme Court finally decided the issue in 1973 in *Keyes v. School District No. 1*. The *Keyes* case, originally filed by African Americans in Denver, forced the Supreme Court to decide how to treat Mexican American children in the desegregation process. Denver had a history of de jure segregation of blacks; about one-sixth of the school population was black and one-fourth was Mexican American. The Supreme Court had to decide whether to desegregate only the blacks or to recognize Mexican Americans also as an illegally segregated group and desegregate each minority with the Anglo students. That is, the court had to define Mexican Americans as part of the white population and pair them with black students, or define them as an identifiable minority and pair them with Anglo students. To assign them the status of identifiable minority, the Supreme Court judges would have to conclude that Mexican Americans as a group had been subjected to a system of pervasive official discrimination. The court decided that for desegregation purposes this group was constitutionally entitled to recognition as an identifiable minority.[41]

These rulings, in effect, linked the Mexican American struggle to the national campaign against school segregation.

This legal victory was short-lived. Within a year, the national desegregation forces, including Mexican American groups, confronted a dilemma because of the *Lau v. Nichols* decision of 1974.[42] This decision encouraged the development of bilingual education, a strategy requiring the segregation of children on the basis of language. Federal legislation and the federal executive branch of government also supported the establishment of bilingual education in the public schools.[43]

For two years, these two different strategies clashed. Desegregation policies mandated the dispersal of Mexican American children throughout the district as a reform strategy. Bilingual education mandates called for an opposite strategy. Bilingual education required the concentration of these children on the basis of language. Although an alternative remedy was proposed, bilingual education within desegregation,[44] by 1975 the court ruled that desegregation took precedence over bilingual education mandates.[45]

Mexican American activists continued to file additional desegregation cases throughout the country or to seek intervention in ongoing ones.[46] Many, however, gradually abandoned desegregation as a remedy and embraced bilingual education as a more appropriate strategy for improving the education of Mexican American and other Latina/o groups in the country. Significant opposition to integration by whites, the increasing burden of desegregation by minority communities, and the increased dependence on bilingual education as a more effective strategy of reform encouraged this action.

By the 1980s, desegregation declined as a viable strategy of school reform.[47] In the meantime, segregation increased and by the early twenty-first century, Latinas/os were the most segregated group in the country.[48]

Contesting Unequal Funding of Public Schools

Unequal funding of schools was another form of discrimination Mexican Americans contested. For decades, schools serving these children had been underfunded, overcrowded, and inferior. During the 1960s, some of these inequalities were remedied as a result of demands from community groups and an influx of federal funds. The buildings, in many cases, were replaced with more modern facilities, qualifications of teachers increased, and per-pupil expenditures improved. Despite the increased funding and channeling of resources to Mexican origin schools the source of inequality—the state funding of public education—remained in place. In the late 1960s activists targeted state financing of public education and challenged it in the courts.[49]

The two most important cases Mexican American parents supported or filed in the late 1960s were in California and Texas—*Serrano v. Priest* and *Ro-*

driguez v. San Antonio Independent School District, respectively.[50] These cases exemplified the two major approaches taken by activists set on challenging inequities in school finance. Those in California pursued their strategy in the state courts; activists in Texas took their case to the federal courts. During the 1970s, the California Supreme Court ruled on behalf of Mexican American plaintiffs in the California case. The US Supreme Court, in contrast, ruled against them in Texas.

THE STRUGGLE IN CALIFORNIA

Mexican American parents filed a class action school finance lawsuit against the state of California in 1968. This lawsuit began a year earlier when John Serrano, a Los Angeles parent, complained to the principal of the inferior services available at his son's school. He was told that the school district could not afford more or better instruction and counseled him to move to one of the wealthier nearby districts. The senior Serrano viewed this advice as well intentioned but worthless because he was unable to move. Instead, he joined with others and brought suit against state officials.[51]

The suit, *Serrano v. Priest,* challenged the manner in which California financed its public school system. It alleged that the system of financing public elementary and secondary education violated the equal protection provisions of the US and California constitutions. Mexican American parents, that is, the plaintiffs, alleged that the heavy reliance on revenue from local property taxes resulted in substantial disparities in per-pupil expenditures from district to district throughout the state, and that these disparities resulted in unequal educational opportunities among school districts. On January 8, 1969, the superior court in Los Angeles dismissed the case on the grounds that the alleged disparities in financing the public schools were not unconstitutional.[52]

Mexican American parents appealed, and on September 1, 1970, the appeals court affirmed the earlier judgment of dismissal. It also argued that the parents did not state cause of action under the equal protection clause of the Fourteenth Amendment of the US Constitution or of the state constitution.[53]

The case was appealed to the California Supreme Court. This court, on August 30, 1971, reversed the lower court and held that if the alleged disparities existed, the system would be in violation of the US and California constitutions. The case was then sent back to the lower court to determine whether expenditure disparities did in fact exist and whether those spending disparities resulted in unequal educational opportunities afforded children among California school districts.[54] The lower court ruled in terms of the concept of fiscal neutrality, that is, the quality of education (as far as it was defined in terms of money) could not be a function of wealth, other than the wealth of the whole state.[55]

Before the trial on the factual issues was completed two significant events affected the case. First, the California legislature in November 1972 enacted Senate Bill 90. This bill significantly increased the amount of state financial assistance to local school districts.[56] Second, the US Supreme Court in March 1973 ruled on *Rodriguez v. San Antonio Independent School District*, the Texas school finance case. In this case, the Supreme Court ruled that while imperfect, the system of school finance in Texas was not unconstitutional.[57]

In 1974 the trial judge who reheard the *Serrano* case declared the school finance system unconstitutional despite significant changes made to it by the state legislature. Because of the Supreme Court ruling on *Rodriguez*, the district court was forced to rely strictly on the California constitution.[58]

The trial court decision was appealed to the California Supreme Court, and in late December 1976 it reaffirmed the lower court's ruling. The Supreme Court declared California's school financing system to be in violation of the state constitution's "equal protection" provision and ordered the legislature to develop new methods of school financing that did not violate the equal protection clause.[59]

This ruling eventually led to significant changes in how the state funded local schools. Unfortunately, other factors complicated the implementation of this new law and led to greater inequities in school financing.[60]

THE STRUGGLE IN TEXAS, 1967–73

Mexican Americans in Texas, unlike activists in California, filed a class action lawsuit in federal, not state court. *Rodriguez v. San Antonio Independent School District*, originally filed in the summer of 1968, focused on the disparities in the funding of schools in wealthy and poor districts. In this case, the Mexican American plaintiffs charged that the system of financing the schools was unconstitutional and deprived poor children of an equal educational opportunity.[61]

On December 23, 1971, the federal district court ruled in their favor and ordered the state to develop a more equitable system within two years.[62]

Local school officials appealed this decision and in late March 1973 the US Supreme Court reversed the lower court's ruling.[63] In a 5–4 decision it argued that the state's public school finance system was constitutional. The court

8. *Vilma Martinez, president of* MALDEF, *getting an award, 1979. Courtesy* MALDEF *Special Collections, Stanford University, Stanford, California.*

9. *Vilma Martinez and Mario Obledo, cofounder of* MALDEF, *discussing strategy on lawsuits, unknown date. Courtesy* MALDEF *Special Collections, Stanford University, Stanford, California.*

found, among other things, that (1) the Texas system did not disadvantage Mexican Americans as a suspect class nor was it dependent on the relative wealth of individuals in any district since there were rich and poor in both wealthy and poor districts; (2) the Texas system of finance did not interfere with a fundamental right (the US Constitution was deemed not to guarantee education as a fundamental right); and (3) although the Texas school finance system was admittedly imperfect, it was a rational way to finance schools.[64]

This case spurred the state legislature to initiate changes in how the state financed its public schools. In June 1973, the state legislature enacted House Bill 1126. This bill changed the manner of funding the public school system. For over a decade, this bill remained in effect.[65]

Mexican Americans' struggles against unequal schools temporarily ended after the passage of HB 1126. This bill, however, did not resolve the issue of inequality nor did it stop Mexican Americans from continuing their efforts to equalize funding for the public schools.[66] In 1984, Mexican Americans reinitiated the struggle for equal schools.[67] In this year MALDEF, representing Edgewood Independent School District and twelve other poor districts, filed another suit to overturn the Texas school funding system. Unlike the last time, they filed in the state not federal court. They also utilized a new legal argument that emphasized the equal protection analysis and the education clause of the state constitution.[68]

The case was originally known as *Edgewood Independent School District v. Bynum*. The lawsuit challenged the constitutionality of the Texas school finance system under the state constitution and sought relief under Texas constitutional provisions for "equal protection" and an "efficient system of public free schools." This case did not make it to trial because of the school finance reforms the Texas legislature initiated in July of the same year. The education reform bill, House Bill 72, made significant equity improvements in the state's school finance system.[69]

The following year, MALDEF refiled the case as *Edgewood Independent School District v. Kirby* (*Edgewood I*). It challenged the newly enacted system on the same "equal protection" and "efficiency" arguments made the previous year.

In 1987 the Travis County District Court ruled in favor of MALDEF and declared that the state school financing system was in violation of the state constitution. The case was appealed and reversed the following year. Aggrieved parties appealed this decision to the state supreme court. In 1989, the supreme court reversed the lower court's decision and ruled that the state's system of public school financing was unconstitutional. Its decision included an injunction that prohibited the state from funding the public school system after May 1, 1990, unless the legislature remedied the constitutional problems in the existing system.[70]

The legislature responded to this mandate by passing Senate Bill 1, a comprehensive set of reforms that modified the way in which the schools were funded.[71]

The district court found this new school financing plan unconstitutional on September 24, 1990. It required the legislature to adopt yet another program for school financing by September 1, 1991. If the legislature did not come up with one the court would impose its own plan. In the meantime it did away with the supreme court's injunction in order to give the state more time to comply with the court's ruling.[72]

In 1991, the Texas Supreme Court reviewed both the district court's decision and Senate Bill 1. In *Edgewood II* the court once again concluded that the Texas method for financing public education was unconstitutional. Additionally, the court reinstated its previous injunction, but stayed its effects until April 1, 1991.[73]

Right before the court's new injunction was to take effect, the state legislature passed a new school finance bill. This bill came to be known as the "Robin Hood" plan because it took money from the property-rich school districts and gave it to property-poor school districts. More specifically, the law shifted funds from property-rich school districts to property-poor districts, imposed a minimum property tax rate, and increased state aid to education.[74]

Several property-rich districts were dissatisfied with the new school finance law and went to court to challenge its constitutionality. The district court ruled against them and upheld the Robin Hood plan.[75]

For about a decade the Robin Hood law remained in effect without any major challenges. This changed in 2001 when residents of property-rich districts who opposed sharing their wealth with property-poor districts again filed suit in state court challenging the constitutionality of the Robin Hood law. Unlike a decade earlier, the court ruled in their favor and requested that the state legislature resolve this matter.[76] Since then legislators have taken a variety of steps to deal with the issue of unequal funding of public education, but by 2009 the problem was still unresolved.

This brief overview of legal challenges to school finance suggests that during the past several decades Mexican Americans played key roles in these struggles. Although their roles decreased over time, especially after 1994, they have been unrelenting in pressuring the state legislatures and the courts to reform public school systems throughout the country. While the matter of unequal schools is still unresolved, the community's intentions are not. Mexican American parents have been and are committed to ensuring that public officials provide all children, including their own, access to quality education through an equitably funded public school system.

Contesting Administrative Bias:
Focus on Testing

Another form of discrimination activists and educators challenged in the courts during this period was administrative bias in the schools, especially testing. Legal challenges to testing were extremely complex and multilayered, but they generally revolved around three central issues: the linguistic and cultural biases in testing, the misuse of standardized tests for placement of children in special classes or for admission to postsecondary educational institutions, and the inappropriate uses of tests, particularly the setting of minimum scores and the basing of decisions solely on one test score. The latter is commonly known as high-stakes testing.

Contemporary struggles against administrative bias began in the late 1960s and early 1970s. The emphasis was on challenging the biases and misuses of tests with linguistically and culturally distinct school age children.

Two major forms of contestation emerged during these decades—legal and scholarly.

Between 1968 and 1972 Mexican American activists in California and Arizona mounted legal challenges to the placement of culturally distinct children in low ability or special education classes on the basis of biased or invalid tests. Special education classes were for those individuals classified as mildly retarded. These were known as EMR or "educable mentally retarded" classes. For decades ethnic Mexican children had been identified as slow learners and placed in low ability or EMR classes. Standardized tests, especially group intelligence tests, were the means used to identify, classify, and place them in these special classes. This practice eventually led to their overrepresentation in low ability tracks, especially in EMR classes.[77] In California a local district court reported in the late 1960s that three out of every one hundred Mexican American students were assigned to classes for the mentally retarded, but only one and one-third of every one hundred other whites were assigned. "It is considered statistically impossible that this could occur by chance—, odds exceed one in one hundred billion," the court noted.[78]

In the late 1960s, community activists began to challenge the testing practices of schools with significant numbers of Mexican origin children. Four lawsuits challenging the uses of tests to place these children in EMR classes were filed in the late 1960s and early 1970s: *Arreola v. Board of Education* (1968),[79] *Diana v. State Board of Education* (January 1970),[80] *Covarrubias v. San Diego Unified School District* (1970),[81] and *Guadalupe v. Tempe Elementary School District* (1972).[82] Three of these cases were filed in California (*Arreola* in Santa Ana, the *Diana* case in Soledad, and the *Covarrubias* lawsuit in San Diego) and one in Arizona.

While the specifics of the cases differed, the arguments and the results were similar. The arguments in the *Diana* case illustrated the strategy lawyers used for the Mexican American community and the outcome of this case. In *Diana*, MALDEF contended that the IQ tests were biased and that the state discriminated against Mexican Americans by using them. The court agreed with MALDEF and ruled that the inherent cultural bias of the tests discriminated against these children. The state Department of Education settled out of court and in 1973 agreed to a five-year settlement known as a consent decree.[83]

Other lawsuits challenged the uses of standardized tests to place ethnic Mexican children in low ability classes or tracks. Some of the better-known cases were *Ruiz v. State Board of Education*, No. 218294 (Superior Court of the State of California, Sacramento, 1971), *Arellano v. Board of Education, Los Angeles Unified School District,* No. C27836 (Superior Court of the State of California, Los Angeles, 1973);[84] *Lora v. Board of Education of the City of New York,* (n.d.);[85] *Morales v. Shannon* (1975);[86] and *Hernandez v. Stockton Unified Sch. Dist.* (1975).[87] The latter two cases dealt with desegregation of the schools but often involved the legality of ability group practices, which had a segregative effect. The first three focused on challenging the use of standardized tests to place Mexican origin students in low ability groups. In most cases, the community won its lawsuit and managed to get some reforms in the tests themselves or in the uses of these tests for placement purposes.[88]

These lawsuits, part of a larger movement against discriminatory use of testing against minority children, played a key role in the development of federal, state, and local school policies and procedures more sensitive to the cultural and linguistic issues involved in the testing and placement of ethnic Mexican students in special classes during the 1970s and 1980s. In California the impact was significant. The state legislature, for instance, modified existing laws or enacted new ones aimed at promoting significant organizational and programmatic changes in the schools relating to the use of standardized tests with racial and ethnic minority children. Comprehensive policies and procedures also were developed to implement these changes. These actions temporarily led to a decline in the number and percentage of Mexican American and black children in EMR classes during the following decade.[89]

The lawsuits also impacted national developments. With respect to Mexican Americans, they contributed to the development of the May 25 memorandum and the official guidelines stating the federal government's position on quality education and on linguistically and culturally different children. This directive became one of the most important mechanisms the federal government used to remedy some of the adverse effects of rigid ability group and curricular tracking during the latter part of the twentieth century. More specifically it contributed significantly to the movement to provide parents and children assigned to special education classes procedural due process guarantees as well as schooling in the least restrictive environment.[90]

The lawsuits likewise helped to shape the nondiscriminatory mandate of Public Law 94–142, the Education for All Handicapped Children Act of 1975, and encouraged national organizations to call for a halt to all standardized testing.[91]

Scholarly contestation of testing emerged during the 1960s and continued throughout the next several decades. Scholarly critiques of testing were quite complex and dealt with several issues. In general, scholars criticized the origins of intelligence testing of ethnic Mexican children in the early part of the twentieth century,[92] cultural biases in intelligence tests,[93] explanations of differences in test scores,[94] the uses and misuses of standardized tests,[95] and both the overrepresentation of Latinas/os in special education classes and their underrepresentation in gifted and talented ones.[96] Most of these scholars also developed practical alternatives to traditional assessment. Two of the most important ones were nondiscriminatory assessment and "dynamic" assessment.[97]

Toward the latter part of the 1990s and into the early twenty-first century, many of these scholars extended their critiques to high-stakes testing and its adverse impact on Latinas/os in the public schools. In most cases scholars challenged the assumptions and negative effects of state testing policies.[98]

High-stakes testing was also challenged legally and politically in the late 1990s, especially in Texas. In the fall of 1999, for instance, Mexican American activists in Texas challenged the use of high-stakes testing by the Texas Education Agency.[99] In *G.I. Forum v. Texas Education Agency* the court ruled against the community and did not find that high-stakes testing was unconstitutional.[100] Mexican Americans also joined others in opposing Senate Bill 4, an antisocial promotion bill incorporating high-stakes testing and passed by the Texas state legislature with the support of then-governor George W. Bush in 1999.[101]

In the early twenty-first century, the struggle against high-stakes testing became national in scope because of the passage of the No Child Left Behind Act of 2001. Mexican American scholars, community activists, and civil rights organizations continued to play a highly visible role in this effort.[102]

Contesting Exclusion from the Curriculum

Mexican American parents and community organizations throughout the country also filed lawsuits against the exclusion of Latina/o students from the curriculum. This was especially the case with those who had little if any fluency with English. In the 1960s and 1970s these students were known as non-English speakers (NES) or limited-English speakers (LES). During the 1980s and 1990s they were known as limited-English proficient (LEP) children. In the twenty-first century, these children are referred to as English language learners (ELLS).

Litigation struggles against the exclusion of ELLS from the curriculum began in 1972. In this year, Mexican American parents in Portales, New Mexico, filed a lawsuit against local school officials for failure to provide appropriate instruction to Spanish-speaking children. Community activists challenged the English-only instructional program in the public schools and demanded a quality bilingual education program.[103] This case came to be known as *Serna v. Portales Municipal Schools.*[104]

This lawsuit followed in the footsteps of Chinese-speaking parents in San Francisco who challenged the exclusion of their children from the mainstream curriculum in 1970. The parents claimed that the absence of programs designed to meet the linguistic needs of Chinese-speaking children in the schools denied them an equal educational opportunity on constitutional grounds. This lawsuit (*Lau v. Nichols*) became the landmark case in bilingual education. In 1974 the Supreme Court ruled that local school officials violated the rights of Chinese-speaking children by failing to provide them with instruction in a language they understood.[105]

The *Lau* decision had a significant impact on the education of Mexican Americans and all those children who spoke a language other than English. It raised the nation's consciousness of the need for bilingual education, encouraged additional federal legislation, energized federal enforcement efforts, and aided the passage of state laws mandating bilingual education. It also impacted ongoing lawsuits and spawned several more.[106]

Lau v. Nichols impacted the Tenth Circuit Court of Appeal's ruling in the *Serna* case.[107] Noting that *Lau* and *Serna* were almost identical, the appeals court declined to decide the case on constitutional grounds and ruled on the basis of Title VI statute. The court ruled that the English-only program violated the students' rights to an equal educational opportunity and ordered a bilingual educational program be provided.[108]

The *Lau* decision encouraged several other communities to file lawsuits. In Patchogue-Medford, Long Island, Puerto Rican parents sued the local district under *Lau* to disclose its student records. The court in *Rios v. Read* (1977) probed the obligations imposed on school authorities toward ELL students. It then ruled that local school officials had to provide an effective bilingual education program for them.[109]

Several years later, the Fifth US Circuit Court of Appeals ruled in *Castaneda v. Pickard* (1981) that "good faith" efforts by school districts in serving ELLS are not sufficient. It established a "three-prong test" to ensure that local officials were meeting their obligations: programs had to be based on a sound educational theory, supported by adequate resources including trained personnel, evaluated for effectiveness, and restructured if necessary. *Castaneda* became a cornerstone of civil rights enforcement for the next several decades.[110]

During the 1970s and 1980s, Mexican American parents won most of their cases. Their one major loss occurred in Arizona in 1975. In *Otero v. Mesa County Valley School District No. 51,* Mexican American parents claimed that the programs provided for their children were inappropriate and violated their rights under Title VI and the Equal Protection Clause. Basing their arguments on the Cardenas-Cardenas Theory of Incompatibilities, they claimed that their children failed because of the incompatibility between the Mexican American working-class-based characteristics and the Anglo middle-class-based school policies and programs. The court rejected this argument and the theory of incompatibilities. It ruled that the Fourteenth Amendment did not require school districts to offer bilingual-bicultural programs. It also added that the Cardenas-Cardenas Theory of Incompatibilities was "illogical, unbelievable and unacceptable." Ethnic Mexican students had low academic performance not because of these incompatibilities but because of socioeconomic factors, it noted.[111]

School Access: Challenging the Formal Exclusion of Undocumented Students

Since the nineteenth century, the presence of immigrant children has had a significant impact on American public life, culture, economy, and education. With respect to education, it has raised concerns about what should be taught to these children and how it should be taught to them. Their presence, in other words, has raised significant questions about language, culture, class, and gender—what language should be used as a medium of instruction in the schools, how can the schools transform non-English-speaking children into American children, what values should be taught, when should academic subjects be introduced in English, should girls be taught the same subjects and in the same classroom as boys, should working-class immigrants be taught differently than middle-class citizens? The central task, however, has been that of assimilation. "Facing public education," noted David Tyack, "was the task of transforming these millions of newcomers—speaking dozens of languages, clinging to diverse folkways, owing multiple loyalties—into one people: e pluribus unum."[112]

Immigrant children continued to enroll in the public schools in the latter half of the twentieth century and to raise significant questions about lan-

guage, culture, and class. A new issue, however, emerged in the 1970s—that
of school access, especially of undocumented Mexican immigrant children,
that is, children who were in the US public schools without any documents.
Should public schools educate immigrant children without any documents or
should they exclude them from the public schools because of their immigration status? This became a significant public issue in the 1970s as a result of
the actions legislators and educators in Texas took.

In Texas, the issue of the education of undocumented children emerged
in the mid-1970s when legislators enacted a law barring these children from
receiving without charge educational services. Prior to this year, Texas did
not have a set policy dealing with the education of undocumented children.
In the absence of such a policy and because of increased enrollment of large
numbers of Mexican immigrant children, including those without any documents, several school districts, especially those residing along the border
or in metropolitan areas, began to exclude them. Most of them argued that
these children were draining the limited resources of local districts to educate American born or naturalized children.[113]

In 1975 the commissioner of education requested a clarification on this
issue from the Texas attorney general. The attorney general responded by
issuing an opinion holding that all children were entitled to attend the public schools. Most legislators opposed to this opinion quickly moved to undermine it. Within a month after the opinion the Texas legislature amended
the public school law in order to officially exclude undocumented children
from receiving a free public education.[114] The existing law stipulated that
"all children" who were between the ages of six and twenty-one were entitled to the benefits of a free public education. The amended school law was
changed to state that "all children who are citizens of the United States or
legally admitted aliens" and were between the ages of six and twenty-one
were entitled to a free public education.[115] Public officials argued that this
law was necessary because of the negative impact that a massive increase
of "illegal alien children," particularly from Mexico, was having on the
public schools and on the local districts' abilities to educate American
children.[116]

LEGAL CHALLENGES
The law was challenged in the courts several years after its enactment.[117] Between 1977 and 1979, countless communities filed lawsuits challenging the

constitutionality of the Texas statute, known as section 21.031 of the Texas Education Code.

HERNANDEZ CASE, 1977   The initial complaint challenging the constitutionality of the amended statute occurred in Houston in February 1977, after activists failed to get relief from state school officials, especially the state board of education. The parents of "illegal alien children," that is, the parents of children who were denied admission to the Houston Independent School District (HISD), filed an administrative complaint with the state board of education challenging the constitutionality of the statute providing for tuition-free public school education for citizens or legally admitted aliens. The state board of education rejected their complaint and argued that section 21.031 was constitutional.[118]

Soon after this action, the parents of these children filed suit in state district court. They argued that the exclusionary provision of the state's admission law was unconstitutional. In *Hernandez v. Houston Independent School District* the district court ruled in favor of Houston school officials when it affirmed the order of the state board of education and decreed that section 21.031 was constitutional. The court held that: "(1) since denial of free public education is not a denial of a 'fundamental right,' the statute would not be subjected to 'strict judicial scrutiny,' (2) the statute bears a rational relationship to a legitimate state purpose; (and) (3) the fact that the state has provided tuition-free education for citizens and legally admitted aliens does not require the state to provide free schooling to illegal aliens."[119]

On November 16, 1977, the Court of Civil Appeals of Texas in Austin affirmed the district court's ruling.

DOE V. PLYLER, 1978   After the serious setback in state court, activists decided to sue in federal court. Leading this effort was Peter Roos, one of the lawyers for MALDEF. Roos developed a long-term strategy for challenging the exclusionary provision of the state law. He systematically sought out the plaintiffs for this case, fought against intimidation of undocumented immigrant plaintiffs, and enlisted the support and assistance of other groups and individuals in this lawsuit.[120]

Roos found four undocumented immigrant families willing to risk their status in the United States in order to challenge the state statute prohibiting their children from receiving a free public education. In September 1977, these four undocumented immigrant families with the help of MALDEF sued the Tyler Independent School District for denying their children access to a free public education and for charging each of their children $1,000 tuition.[121]

A year later, on September 14, 1978, the judge ruled in *Doe v. Plyler* that the statute was in violation of the equal protection clause of the US Constitution. The Tyler Independent School District was permanently enjoined from denying undocumented children access to free public education. Although this ruling applied solely to the Tyler school district, it became a significant case, because for the first time in the history of this country a federal court had ruled that undocumented children were entitled to free public educational services.[122] Tyler school officials soon thereafter filed an appeal.

IN RE: ALIEN CHILDREN, 1980   The *Doe v. Plyler* outcome encouraged other communities to file lawsuits challenging the constitutionality of the state law. Within a two-year period, close to a dozen communities in different parts of the state filed lawsuits.

One of the most important lawsuits, because of its size, occurred in Houston. In September 1978, a group of local attorneys and a California-based public interest law firm led by civil rights lawyer Peter Schey filed a lawsuit against HISD challenging the constitutionality of section 21.031. Soon thereafter four additional complaints were filed in the Southern District of Texas and two in the Northern District. The Eastern District court that had decided *Plyler* faced an additional six cases after the ruling. Unlike the Tyler case, which only sued the particular school district, these lawsuits included the state of Texas, the Texas Education Agency (TEA), the governor of the state of Texas, and the commissioner of education.[123]

All of these new cases eventually were consolidated on November 16, 1979, and referred to Judge Woodrow Seals of the US District Court for the Southern District of Texas.[124] The *Plyler* case, however, was not consolidated and remained independent. This combined lawsuit came to be known as the In re Alien Children Education Litigation case.[125] On January 11, 1980, the US Department of Justice filed a motion to intervene on behalf of the undocumented children, asserting that the statute violated the equal protection clause of the Fourteenth Amendment of the US Constitution. On February 1, 1980, the court granted the motion to intervene.[126]

A hearing was conducted in February and March 1980. On Tuesday, July 22, 1980, Judge Seals ruled that the statute barring the children of un-

documented aliens from attending Texas public schools was unconstitutional. The statute, he noted, violated the Equal Protection Clause of the
Fourteenth Amendment. He argued that absolute deprivation of education
should trigger strict judicial scrutiny. The court determined that the state's
concern for fiscal integrity was not a compelling state interest, that exclusion
of these children had not been shown to be necessary to improve education
within the state, and that the educational needs of the children excluded from
education were not different from the needs of those included. The statute,
the court further noted, was not carefully tailored to advance the asserted
state interest in an acceptable manner.[127] The state of Texas immediately filed
an appeal.[128]

COURT OF APPEALS, 1980   While the appeal of the district court's decision on In Re was pending, the court of appeals rendered its decision in the
Plyler case. In October 1980, it upheld the district court's injunction and affirmed the lower's court's ruling. Tyler school officials once again appealed
this decision to the US Supreme Court. A few months after this decision the
Fifth Circuit Court affirmed and accepted the consolidated Houston cases.[129]

SUPREME COURT RULING, 1982   In May 1981, the US Supreme Court
agreed to hear the *Plyler* case. Sometime later it combined the Texas appeals
of both cases, the *Plyler* and *In re Alien Children*. The combined cases assumed the name of *Plyler v. Doe*.[130] In 1982, the Supreme Court ruled that it
was unconstitutional to deny these children access to free public education.

RESPONSES TO *DOE*   The attorneys, parents, and community groups
were ecstatic about this victory. The decision, noted Peter Schey, one of the
attorneys arguing the case, "was received by our clients with joy and tears."
"Our long battle in federal court to establish that undocumented children are
persons under our Constitution and entitled to some level of protection by
the Bill of Rights has finally found acceptance in the Supreme Court of this
country," he further added.[131]

Despite its significance, *Plyler,* as Michael A. Olivas noted, has not substantially influenced subsequent Supreme Court immigration jurisprudence
in the twenty-five years since it was decided. Still, this case has been important in extending the benefit of the equal protection clause to noncitizen
immigrants and in ensuring access to educational opportunity.[132] As a result
of the *Plyler* ruling, public schools may not deny public school admission

to a student on the basis of immigration status, treat a student differently to determine residency, engage in any practices to "chill" or hinder the right of access to school, require students or parents to disclose or document their immigration status, or ask students or parents questions that may expose their undocumented status.[133]

Decades after its ruling, the *Plyler* case was impacting local, state, and national developments. In the 1990s it was used as a defense against the implementation of Proposition 187 and against the enactment of federal legislation with exclusionary provisions. Proposition 187 was a ballot initiative California voters passed in 1994 that would have denied virtually all state-funded benefits, including public education, to undocumented aliens. The federal courts ruled this proposition unconstitutional on the basis of the arguments in the *Plyler* case. Others used the case as a way to effectively oppose a federal bill with a provision allowing states to charge tuition to undocumented students or to exclude them from public schools. The *Plyler* case also has been used as a means to extend higher education access to undocumented students. Although activists have a long way to go, they have opened the door wider to undocumented students wishing to attend institutions of higher education.[134]

Opposing School Closures

A final area of contestation involved school closures. In the 1970s, declining enrollment, runaway inflation, and fiscal austerity led to the closure of over seven thousand public schools, affecting 80 percent of the nation's school districts.[135]

A significant proportion of racial/ethnic minority schools were targeted for closure.[136]

Several reasons were given for closing schools located in ethnic Mexican communities. One of these was fear of white flight. The school board in Santa Barbara, California, for instance, voiced the following when considering closing one of the white schools with declining enrollment.

The schools' residential area is one of the highest socioeconomic areas in the city. Maintaining this area as a predominantly public school attendance area is important to the District. Unless the District can attract and hold these upper middle class areas the entire Elementary School District is in danger of becoming more ethnically and socioeconomically segregated.[137]

This fear, coupled with disregard of the community's concerns, led to the decision by the local board to close the Mexican American, instead of the white, school. Both of these schools had high enrollment, but the white schools had begun to experience declines in student enrollments. No such decline had occurred or was expected to occur in the segregated Mexican American schools.[138]

The school board's rationale for not closing any white schools in Santa Barbara did not sit well with ethnic Mexican parents. Many of them decided to boycott the public schools. They also unsuccessfully filed a lawsuit arguing that the rationale for closing minority schools was arbitrary and discriminatory based upon the suspect classification of wealth.[139]

Other communities in different cities opposed to the closing of their schools likewise filed lawsuits. In *Castro et al. v. Phoenix Union High School District No. 210 et al.*, parents were successful in their efforts.[140]

The school closure cases, while minor, are extremely important ones because they suggest, as Richard Valencia noted, "a new form of denial to education . . . that was not there previously."[141] These cases, as well as all the others, suggest that the community's resolve to fight specific forms of discrimination was relentless and passionate.

CONCLUSION

The legal struggle against discrimination, as shown above, was highly complex, extremely diverse, and of long duration. Before the 1960s, the historic struggle against educational discrimination was mostly one against school segregation. In the post-1960s years, this struggle was expanded to include a variety of exclusionary and discriminatory policies and practices in school access, school finance, administration, and instruction. The attack against various forms of discrimination in the schools was comprehensive, systemic, and unyielding. Some of these struggles lasted for a couple of years. Among these were those against school closures, school segregation, and denial of access to undocumented children. Others lasted longer and continue to be challenged by Mexican American parents and community groups. Among the policies that continue to be contested are school finance and access to the curriculum via language and testing, especially high-stakes testing.

Throughout this period, community groups and individuals have had significant successes and some failures. Some of their struggles have led to significant changes in the ways that public school officials classify and educate

TABLE 2.1. A SELECT LIST OF POST–CHICANO MOVEMENT PROTEST ACTIVITY, 1976–2008

1976	Protest Bakke decision.
1985	UCLA students protest fraternity (Beta Theta Pi) racist theme party.[142]
1987	Over 7,000 march to Sacramento, California for education.[143]
1988	Students hold sit-in to protest tuition increases at University of New Mexico.
	Students protest against racism and for diversity at UCLA.[144]
1989	In October, students walkout of Austin H.S. in Houston, Texas.
1990	UCLA students protest the dismantling of Chicano Studies major at chancellor's office.[145]
1991	April, Latinos in Milwaukee, Wisconsin, demand at hearing that bilingual education not be cut.[146]
1997	October 30, Indiana University expelled a fraternity for sending pledges on a scavenger hunt for photos of "any funny-lookin' Mexican."[147]
1998	April 29, LULAC, alumni and others protest Baylor University sorority Mexican theme party where students were dressed as gangsters and pregnant women.[148]
2000	May 17, a coalition of groups files a class action lawsuit alleging that California has failed to ensure basic educational equality under the state constitution.[149]
2003	February 10, students protest the University of New Mexico's failure to adequately fund the Chicano Studies program.[150]
	September 29, students at Pitzer College in Claremont, California meet with president to discuss concerns about failure to keep Latino assistant dean of students, issues of diversification, and exclusion of community in strategic planning.[151]
2004	During October and November students protest name change at the UNM from Chicano Studies to Southwest Hispanic Studies without informing students or community.[152]
2005	February 1, Latino activists support Ward Churchill and oppose efforts to oust him from teaching for making critical comments about 9/11.[153]
	February 4, a few activists protest the censoring of *Bless Me Ultima* and requests by parents in Norwood, Colorado, to burn the book.[154]
	February 4, activists protest filing of bill to repeal top 10% law in Texas passed in 1997 in response to federal judge ruling against the use of race in admissions to college.[155]
	February 25, activists protest Young Conservatives "Catch an illegal immigrant game" at UNT in Dallas.[156]
	March 2, activists protest the UT administration's denial of tenure for one of the Latino community's favorite professors—Barbara Robles.[157]
	March 3, protesters confront UT conservative group in campus.[158]
	May 4, protesters tell of riot police brutality of 80 students at UC Santa Cruz.[159]

TABLE 2.1. (*CONTINUED*)

November 2, Students struggle for establishment of BA program in Chicano Studies at California State University at Channel Island.[160]

November 16, Students celebrate approval and establishment of new doctoral program in Chicano/Latino Studies at MSU.[161]

2006   February 20, a variety of student groups protest the effort to dismiss and take away the tenured professorship in Spanish and Chicana/o Literature of Dr. Manuel de Jesus Hernandez, a former National NACCS Chair.[162]

In March and April students, parents, and community activists protest immigration legislation and march in support of immigrant rights.[163]

November 8, racist video causes uproar on A&M campus at College Station, Texas. The video depicted a mock master-slave scene complete with shoe polish blackface, a banana, and simulated sexual abuse.[164]

2007   September 23, activists protest the exclusion of Latinos from Ken Burns video on WWII in front of KPBS Studios at SDSU, in Austin, Texas, and in other cities.[165]

November 8, Latinos protest imbalanced Latino historical exhibit at Texas A&M University[166]

November 10, activists support Columbia University hunger strikers to protest the university's lack of diversity and to transform the university's institutional culture of institutional racism and negligence.[167]

November 17, a meeting is called to discuss exclusion of Latinos from textbooks at TSHA conference in March.[168]

2008   February 21, activists protest the exclusion of Tejanos from Texas history.[169]

During February–March, activists protest lack of Latino input on curriculum at Texas State Board of Education meetings.[170]

March 11, activists call for a boycott of Go Tejano Day in Houston.

March 5–8, a meeting held to discuss exclusion of Latinos from textbooks at TSHA conference in March.[171]

April 11, activists encourage hiring of full-time tenure track professor for Chicano Studies and support for two outreach programs at Ohlone College in Fremont, Cal.[172]

April 16, activists protest proposed Arizona legislation to ban the denigration of American values and the teachings of Western Civilization and to bar "race-based" organizations such as MECHA from schools and colleges.[173]

2010   November, students protest SB 1070 (anti-Mexican legislation) and HB 2281 (anti-ethnic studies bill).[174]

2011   April 27, high school students take over Tucson school board to protest dismantling of ethnic studies program.[175]

April 27, UCLA students launch hunger strike to protest ethnic studies staff cutbacks.[176]

culturally and linguistically distinct children, whereas others have had either limited impact or no significant impact on local school policies and practices. Still the struggle to eliminate discrimination in education is a testament to the fierce determination in activist communities to ensure that the children receive a form of learning that is equitable and excellent.

The complex struggle against discrimination, while admirable, was only one aspect of the community's quest for quality education. Mexican Americans engaged in other types of struggles to achieve their goals. The following chapter indicates that they also advocated for school reforms aimed at meeting the educational, linguistic, and cultural needs of their children.

THREE

Advocacy

Т he quest for education was not only about eliminating discrimination in the schools. It was also one of assertive advocacy. Mexican Americans wanted schools that were free from discrimination, that reflected their communities and their cultural heritage, and that met their academic needs and political interests. The struggles on behalf of power, access, quality instruction, and pluralism reflected these desires.

POWER

Mexican American parents and community activists have engaged in many different types of struggles since the 1960s. One of the most important dealt with gaining power in order to make decisions about the education impacting their own children. The quest for power has been reflected in the struggles aimed at promoting community access to important decision-making positions in three major areas of public education: school governance, educational administration, and teaching. Prior to the 1960s, this strategy was aimed primarily at the K-12 public school system. Afterward, efforts were expanded to the postsecondary level and to the federal level.[1]

The struggle for power in education has been ongoing for decades, but it took new forms in the 1960s. As early as 1963, for instance, Mexican Americans mobilized to take over structures of power in Crystal City, a small rural community in central Texas. Although activists succeeded in wresting control from a dominant Anglo elite in that city, they were only able to maintain power for two years. The dominant groups in that city organized a major campaign against Mexican American activists and voted them out of office two years later.[2]

10. (right) Angel Noe González, superintendent of Crystal City Independent School District, 1970–74. Courtesy José Angel Gutiérrez Papers, Nettie Lee Benson Latin American Collection, University of Texas Libraries, the University of Texas at Austin. (Kelly Kerbow Hudson, Archival Processing)

11. School board meeting with students and parents expressing anger over firing of Amancio Cantú, school superintendent in September 1975. Courtesy José Angel Gutiérrez Papers, Nettie Lee Benson Latin American Collection, University of Texas Libraries, the University of Texas at Austin. (Kelly Kerbow Hudson, Archival Processing)

In the late 1960s, and largely as a result of the emergence of the Chicano and Chicana movement, activists began to agitate for controlling the schools as part of a larger plan for liberation in the United States. In 1969 and 1970, several of them won control of two local school districts in two cities of the Southwest—Cucamonga, California, and Crystal City, Texas. These victories, especially the latter, served as beacons of hope for Mexican American activists throughout the country that educational change was possible.

The "revolution" in Cucamonga occurred as a result of an energetic and arduous campaign a determined group of ethnic Mexican activists waged. Cucamonga, a small rural community outside of Riverside, California, was similar to many other communities in the Southwest with significant numbers of Mexicans and Anglos. In this city, Mexicans were poor, socially segregated, exploited, and denied political representation in local government.

12. Students mobilizing on behalf of superintendent Amancio Cantú, fired by local school board in September 1975. Most of these students were supporters of a community-based organization, Ciudadanos Unidos, and aligned with the leadership of José Angel Gutiérrez in Crystal City. They called themselves "Gutierristas." Courtesy José Angel Gutiérrez Papers, Nettie Lee Benson Latin American Collection, University of Texas Libraries, the University of Texas at Austin. (Kelly Kerbow Hudson, Archival Processing)

13. A packed school board meeting at the Fly Cafeteria in one of the local schools, Crystal City, 1975. Courtesy José Angel Gutiérrez Papers, Nettie Lee Benson Latin American Collection, University of Texas Libraries, the University of Texas at Austin. (Kelly Kerbow Hudson, Archival Processing)

Two segregated school districts existed in this city, one white (88 percent) and one Mexican (99 percent). Despite this segregation, Anglos dominated all positions in both districts, including the school board, administration, and teaching. Even the janitors in the Mexican district were Anglos. Those in power mandated an Anglo-centric curriculum and an English-only school language policy. They also had insensitive teachers and discouraged Mexican parental involvement. High illiteracy and dropout rates characterized the education of Mexican origin children in the Cucamonga schools.[3]

Conditions began to change once activists formed the Mexican American Political Association (MAPA) on March 12, 1968. For the next nine months MAPA held meetings in the community to dispel distrust and promote unity. It initiated action projects such as community cleanups, scholarship dances, and public forums. In January 1969, the mapistas, as MAPA members were known, presented several demands to the local school board, but they were ignored. Local board indifference encouraged the organization to run three candidates for the upcoming school board elections. Although contested, this decision ensured that if all of their candidates won they would gain control of the five-member board and initiate significant changes.[4]

In March MAPA organized for the elections. With the support of college students it identified the candidates (two workers, one librarian), conducted a successful voter registration project (Mexican American voter registration jumped from 40 percent to 48 percent), an educational awareness campaign (informed the community to support the slate and don't antagonize Anglos), organized by block and sections, raised funds in the community, and implemented an effective get out the vote (GOTV) campaign. On April 14, 1969, the three candidates won. Low Anglo and high Mexican American voter turnout led to their success. Anglos were shocked but not necessarily hostile to the takeover. "Los tres" (the three new candidates) assumed office in July.[5]

Once in office they began to implement a bilingual education program but were unable to increase the hiring of Mexican American teachers or build a new ballpark for school children because of opposition from the superintendent. For close to nine months the superintendent acted as an obstacle to their change agenda.

During the first two months of 1970, MAPA board members abandoned their cautious approach and became more militant.[6] With support from college students and community members they attacked the superintendent in two well-planned meetings. Their militancy silenced Anglos and eliminated the superintendent's oppositional tactics, but it fomented divisions among Mexican Americans. Some community members accused the mapistas of being outsiders and of creating conflict within the Mexican American community. Despite this division, MAPA was able to elect another Chicano to the school board in the following election. By 1972 then four out of five school board members were Mexican Americans. Their dominance enabled them to proceed with the changes they wanted to initiate in order to improve the education of Mexican American schoolchildren. Control of the local school board eventually led to the development of a comprehensive bilingual edu-

cation program, the hiring of bilingual teachers, administrators, and a superintendent, the establishment of a free lunch program, the building of a
ballpark, control of the parent teacher association, greater Mexican American parental involvement, and the declaration of September 16 (Mexican
Independence Day) as a school holiday. "La Raza of Cucamonga has been
awakened and politicized," noted Armando Navarro.[7]

With MAPA's victory on April 14, 1969, the Cucamonga School District
became the first in California and probably in the nation to come under the
control of militant Chicanos. Once in control, they began to implement significant changes in the ways schools taught Spanish-speaking children and in
the curriculum utilized to teach them.[8]

Nine months after the Cucamonga takeover, Mexican American activists
in Crystal City, Texas, followed in their lead. Unlike activists in Cucamonga,
those in Crystal City were more organized and successful. They not only
gained control of the local school board but also of the city council and
county commissioner's court.

With the help of the Mexican American Youth Organization (MAYO), local community groups, and eventually La Raza Unida Party (LRUP), activists
mobilized the community and conducted effective voter registration drives
to get out the votes. Because of these efforts, they won all of the local offices
and used their positions to initiate significant reforms in social, economic,
and educational policy. Some of the major changes in education that activists
made included, among many others, the replacement of Anglo administrators with Mexican American ones, the hiring of Spanish-speaking teachers,
the increased participation by parents and students in school decisions, increased federal funding of school programs, the establishment of bilingual
education programs to increase academic achievement, and the valuing and
recognition of Mexican patriotic and cultural holidays. It also included support for César Chávez and opposition to the war in Vietnam.[9]

Although Crystal City Anglos opposed the variety of changes Mexican
American activists initiated, they were not successful in dislodging them
from power. These activists, however, lost power due to what Armando Navarro called the "politics of self-destruction." The various factions within
the coalition that won power in 1970 engaged in bickering, infighting, and
bitter power struggles. The ultimate result was the replacement of Mexican
American radicals interested in social and educational reform with a group
of politicians more interested in restoring social and political order in that
city. The effort to bring about social, economic, and educational change

TABLE 3.1. CHICANA/O AND LATINA/O SCHOOL BOARD MEMBERS IN THE UNITED
STATES, 1984–2007

	Total	Male	Female
1984	555	403	152 (27%)
1991	1588	1128	460 (29%)
1996	1240*	n.a.	n.a
2007	1847	n.a.	n.a.

Source: National Roster of Hispanic Elected Officials (Washington, DC: National Association of Latino Elected and Appointed Officials, 1984), xi–xii; *National Roster of Hispanic Elected Officials* (Washington, DC: National Association of Latino Elected and Appointed Officials, 1991), viii–ix. For 1996 and 2008 see naleo.org/downloads/NALEOFactsheet07.pdf (accessed December 16, 2009).

*new procedures for tabulating the number of Latina/o school board members accounted for the loss between 1991 and 1996. Phone interview with Salvador Sepulveda, *Program Associate*, NALEO Educational Fund, January 4, 2010.

through militancy and confrontation was replaced with accommodationism and integrationism into the existing social order.[10]

The election of militant Chicano activists to two local school districts in the Southwest led to the disruption of the historic pattern of exclusion from school governance common in the Southwest since the nineteenth century. It also led to the development of a pattern of inclusion. This was reflected in the increasing numbers of ethnic Mexicans elected to local school boards in the years after the initial takeover of Cucamonga and Crystal City schools. By 1984, for instance, 555 Mexican American and other Latinas/os had been elected to these positions. Their numbers continued to increase over the next two decades. By 2007 a total of 1,847 were part of the governance structures of local schools throughout the country.

The increase in school board representation was highly uneven and limited to certain parts of the country. As indicated in chapter 1, this led to control of many small school districts throughout the country but only moderate representation in large urban school districts such as those in Los Angeles and Houston. Demographic projections, however, suggest that the Latina/o population will increase over time and so will probably their numbers in school governance structures.

The struggle for power was not only limited to gaining control of local school boards. It also applied to other positions of influence within the school district, including the selection of superintendents and principals. It even applied to the hiring of individuals for teaching and other professional positions.

In a few cases the struggle for access to these positions stirred up unfortunate tensions between Mexican Americans and African Americans. In major urban areas such as Houston, Los Angeles, and Chicago, for instance, the struggle to select a superintendent during the 1980s and 1990s created tensions between these two groups.[11]

Tensions continued into the early twenty-first century, especially when it dealt with selecting principals and teachers for schools undergoing significant racial and ethnic transformations or with schools that had also undergone that change, either from black to brown or from brown to black.[12]

ACCESS

Activists also struggled for full access to public education.

During the post-1960s, most students had gained access to the elementary and secondary grades but there were at least three lingering issues. One of these pertained to the out of school population. While the majority of ethnic Mexican school-aged children were enrolled in the schools, a small percentage were not. The out of school population increased in the early twenty-first century because of the influx of Mexican and other Latina/o immigrants from countries where schooling was not available or for economic and social reasons.[13]

Another issue focused on the occasional exclusion of groups of students, especially immigrants. In the late 1970s, for instance, Texas school officials passed a law prohibiting undocumented Mexican immigrant children from enrolling in the public schools. Mexican American activists legally challenged this law in the latter part of the decade. In the early 1980s, they finally won legal access of undocumented immigrant children to the public schools.[14] In the 1990s, several states, including California and Arizona, sought to exclude undocumented immigrant children from the public schools through the passage of several propositions. Activists took public officials to court and reaffirmed their right to a free public education.[15]

A final issue dealt with access of Mexican origin children to special educational programs. In the 1960s and early 1970s, parents and community groups fought for gaining equitable access to compensatory and remedial programs.[16] In the 1970s and 1980s, they focused on gaining access to the regular curriculum through bilingual education and migrant education programs.[17] In the 1990s, they expanded their concerns to include gaining access to pre-kindergarten classes.[18] This struggle was extended to full day pre-kinder classes in the following decade as illustrated by the support of the National Council de La Raza (NCLR), the largest national Latina/o civil rights and advocacy organization in the United States, for passage of the Improving Head Start Act of 2007. This bill, NCLR noted, "will significantly expand access to the nation's premier early childhood and education program for Hispanic children, who represent the fastest-growing segment of the Head Start eligible child population."[19] Toward the latter part of the twentieth century and in the early part of the twenty-first century, activists, parents, and community organizations also focused on gaining equitable access to academically enriching programs such as advanced placement and both regular and bilingual magnet and vanguard programs.

At times the struggle took different forms because of political circumstances and organizational resources. One such example occurred in Houston. In the mid-1970s, for instance, Mexican American activists opposed the establishment of the magnet and vanguard programs as a means to desegregate the schools. By the early 1980s, they embraced these programs and fought to have their children gain access to them. In the early 1990s, they fiercely defended these programs and opposed the elimination of race as a mechanism for admittance into these classes.[20]

At the postsecondary level, students, parents, and community activists demanded access to higher education and significant changes in the governance, administration, and content of public universities and colleges. The struggle for higher educational opportunities for Mexican Americans in the United States was a long one involving many individuals and multiple actions. After the 1960s it went through several overlapping stages: demanding access (1960s–70s), retrenchment and resistance (1980s), institutional setbacks and advances (1990s), and continued struggle (twenty-first century).

Demanding, Creating, and Strengthening Access, 1960s–70s

Mexican American students and organizations had been seeking higher educational opportunities at the local and state level since the nineteenth century, but in the 1960s they became more forceful.[21] Many individuals took over buildings, demonstrated on campus, and engaged in a variety of direct actions to demand not only the recruitment of students and faculty to universities but also the establishment of Chicana/o controlled colleges, departments, or research centers, and the development of Mexican American classes.[22]

Partly because of their activism, the enrollment of Mexican American students in the universities increased gradually. As their numbers increased, students pressed for the creation or expansion and control of student support programs such as Educational Opportunity Programs (EOP) in California or of Mexican American Studies programs in other parts of the country.[23]

The push for control of these programs placed ethnic Mexicans at odds with white and black administrators, whose overriding emphasis was on recruiting black students. In a few cases, competition for resources led to the dual administration of EOP programs, one controlled by Mexican Americans and one controlled by blacks or white liberals. The desire for student control of university programs also occasionally led to conflict with Mexican American administrators who opposed these efforts.[24]

During the latter part of the 1970s, youth activists increasingly turned to institutional mechanisms such as Educational Opportunity Programs (EOP) and Chicana/o Studies programs or centers to increase student access to higher education and to improve their retention in these institutions. Activists also supported the establishment of affirmative action and special admission policies that encouraged the recruitment of Chicana/o students and faculty to colleges and universities.[25]

Private foundations, especially Ford, Carnegie, and Rockefeller, supported many of these reforms and developed their own initiatives aimed at improving minority access to and retention in higher education. These efforts paralleled their support of Historically Black Colleges and Universities (HBCUs) and of the NAACP's legal struggles against racial discrimination.[26]

In a few cases, Mexican American activists established their own institutions of higher learning. Their intent was to develop viable alternatives to conventional institutions that "have historically failed to respond to the educational needs of Chicanos."[27] The establishment of these universities soon led to discussions of the need to create an organization of institutions to promote their growth in American higher education and to increase the recruitment and retention of Latina/o college students.[28]

Retrenchment and Resistance: The 1980s

The 1980s was a decade of retrenchment and resistance. In this period, Mexican American progress in higher education came under attack. University enrollment stalled; student support services were cut back; Chicana/o-controlled colleges, departments, and centers closed or scaled back; affirmative action programs were contested; and students were physically attacked or ridiculed on campus as the climate became more conservative.[29]

Activists responded to these developments in several ways. Some took to the streets and protested the growing attacks against these programs, services, and Chicano Studies curricula.[30] Significant mobilization also occurred around specific incidents of racism on campus.[31]

Others sought legislative reforms aimed at increasing Chicana/o access and retention. Several bills were introduced in the early 1980s in Congress to provide direct aid to institutions with high concentrations of Latina/o students and to increase funding for upward bound programs and for teacher preparation for these students. Although they were not passed, these pieces of legislation opened the way for successful bills in the 1990s.[32]

In a few cases community organizations took the litigation route. In the late 1980s, for instance, the League of United Latin American Citizens (LULAC) and MALDEF joined forces to file a lawsuit in Texas challenging the discriminatory practices of institutions of higher learning. Although they lost the case (*LULAC v. Ann Richards*, 1987), this lawsuit served as a major motivation for channeling funds to institutions of higher learning located along the South Texas–Mexican border that eventually benefited Mexican origin students residing in that part of the state.[33]

Private groups responded by increasing their support for college students. The Ford Foundation, for instance, provided more funds for higher education assistance and established the minority postdoctoral fellowship program in 1985.[34]

Individual scholars and Chicano think tanks responded by focusing public attention on the status of Latina/o college students. They conducted a slew of studies analyzing the problems these institutions faced and proposed a variety of solutions to improve higher education access.[35] Some of these scholars challenged specific issues that negatively impacted student access to colleges and universities. Among two of the most important were the role of standardized testing in college admission and the discourse of "reverse discrimination" popularized by the Supreme Court decision in *Bakke v. Regents of the University of California* (1978).[36]

Institutional Setbacks and Progress, 1990s

During this decade Mexican Americans continued to lose ground in access to higher education, especially after the adoption or passage of several rulings and ballot initiatives negatively impacting affirmative action programs in California and Texas. These actions directly affected the quality of Mexican origin schooling in general and access to higher education in particular.

In 1995, the Regents of the University of California adopted a new admissions policy (SP1) that ended affirmative action in the University of California system. The following year, Californians voted in favor of Proposition 209, the self-labeled "Civil Rights Initiative" that ended affirmative action in public higher education throughout California.[37] That same year, the Fifth Circuit Court of Appeals ruled in *Hopwood v. State of Texas* that the use of race/ethnicity and gender in undergraduate and graduate admission in institutions of higher education was illegal. The Fifth Circuit's jurisdiction included Texas, Louisiana, and Mississippi. In 1997, Texas attorney general Dan Morales expanded the impact of this decision to include not only admissions but also financial aid, scholarships, and student and faculty recruitment and retention.[38]

Activists in California and in Texas vigorously opposed these developments. In California, large numbers of Chicana/o students, grassroots organizations, and professionals, in cooperation with a host of other minority and nonminority groups, protested these measures in the streets and in the courts.[39] In Texas, activists responded legislatively to the *Hopwood* case. In 1998, two years after the *Hopwood* ruling, political leaders in the state, supported by Chicana/o activists, enacted what came to be known as the Top Ten Percent Plan. Under this plan, all seniors in the top 10 percent of their class in the state of Texas were guaranteed automatic admission to the state university of their choice. Since significant numbers of these students were minorities, they tended to benefit from this legislation.[40]

Occasionally, activists in the community struggled for the establishment of higher education facilities in their own communities. In a few cases, they succeeded in getting public officials to establish a university that would benefit Mexican origin students living in the inner city.[41]

While Chicanas/os were experiencing setbacks in a variety of states, a different story with respect to access to higher education unfolded at the national level. In this case, activists succeeded in getting federal recognition of institutions highly impacted by Latina/o enrollment. These institutions, known as Hispanic-Serving Institutions (HSIs), were modeled after the historically black colleges and universities (HBCUs). Because of the enormous historical, social, and political differences between the two groups, however, the higher education model utilized by and for African Americans did not serve the specific needs of Latinas/os in higher education. Latinas/os required a different type of institution to serve their needs. The HSI became that model—a unique and powerful instrument for recruiting Latina/o students and faculty to the university and for improving the quality of institutions of higher learning serving them.[42]

The push for recognition of HSIs was led by the Hispanic Association of Colleges and Universities (HACU), an organization established by Latina/o impacted institutions of higher learning in 1986. HACU began to lobby the federal government during the 1980s, and in the early 1990s succeeded in getting such a designation. This was reflected in the 1992 reauthorization of the Higher Education Act of 1965. This bill provided a definition of HSIs, the requirements for attaining this status, and provided limited funding. Six years later in the 1998 reauthorization of the same bill, the requirements for becoming an HSI were relaxed and funding increased significantly. In this latter year, the HSIs also received a separate designation in federal legislation. This designation was embodied in Title V of the 1998 reauthorized Higher Education Act of 1965. Separate designation acknowledged a distinct identity within federal discussion of higher education.[43]

Continued Struggle in the Twenty-First Century

During the first decade of the twenty-first century, Chicana/o and Latina/o activists made advances in certain areas but lost ground in others. They continued to make progress in getting financial support for the strengthening of HSIs in the country and in facilitating their growth over time. Although still severely underrepresented, their numbers steadily increased. These advances came despite the new challenges to access mounted by conservative legislators throughout the country, the lack of significant reforms in facilitating transfers from two-year to four-year colleges, the rapid increase in college tuition, and the decrease of federal funding for college students.[44]

The constant albeit slow increase in student access to postsecondary education did not apply as readily to those who had an undocumented status. As larger numbers of Mexican origin students graduated from high school and attended college, the problem of undocumented student access to colleges and universities emerged. Civil rights activists looked to the 1983 Supreme Court ruling in *Plyler v. Doe* for possible resolution of this new issue. The *Plyler* case dealt with the exclusion of undocumented students from elementary and secondary education in Texas. The Supreme Court ruled in this case that it was unconstitutional to deny undocumented students access to public education. Activist lawyers sought to extend this ruling to the postsecondary level in the late 1980s and early 1990s, but with mixed results.[45]

In the early twenty-first century, several states began to deal with this issue. Texas led the way. In 2001, the Texas legislature enacted H.B. 1403 establishing the right of undocumented college students to establish resident status and pay in-state tuition in the state's public colleges. Other states soon enacted similar laws.[46]

Encouraged by these developments, congressional leaders formulated and sought the enactment of similar bills to facilitate and increase higher educational access for undocumented college students. The first bill, coauthored by the conservative Utah senator, Orrin Hatch, was called the Development, Relief, and Education for Alien Minors (DREAM) Act. This bill, drafted in 2003, sought to remove a provision from federal law that discouraged states from providing in-state tuition status to undocumented college students. It also allowed undocumented students the opportunity to regularize their federal immigration status if they met certain educational requirements or if they served in the US military for two years. Because of opposition from conservative legislators the DREAM Act was not enacted into law.[47] Since then the DREAM Act, in modified form, has been introduced in Congress several times, but it has not passed.[48]

The quest for Chicana/o and Latina/o access to elementary, secondary, and postsecondary education, as indicated above, has been unrelenting, constant, and intense. It has been led by those who desired and envisioned a more equitable system for all public school children regardless of nationality, class, or immigration status.

QUALITY INSTRUCTION IN THE CONTEMPORARY PERIOD

Another major strategy Mexican Americans advocated focused on promoting or improving quality academic instruction. Activists used two major approaches in their struggle for quality instruction. One of these focused on developing or gaining access to innovative curricular and instructional programs aimed at improving the academic achievement of Mexican origin students; the other focused on promoting comprehensive school reforms to ensure the same goal.

Innovative Reforms and the Struggle for Quality Instruction

The historic struggle for quality instruction in particular and the push for more responsive schooling in general intensified after the 1960s. Unlike decades earlier, when the majority of educators, scholars, and policy makers were Anglos, in this period an increasing number of them were Chicanas/os. These individuals were quite diverse and included community activists, practitioners in the schools, intellectuals, and researchers working together to improve the schools serving Chicana/o children.

The initial crop of activists publicly emerged in the late 1960s and presented their works in a variety of state, regional, and national conferences.[49] During the 1970s and 1980s a new crop of activist educators emerged as leaders and played important roles in promoting school reform in general and in struggling for a differentiated curriculum geared toward meeting the diverse needs of Mexican origin students. Among some of the more influential educators and activists of the 1970s and 1980s were individuals such as Carlos E. Cortés, Alfredo Castañeda, Jose Cardenas, Josué González, and Beatriz Arias.[50]

The new activists included not only hundreds of committed laypersons, scholars, teachers, principals, and administrators but also organizations such as the Mexican American Legal Defense and Educational Fund (MALDEF), Intercultural Development Research Association (IDRA), National Association for Bilingual Education (NABE), Mexican American School Board Association (MASBA), the Southwest Educational Development Corporation, and the Advisory Committee on Mexican American Education of the US Office of Education.[51] The latter organization was headed by Armando M. Rodriguez in 1969 and became instrumental in pushing the reform agenda for Chicana/o children at the national level.[52]

In the 1960s, Mexican American activists struggled for and either promoted, supported, or helped establish a variety of curricular innovations aimed at improving the low academic achievement of Mexican origin children in the public schools. Among the most popular were early childhood, migrant, bilingual, and adult education programs.[53] These programs enjoyed widespread support by scholars, educators, community activists, and organizations such as the Southwest Educational Development Corporation and the National Advisory Committee on Mexican American Education of the US Office of Education.[54]

Despite the existence of various worthwhile curricular programs, many

activists began to concentrate on bilingual education by the following decade. Bilingual education was viewed as the best means for bringing about
significant changes in the way the schools educated these children and in
addressing their linguistic, cultural, and academic concerns. The central
purpose of this curricular innovation was to improve the academic achievement of children viewed as limited in their English proficiency. Today these
children are referred to as "English language learners" (ELLS). Academic
achievement would be improved by ensuring the equal access of ELLS to the
mainstream or standard curriculum. The vast majority of these reforms were
concentrated in the elementary grades.[55]

In the mid- and late 1980s activist scholars expanded the discourse on
Chicana/o and Latina/o education and went beyond both language and bilingual education to other concerns and reforms. For over a decade, since the
passage of the federal Bilingual Education Act of 1968, scholars had focused
on language issues in the education of these students and on the establishment and strengthening of bilingual education throughout the country. In
the 1980s, they began to systematically explore factors other than language
that impacted their education and to consider a variety of other curricular
and institutional reforms that would benefit them in the schools. The publication of *Beyond Language: Social and Cultural Factors in the Schooling of Language Minority Children* by the Evaluation, Dissemination, and Assessment
Center at California State University in Los Angeles in 1986 was indicative
of this trend. In this publication, scholars and activists argued that Latina/o
underachievement was due to a host of social and cultural factors other than
language. Among some of the most important identified as impacting their
education were teacher attitudes toward minority groups, cultural values,
parental involvement, group attitudes toward education, historical experiences, language use patterns, and self-identity. Educational programs, in
order to positively impact the academic achievement of these students, the
authors asserted, had to address these concerns in a systematic fashion. Effective school reform, in other words, needed to go beyond language and
beyond bilingual education.[56]

Educators and scholars not only expanded the discourse on underachievement, they also shifted the emphasis of their concerns away from ELLS in
the elementary grades to secondary school-age students who were relatively
proficient in English, but still underachieving. Most of these students, as the
National Commission on Secondary Schooling for Hispanics' report titled
Make Something Happen (1984) noted, attended segregated and overcrowded

inner-city schools, had poor school achievement levels, were disproportionately tracked into vocational and general education programs, dropped out
of school in large numbers, and had low college enrollment. They attended
large impersonal urban schools and their needs were different from those of
English language learners in the elementary grades. These students required
different types of curricular and instructional programs than those in the
elementary grades and more personal attention and support from adults and
from school officials.[57]

The shift from bilingual education in the elementary grades to underachievement in secondary schools was slow. It occurred in the context of
acrimonious debates over bilingual education, affirmative action, and desegregation and a new national concern with the quality of public education.[58]
Beginning in 1983 with a national report noting that the nation was at risk
because of declining academic competitiveness, this movement soon over-
whelmed the equity struggles of the Latina/o community. The 1983 report,
A Nation at Risk, sponsored by the National Commission on Excellence in
Education, urged immediate improvement in the nation's schools and led to
the emphasis on excellence or quality education including: improved standards, a more rigorous curriculum, and accountability.[59] Although this report called for excellence or quality education, many activists and their allies raised questions about its relationship to equity concerns. Peter Roos, a
strong advocate of quality instruction for Latinas/os, for instance, analyzed
the tensions between traditional views of equality and the proposed concepts
of quality. He called not only for quality education but for equity as well.[60]

Working within this context of a national call to action, Chicana/o and
non-Chicana/o activists pressured or compelled federal and state officials to
form special committees or enact legislation to investigate and address the
issue of improving the quality of education for Latina/o youth.[61] Emphasis
in most cases, as noted in *Make Something Happen* (1984), was on publicizing
the devastating impact that high dropout rates and low school achievement
levels were having on minority communities and on American society. This
report likewise proposed recommendations to address these concerns and
encouraged local and state leaders to promote significant reforms, including
curricular changes, to ensure academic success.

The nature of the struggle during the latter decades of the twentieth century thus changed, without great fanfare, from one demanding access to a
differentiated curriculum to one aimed at getting access to a rigorous one. At
the elementary level, activists and scholars interpreted this shift to mean get-

ting access to a rigorous curriculum through quality bilingual education.[62] At the secondary level, they focused on getting access to both a college preparatory and an accelerated curriculum comprised of magnet, gifted and talented programs and advanced placement classes.[63]

Many of these activists contested the continuing disproportionate number of Chicana/o and Latina/o students being provided an average or below average curriculum. Most of the students receiving a below average curriculum were enrolled in slow learning and low ability classes or else in classes for students with mental retardation. In an effort to eliminate the large numbers of Latinas/os being provided a below average curriculum, activists challenged the methods of testing, labeling, and selecting students for these types of classes. They utilized the courts, legislation, executive action, and in some cases, political struggles at the local level to challenge these procedures and processes.[64]

Despite the diversity of approaches and strategies and the multifaceted nature of these curricular struggles, the dominant one revolved around quality bilingual education. This specific curricular innovation was supported for various reasons. It continued to be viewed as the most important means for bringing about significant change in the education of linguistically and culturally distinct children. It united all educators around several central themes in the education of Latinas/os, especially language and culture. It addressed the linguistic, cultural, and academic concerns of these children. For these and other reasons, the quest for access to a rigorous curriculum through quality bilingual education intensified over time. (For an elaboration of this struggle see the next chapter.)

Comprehensive School Reform and the Struggle for Quality Instruction

Chicana/o and Latina/o educators and activists did more than simply promote curricular reforms or innovations. During the 1990s, a select group of educators and community organizations began to promote comprehensive reforms of schools educating Latina/o students. Many of these individuals had bold visions of school change and were successfully initiating curricular, instructional, and administrative changes from within the schools aimed at transforming underachieving schools and districts into high achieving ones. Among the new visionaries during the 1990s and early twenty-first century were Joseph Fernandez and Ramon C. Cortines, both chancellors of New York City during the 1990s; Abe Saveedra, superintendent of the Houston

Independent School District; Michael Hinojosa, superintendent of the Dallas Independent School District; and Hector Montenegro, superintendent of Ysleta Independent School District.

Representative of these new activists was Joseph A. Fernandez, one of the most important and controversial leaders in the field of education during the 1990s. Fernandez was born in New York City during the 1930s, became a dropout in the 1940s, joined the Air Force in the 1950s and then got his GED, BA, and PhD with assistance from the GI Bill. The college degrees were in education. He began teaching in the Dade County Schools in Florida in the late 1960s, got involved in school politics during that period, and soon moved up in the system. By 1975 he had advanced to principal and soon thereafter became superintendent of Dade County Schools. While superintendent of a largely Latina/o school district, he began to lay the groundwork for a number of pilot programs and satellite schools that soon evolved into a comprehensive approach to school reform. In 1990, he became chancellor of the New York City public schools and proposed a comprehensive set of reforms to restructure the New York public school system. This reform program focused on teaching and learning, not governance or administrative issues. Although he did not get to fully implement his program because of political opposition to some of his decisions, especially a condom distribution policy, a pro-homosexual curriculum, and his published memoirs indicating he had used heroine in his earlier years, he set the stage for the most ambitious school restructuring program in the country.[65]

Other Latina/o superintendents followed in Fernandez's footsteps and soon took over the reins of mostly minority school districts and began their ambitious programs of comprehensive school reform. One of the most successful during the early twenty-first century was Hector Montenegro, superintendent of the Ysleta Independent School District (YISD), a small rural community in West Texas. He assumed leadership of the YISD, a low-performing district with a large number of ELL students from low-income families and transformed it into one of the highest performing districts in the state. The district's transformation was achieved by focusing on a variety of comprehensive school reform strategies Montenegro developed over a thirty-year period of teaching and administrative work.[66]

Community organizations also proposed comprehensive school reform plans aimed at promoting quality instruction in particular and improving Chicana/o school success in general. One of these was IDRA, Intercultural Development Research Association. For over four decades, this organization had been in the forefront of school reform and had consistently fought for quality education in American life. In the early twenty-first century, IDRA developed the Quality Schools Action Framework (QSAF). This school reform plan, developed in collaboration with schools and communities in Texas and other parts of the country, offered a model for assessing school outcomes, identifying leverage points for improvement, and focusing on and effecting change.[67]

The model was based on three premises. The first suggested that if the problem were systemic, then the solution had to address schools as systems. The second was that if educators supported student success, then they had to develop a vision that sought outcomes for every child. School success, IDRA noted, was for all children "no matter where they come from, no matter the color of their skin, no matter the side of town they come from, no matter the language they speak." And the third premise of this framework was that schools were not poor because children in them were poor or black or brown. Schools were poor because districts had poor policies, poor practices, and inadequate investments.[68]

PLURALISM

A final strategy activists advocated during these years focused on struggling for pluralism, that is, for the valuing and utilization of the Chicana/o children's historical and cultural heritage in the schools. Prior to the 1960s, the vast majority of schools throughout the country omitted or distorted the historical heritage of ethnic Mexicans in the textbooks and sanctioned the devaluation of their culture in the classrooms and in school activities. During the 1960s activists protested these policies and practices and demanded the inclusion, valuation, and recognition of their historical and cultural heritage in the schools, textbooks, classes, and extracurricular activities.

Contesting Cultural Omission or Distortion

During the 1960s and 1970s activists contested the culturally exclusive policies and practices of local schools and demanded the inclusion of their heritage in the textbooks. Most of the textbooks in these decades said little if anything about the role and contributions of Mexican origin individuals or about any other Latinas/os. Moreover, if any comments were made it was only about Mexican Americans and, as the US Commission on Civil Rights noted in the early 1970s, they usually tended to be "negative or distorted in nature."[69]

The most celebrated case of contestation in this period took place in California when the Textbook Task Force of the Mexican American Education Commission in 1971 "unequivocally" rejected all the basic social science textbooks being considered for adoption by the California State Board of Education.[70] None of the basic texts, according to the task force, met the legal criteria for adoption by the state. Furthermore, it noted that contrary to state law the textbooks under consideration by the board demeaned and misrepresented the role and contributions of most minority groups, including Mexican Americans.[71]

Other minority groups, educators, and organizations, including a new task force of twelve ethnic scholars the state board established, also voiced their opposition to the textbooks.[72] Although textbook publishers made some minor changes, most of the members of this new ethnic task force argued that "the underlying racism of the books was intact and the damaging effect on children had not been diminished."[73] Despite this opposition the board adopted the social science textbooks in March 1972.

Individuals also protested the lack of Chicana/o heritage in the college textbooks, especially those focusing on history. In the early 1970s, for instance, the historian Abraham Hoffman noted the omission of the Mexican American experience in American history textbooks. Hoffman examined the quantity and quality of Mexican American content in a dozen American history surveys published between 1968 and 1971 and concluded that despite the growth of minority militancy in general and community protests in particular American history texts tended to ignore the historical presence and contributions of Mexican Americans or only made "the most elemental references" to them. His investigation of Chicana/o content in American history textbooks, he stated, "was an almost futile exercise in page-turning."[74]

For the next several decades scholars continued to criticize the history profession for failing to include the experiences and contributions of Chicanas/os in the textbooks. Antonia Castañeda, a well-known feminist historian, noted in 1990 that the omission and distortion of Mexican American history, especially that of Chicanas, continued during the 1980s despite the introduction of a multicultural approach to Western history by two feminist scholars in the early part of this decade.[75] Although more sensitive to minorities and women this approach failed to significantly incorporate the experiences of poor working-class Chicanas and other women of racially mixed backgrounds into the histories of the West.[76]

Chicana/o historians continued to critique the field of American history at the turn of the century for its failure to adequately and effectively incorporate the varied experiences of Mexican Americans into the national narrative. In an examination of eight national historical surveys published between 1994 and 1999, for instance, two scholars noted that while these textbooks provided more information on Latinas/os, they failed to develop a consistent narrative around this information, to incorporate individual stories of these individuals, especially women, and to deal with all the contradictions and complexities of this group. Latinas/os were too frequently reduced to numbers or faceless statistics who wandered in and out of the text.[77]

Mexican American Culture and Curricular Reform

Schools, universities, and publishers responded differently to the demands for curricular relevance, that is, for the inclusion of the histories and cultures of minority groups in general and of Mexican Americans in particular in the curriculum. Schools and universities quickly established a few courses on the histories and cultures of specific ethnic minority groups. These types of courses, for the most part, were haphazardly put together and were taught without the appropriate curricular materials and textbooks. Publishers also hurriedly incorporated some ethnic content into their textbooks, but their efforts were limited and inaccurate.[78]

The need for information on the historical, cultural, and contemporary experiences of ethnic minority groups led to two thrusts in the creation of Mexican American studies at the elementary and secondary level. One thrust focused on the creation of Mexican American history textbooks for the elementary and secondary curriculum. The second thrust was pedagogical in nature. It involved the development of approaches to incorporating Mexican American history and culture into the mainstream curriculum and of strategies for teaching this content in the classrooms. The former dealt with curricular development, the latter with pedagogical matters.

Creating Mexican American Ethnic Content in the Public School Curricula

The initial phase of the movement to integrate Chicana/o content into the public schools began with the creation and development in the late 1960s and early 1970s of a Mexican American curriculum, that is, a set of materials and textbooks that focused specifically on the cultural, historical, and contemporary experiences of this group. The rationale for this curriculum was similar to the ethnic studies efforts of the early twentieth century. It was aimed at

14. Folkloric dancers, Crystal City Independent School District, 1970. Courtesy José Angel Gutiérrez Papers, Nettie Lee Benson Latin American Collection, University of Texas Libraries, the University of Texas at Austin. (Kelly Kerbow Hudson, Archival Processing)

improving the thinking and self-esteem of ethnic minority group students, in this case, Chicanas and Chicanos. Activists believed that these students were being miseducated, indoctrinated, or worse, "colonized" because they were being taught about Anglo American or European civilization at the expense of their own great civilizations and cultures.[79] Some felt that they were being "de-ethnicized" and their histories, cultures, and languages repressed and suppressed. The suppression and/or devaluation of their heritage had harmful effects and served to deflate their self-esteem. The ultimate consequences of these actions were low academic achievement and high dropout rates.[80]

The development of Chicana/o curricular materials for the elementary and secondary grades was a gradual and relatively small undertaking because of resistance, the nature of the market, and other factors.[81] Most books written during the 1960s and 1970s were for the elementary grades. A few others were written for the secondary grades.[82] In many cases, these publications contained factual errors, overemphasized the Spanish aspects of the Mexican American heritage, failed to discuss the Chicana/o movement, or were too advanced for use in the elementary and secondary grades.[83] Despite these problems, scholars continued to publish these types of works and teachers continued using them.

Integrating Mexican American Content into Mainstream Curriculum

Although the creation of Chicana/o history textbooks for the elementary and secondary grades, while fraught with inaccuracies, was extremely important, the effort quickly shifted from curriculum development to pedagogy. This led to the second phase of the movement for integrating Mexican American content into the curriculum.

The need for ethnic relevancy led to increased demands for assistance from schoolteachers and administrators. How could teachers incorporate Mexican American content into the curriculum given the lack of knowledge and content on this group? These concerns encouraged curricular activists to focus more on how to teach the Mexican American experience.[84] One of the first scholars to move in this direction was Carlos E. Cortés, a young professor of Chicano history at the University of California at Riverside. In the early 1970s he provided one of the earliest articles on teaching the Chicana/o experience in the public schools. In his article Cortés discussed the major obstacles to teaching this experience, proposed new exploratory concepts for analyzing it, and suggested strategies for teaching about this group.[85] Soon, others followed.[86]

Chicanas/os, as I have suggested above, were not acting alone in this period. They worked in conjunction with others interested in ensuring that the experiences, cultures, and histories of other victimized ethnic minority group children were incorporated into the curriculum. Mexican American Studies, in other words, merged with the larger movement for ethnic studies instruction in the public schools.

During the mid-1970s, curricular activists began to reassess their approaches to the teaching of ethnic studies. James Banks, one of the primary architects of this effort, provided the rationale for this new approach. First, he argued, ethnic studies should go beyond providing knowledge about specific ethnic minority groups and their cultural and historical experiences. Instead, it should provide information about all ethnic groups in general and about the role that ethnicity plays in American life.[87] Second, its goals should be different. It should not be primarily aimed at offering a balanced view of the

American past or present, at giving the ethnic minority group perspective, or at providing a form of liberation for ethnic minority group members. It should help students understand the nature of knowledge, develop their ability to make intelligent decisions, and provide them with social action skills to help resolve problems. To help students develop effective decision-making skills, ethnic studies had to help them master higher-level concepts, generalizations, and theory.[88] Third, ethnic studies should be for all students, not simply members of ethnic minority groups. Ethnic studies was evolving into what would eventually became multiethnic and multicultural education.[89]

Two of the most influential scholars in the movement to integrate ethnic content into the curriculum were Carlos E. Cortés and Sonia Nieto. As mentioned earlier, Cortés began his work as a Chicano Studies scholar in the early 1970s.[90] He exemplified what James A. Banks called the first phase of multicultural education—an educator who sought to incorporate the concepts, information, and theories from Chicana/o history into the school and teacher-education curricula.[91]

Using his knowledge of Chicana/o history, Cortés provided teachers with information of factors limiting effective teaching, suggested teaching strategies useful for studying this experience, identified and evaluated supplementary materials to use in these classes, and encouraged the use of local community resources.[92] In suggesting ways in which teachers could utilize Chicana/o history in the curriculum, Cortés officially joined the multicultural education movement.[93]

Sonia Nieto also became one of the leaders of the multicultural education movement in the 1980s. She focused on the history of Puerto Ricans on the US mainland and on incorporating this into the public school and college curricula.[94] Throughout her professional career, Nieto has written on the sociopolitical context of multicultural education, on the process and goal of teaching and learning in a multicultural environment, teaching as a profession, and linguistic and cultural challenges of teacher education. Her research, in essence, focuses on the primacy of language, culture, and race in learning generally and in teaching specifically.[95]

Mexican American and Chicana/o Studies in the Universities

The process of responding to student and community demands for curricular relevance also occurred at institutions of higher learning. Universities and colleges responded in various ways to these demands. Some of them modified their organizational structures and established institutional units to promote the study of Mexican Americans. Others merely established courses on the histories, cultures, and experiences of Mexican Americans and taught them in different academic units. Chicana/o students, staff, and faculty played key roles in the establishment of these courses and institutional units. The institutional units offering courses on these groups on a consistent basis were known as either Mexican American or Chicana/o Studies departments, centers, and programs. Broader-based courses and units were established in the 1990s. The broad array of courses involving a variety of Latina/o groups came to be known as Latina/o Studies and the institutional units responsible for teaching these classes as Latina/o Studies departments, centers, and programs.[96]

Publishers also hurriedly incorporated some ethnic content into their textbooks, especially American history, but, as in the case of those for the public schools, they were insufficient. Chicana/o educators responded to their meager efforts and initiated a movement to create their own textbooks. This effort quickly led to the development of a new field of study that came to be known as Chicano Studies.[97] Chicano Studies in the universities was part of and contributed to the origins and development of the larger ethnic studies movement that emerged in the United States during the same period.[98]

The field of Chicano and later Chicana Studies, while containing many new elements, was part of a long-standing intellectual tradition within the Mexican origin community. The development of Chicana/o Studies units in universities, however, was more recent and usually referred to the establishment of institutional units to teach ethnic Mexican content at the university level. This part of the chapter focuses more on Chicana/o Studies as a field of inquiry than as an instructional unit in the university.

As in the case of developments at the elementary and secondary grades, the evolution of Chicana/o Studies as a field of study occurred in overlapping phases. The first phase was the creation of the field. The second phase was the push to integrate Chicana/o Studies into the mainstream curriculum. Each of these overlapping phases entailed the activism of significant numbers of faculty, administrators, and students, especially the latter, and led to considerable debate within the university and in the larger society. Many of these debates have yet to be resolved.

ORIGINS AND GROWTH OF CHICANA/O STUDIES

Chicana/o Studies had its roots in the first half of the twentieth century, but it flourished and assumed a distinct identity in the post-1960s era.[99] Two major thrusts were apparent in its development.

One thrust focused on the reprinting of important books and research studies written in earlier decades. Among some of the most important studies reprinted during this period were Carey McWilliams's *North from Mexico: The Spanish Speaking People of the United States* (1948), the first major historical study of this group in the twentieth century, and Manuel Gamio's *Mexican Immigration to the United States* (1930), an excellent study of Mexican immigration to the United States during the first three decades of the twentieth century.[100] Arno Press, a well-known publisher, also issued several significant volumes of older works on Chicanos, Cubans, and Puerto Ricans. This series was edited by the well-respected historian Carlos E. Cortés, who was then at the University of California, Riverside.[101]

A second major thrust in the development of Chicana/o Studies was the publication of new works that focused on the experiences and struggles of ethnic Mexican people in the United States. Most of this new research was conducted by Chicanos and Chicanas. This research eventually became the basis for the emergence of this field in the contemporary period.

Chicana/o Studies research in this period, unlike earlier decades, was much more critical of American society and its treatment of Mexicans. It rejected the master narrative developed by mainstream historians and social scientists and created an alternative view of American development in general and of Chicana/o participation in that development in particular.[102] Chicana/o Studies, noted Pedro A. Cabán, "posed epistemic challenges to the hegemony of the disciplines." Because of its oppositional character, it failed to achieve legitimacy in the academy as existing area studies or other disciplines.[103]

Chicana/o Studies research originated in the midst of a vigorous nationalist movement taking place in the late 1960s and early 1970s. It came to be viewed by many of these activists as a means for facilitating Mexican origin liberation against Anglo or Euro-American oppression.

The need for research linked to social and political change led to what Carlos Muñoz Jr. called a quest for paradigm. Muñoz argued that the crisis confronting the community compelled Chicana/o scholars to "develop new paradigms of research and analysis that will adequately deal with the problem of poverty, alienation, and political powerlessness."[104]

Those committed to the development of a Chicana/o Studies paradigm began to conceptualize the ethnic Mexican experience in the context of colonialism. Influenced by the works of Frantz Fanon, Albert Memmi, Robert Blauner, and others, these scholars conceptualized ethnic Mexicans as an internal colony of the United States. This "paradigm" utilized culture and race as major causal factors in the development of the community.[105]

By the mid-1970s, scholars raised significant questions about this paradigm and its potential for interpreting the Mexican American experiences in the United States. Some called for the incorporation of class analysis into this framework.[106] By the late 1970s, women criticized both their exclusion from the discourse and the exclusion of gender as an analytical category in the analysis of the Chicana/o condition. More specifically, they argued for the inclusion and intersection of race, class, and gender in the analysis of Chicana/o Studies.[107]

In the 1980s, those involved in Chicana/o Studies began a serious and systemic push for integration into the mainstream college curriculum as attacks by conservative politicians and immigration from various parts of the Spanish-speaking world dramatically increased.[108] The struggle to make Chicana/o Studies a part of the mainstream curriculum proved to be especially controversial.

INTEGRATING CHICANA/O STUDIES INTO MAINSTREAM CURRICULUM

During the 1960s and 1970s, most of the courses offered in Chicana/o Studies programs tended to be for the benefit of ethnic Mexican students. By the 1980s, many felt that these types of classes as well as other ethnic studies courses should be for everyone, not simply minority students. A new campaign aimed at integrating Chicana/o Studies and other kinds of ethnic studies courses into the mainstream curriculum was initiated. This effort focused on mandating some kind of ethnic or non-Western studies course for all students.[109] This effort expanded significantly during the following decades.

A variety of reasons were given for mandating ethnic studies classes. Among the main ones were the need to reduce prejudice on campus against minorities, to promote intergroup awareness and understanding, and to correct the historical record of Chicana/o and minority group exclusion.[110]

The push for the integration of Chicana/o and ethnic studies into the mainstream curriculum emerged and contributed to the debate over the role of education in the promotion of a common, that is, Western, tradition. Some, such as William Bennett, Alan Bloom, and E. D. Hirsch Jr., advocated a return to a "common curriculum" based on Western culture and great white men.[111] Others, including ethnic studies activists, argued for a diverse or non-Western, nonmale, nonwhite one.[112] Despite the vociferous nature of this debate, an increasing number of universities added ethnic studies or non-Western courses to their curriculum.[113]

Cultural Heritage and the Informal Curriculum

The struggles to include the Mexican cultural heritage in the schools were more successful than the curricular and institutional reforms in the schools and universities. In the late 1960s, the federal government played a positive role in encouraging the acknowledgment and utilization of Chicana/o culture in the schools. Responding to community political pressures for recognition of their culture, Congress, in 1968, authorized and proclaimed September 15 and 16 as "National Hispanic Heritage Week."[114] This proclamation called upon all Americans, especially educators from across the nation, to observe this week "with appropriate ceremonies and activities." Most educators began to celebrate the accomplishments of Mexican origin individuals and Mexican American contributions to the development of the United States.[115] Numerous websites also were created to "help teachers focus attention on the contributions of people of Hispanic heritage to the history of the United States."[116] In 1988, Congress expanded the observances of Chicanas/os and Latinas/os to a whole month.[117]

Federal recognition of National Hispanic Heritage Month thus encouraged the partial institutionalization of Chicana/o and Latina/o cultures in the schools during these decades. The rapid growth of immigration from Mexico and Central and South America during the latter decades of the twentieth century spurred and expanded the inclusion of their cultures in the schools. By the end of the twentieth century, hundreds of thousands of schools and colleges throughout the country celebrated the cultural traditions of Latinas/os during the school year.

CONCLUSION

The quest for equality as shown above focused as much on advocacy as it did on contestation. Mexican Americans consistently and vociferously advocated for changes in the schools that were reflective of their communities, of their ethnicities, and of their interests. They, in essence, sought schools that were inclusive, pluralistic, and provided quality instruction for their children.

FOUR

Advocating for Quality Instruction: The Case of
Bilingual Education

D espite the diversity of curricular struggles, the dominant one revolved around bilingual education. This curricular innovation was
supported for various reasons. It was viewed as the most important
means for bringing about significant change in the education of Mexican origin children.[1] It united all educators around several central themes in their
education, especially language and culture. It also addressed the children's
linguistic, cultural, and academic concerns. For these and other reasons, the
quest for access to a rigorous curriculum through quality bilingual education
intensified over time.

This struggle was waged on multiple fronts—in Congress, the courts, the
executive branch, the streets, the schools, and the universities. It involved
both Mexican American and non–Mexican American individuals and organizations working together or in coalitions, and it was extremely contentious.
It encountered many obstacles, especially national desegregation mandates;
a lack of clarity on approaches, goals, and objectives; a declining activist federal bureaucracy; and political opposition to it by educators, Anglo parents,
and conservative organizations.

CONTEXTUAL FACTORS, 1960–65

A variety of social, political, and educational developments laid the foundation for the establishment of a federal bilingual education policy in the
1960s. Although local education agencies had to deal with the education of
other non-English-language groups such as Puerto Ricans and Cubans, the
Mexican origin student was the central concern of those initially involved in
shaping this policy. Among the most important factors contributing to its de-

velopment during the first half of the 1960s were bilingual research findings, the civil rights movement, federal legislation, and the emerging Chicana/o movement. These contextual forces brought to light questions about non-English-language instruction in the public schools, the federal role in school change, power and pedagogy, and eventually contributed to the enactment of the federal Bilingual Education Act of 1968.

Research on Bilingualism

Research on bilingualism, that is, on the impact and extent of "non-English languages" in American society, influenced many of the arguments that advocates used to support bilingual education policy. This new research questioned several prominent myths in education dealing with intelligence, achievement, and assimilation.

Since the 1920s research on intelligence and achievement had indicated that bilingualism was an obstacle to success. This research showed a negative relationship between dual language capabilities and intelligence. However, in the early 1960s a gradual shift occurred in this literature. Scholars found that bilingualism was an asset to learning in the schools and that it played a positive role in intelligence.[2] More specifically, they found that bilingual children were either equal to or superior to monolinguals on intelligence tests and in other areas of language usage.[3]

Bilingual research studies also questioned the myth of underachievement based on language barriers. These new studies indicated that in conjunction with other reforms, "non-English" or native language instruction, rather than retard school performance, could improve school achievement in general.[4] For instance, Annie Stemmler in 1964 stumbled onto the idea that Spanish language instruction could improve Mexican American children's attitudes toward themselves and toward school. Stemmler found this unexpectedly because her research project initially focused on the impact of all-English instruction on the education of Mexican American children in San Antonio. In order to control for the degree of native language hindrance of English acquisition she used the all-Spanish instruction approach. Instead of hindering learning she found that the Spanish only approach improved school performance and ethnic identity. Based on this finding she wrote that "we became aware of the tremendous positive impact of according Spanish an accepted role in the traditionally English-speaking classroom."[5]

The new studies also indicated that bilingualism could improve second language acquisition in particular. One such study found that Spanish-speaking children instructed bilingually tended to perform as well in English language skills and in the content areas as comparable students taught only in English. At the same time, these children were developing language skills in Spanish. Anglo students in bilingual programs were not adversely affected in their English language development and in the content subjects and were learning a second language, Spanish.[6]

This new research likewise raised questions about assimilation. Traditional theory argued that ethnicity in general and ethnic minority languages in particular would disappear over time as a result of ethnic group assimilation into American life. Research on bilingualism, however, indicated that certain minority groups in the United States maintained their language abilities over time.[7] Bilingualism, in other words, was not disappearing but being maintained and, in some cases, increasing. Much of this was due to the language maintenance efforts among the French-speaking groups in the northeast and the Spanish-speaking population in the Southwest.[8]

Studies on bilingualism reinforced the work of scholars such as Nathan Glazer and Daniel Moynihan who argued that people maintained their cultural identities and felt close affiliation to those of the same group. According to them, cultural and linguistic pluralism was a much more common phenomenon than previously assumed. Ethnic and language minority groups, they noted, were not melting and ethnicity was not declining as rapidly as many scholars had believed.[9]

The Civil Rights Movement

A second factor contributing to the foundations of bilingual education legislation was the civil rights movement. The growing strength of the African American struggle for voting rights, equal employment, and an end to segregation in public facilities, as well as the enactment of civil rights policies, focused attention on the presence of racial discrimination in American life. The civil rights movement also suggested new means for eliminating discriminatory policies and practices, including the use of protest, demonstrations, pickets, and increased federal involvement.[10]

Language scholars and ethnic minority activists strongly supported the civil rights movement. They, however, began to argue that discrimination was not simply based on race but on other factors such as national origin, religion, and gender. In the case of Spanish-speaking children and with respect to bilingual education arguments, civil rights leaders and educators began to emphasize the impact and significance of discrimination based on language and culture. This type of discrimination, many activists and scholars argued, negatively impacted the school achievement of Mexican Americans in particular and language minority children in general.[11]

These activists also began to argue that the federal government had a responsibility for overcoming all forms of discrimination. Like racial discrimination, many of them noted, inequitable treatment on the basis of language and culture could be eliminated in the schools with the support of the federal government.[12]

The War on Poverty Legislation

The enactment of poverty legislation also influenced the arguments for bilingual education. This type of legislation led to a renewed consideration of poverty and educational underachievement especially among language minority groups in general and Spanish-speaking minority children in particular. It also encouraged individuals to look for a stronger federal role in eliminating poverty.

The federal government discovered poverty in the early 1960s and declared war on it. Education became instrumental in winning this War on Poverty. With respect to public education, Congress enacted two major pieces of legislation aimed at developing social and educational programs to meet this federal goal—the Economic Opportunity Act of 1964 and the Elementary and Secondary Education Act (ESEA) of 1965. The former, among other things, required the involvement of poor parents in the development and implementation of federal programs. The latter provided funds to public schools and led to a renewed emphasis on eliminating poverty through education.[13]

Although most liberal activists supported the ESEA, many of them challenged its failure to address the concerns of Mexican American and other Latina/o children. The federal programs encouraged by this legislation, some of these educators and activists argued, were geared toward meeting only the needs of English-speaking students and did not take into consideration the special needs of poor Spanish-speaking children. Compensatory and remedial programs developed under ESEA also failed to recognize the impact that discrimination had on the ethnic identity and scholastic progress of language minority children.[14] Advocates of Mexican American education argued that English-only laws, no-Spanish-speaking policies, unwillingness to hire Mexican Americans teachers, school segregation, and other discriminatory practices had the effect of lowering their self-esteem. This in turn eventually led to the school failure of Mexican origin students.[15]

A few activists, especially language specialists, also argued that English-only laws and practices led to the waste of necessary national language resources that could benefit the country.[16]

Activists and Cultural Pluralism

Finally, the emerging Chicana/o movement became an important ingredient in the rationale for bilingual education. The activists of the 1960s viewed themselves as being culturally victimized, structurally excluded by the dominant society and its institutions, including the schools, and controlled by an Anglo political and economic elite not interested in their academic or societal progress.[17] Unwilling to accept these conditions anymore, they challenged the cultural and political hegemony of the dominant groups and promoted significant reforms in the schools, including bilingual education.

Mexican American activists supported bilingual education for at least three reasons. First, they viewed this program as a strategy for the structural inclusion of those elements that had been historically excluded from the schools in the past—the Spanish language, Mexican culture, and the Mexican origin community.[18] Second, many activists viewed bilingual education as "a vehicle for institutional change."[19] Although a few of them initially were suspicious of this program,[20] most came to believe that its development could lead to the elimination of school discrimination and to significant changes in curricular and instructional policies.[21] This particular view of bilingual education was best summarized by Manuel Ramirez III when he said, "We must view bilingual programs not only as providing opportunities for introducing the Spanish language, Mexican history, and Mexican American history into the system, but as vehicles for restructuring that system to insure the academic survival of Chicano children and the political and economic strength of the Chicano community."[22] Third, many activists saw this reform as a means to deal more effectively with cultural assimilation. Initially, supporters looked at this program as a way to help Mexican American children adjust to the Anglo culture of the school. But over the years, it came to be viewed as a means for preserving the Spanish language and Mexican culture of the ethnic Mexican community. Bilingual education, noted Atilano A. Valencia, the director of related programs for Chicanos at the Southwestern Cooperative Educational Laboratory in Albuquerque, was "a quest for bilingual survival."[23]

Impact of Context on Bilingual Education Proponents

These overlapping contextual factors had significant implications for society in general and for the education of ethnic Mexican children in particular. With respect to the social implications, these studies added new dimensions to domestic issues of civil rights and poverty. More specifically, they extended the definition of discrimination to include language and culture. They also reinforced the notion that poverty had a linguistic dimension. These new studies likewise led to new attitudes toward bilingualism and bilinguals. Non-English languages came to be viewed in a positive light and as a precious resource that should be conserved. Bilinguals also came to be viewed more positively during these years. Finally, these studies seriously questioned the reality of the melting pot theory and provided support for cultural pluralism in American life.

These contextual forces also had educational implications. They led to a reassessment of specific educational practices that had detrimental impact on the ethnic identity and academic performance of poor Spanish-speaking children. Among these practices were English-only laws, no-Spanish-speaking rules, and structural exclusion of Mexican Americans from public education. Finally, they led to the promotion of language and culture-based school reforms such as the hiring of Spanish-speaking teachers, the incorporation of Spanish and Mexican American culture into public education, and the repeal of English-only and no-Spanish-speaking policies.

ENACTMENT

Professional educators took advantage of the confluence of these factors and initiated the contemporary push for federal bilingual education legislation in the mid-1960s. Newly enfranchised Chicana/o activists, civil rights groups, and educational activists soon joined them. The National Education Association (NEA), the largest group of educators in the country, was instrumental in facilitating the work of those interested in improving the education of Mexican origin children through federal legislation. In 1965 it conducted a survey of the education of Spanish-speaking children in the schools throughout the Southwest and published the report the following year. This report publicized the negative impact of the schools on their cultural identity and academic performance. It documented many of the discriminatory educational policies affecting these children and argued that they contributed to low school performance and to alienation from the larger society. Traditional school policies and practices such as rigid "Anglicization" practices, English-only policies, no-Spanish-speaking rules, and cultural degradation, the report argued, led to "damaged" self-esteem, resentment, psychological withdrawal from school, and underachievement.[24]

This report not only documented the major problems confronting educators, it also proposed bilingualism as a solution for improving their education. Bilingualism, it argued, could help overcome decades of cultural degradation caused by rigid assimilationist policies and improve academic achievement.[25] If schools hired Spanish-speaking teachers and adapted their curricular and administrative practices to the cultural and intellectual needs of these children, it further argued, their self-esteem, cultural identity, and school performance would improve.[26]

The findings of this report served several important functions. First, the findings presented a challenge to the dominant ideology of the causes of underachievement. According to existing views, poor school performance was due to the children's cultural background. Minority children, including Spanish-speaking children, the cultural deficit view stated, were not interested in education or did not desire it strongly enough as did other groups. The lack of motivation and desire thus accounted for their underachievement.[27] The NEA report presented an alternative view. Discriminatory as well as traditional and nonaccommodating school policies and practices, not the children's linguistic or cultural backgrounds, it argued, were responsible for underachievement.[28]

Second, the NEA report challenged the dominant belief of assimilation. This belief held that all individuals would eventually abandon their "foreign" languages and cultures and accept the idealized version of "American culture" as embodied in the Anglo-conformity or melting pot idea. Spanish-speaking children, it argued, were not melting and abandoning their linguistic and cultural heritage. This report also questioned whether assimilationism was an appropriate goal for the public schools. Bilingualism and cultural pluralism were more desirable goals than "melting potism," it argued.[29]

Unfortunately, the survey was unable to make a complete break with the dominant explanation of school performance. It still accepted the cultural deficit model as illustrated in the constant recognition of "handicaps" held by the Spanish-speaking children. Although it viewed the children's language as an asset for improving self-esteem and achievement it continued to refer to it as a handicap. This implied that the school's role was to overcome this language handicap by helping children learn English. English acquisition was to come at the expense of Spanish, or so this cultural deficit model implied. Despite these shortcomings, the NEA report represented a viable alternative to dealing with the problem of low achievement among Spanish-speaking children in the Southwest.[30]

Finally, this report helped unify the diverse groups of educators and activists interested in improving the education of Mexican American students in the Southwest. It also began the chain of events that eventually led to the enactment of the federal Bilingual Education Act of 1968 and to the increased participation of Mexican Americans in this struggle.

In late 1966, the NEA sponsored a planning conference to educate national, state, and local policy makers about the problems and solutions delineated in the 1965 survey findings. It also sought to encourage them to enact a federal Bilingual Education Act that would serve the needs of these schoolchildren. Under the guidance and leadership of Monroe Sweetland, conference organizers invited legislators, educators, researchers, and a variety of special interest groups, including Mexican American activists to the Tucson conference. At the conference and through a variety of discussion sessions, participants were informed about the dimensions of the educational problems confronting schools with large numbers of Spanish-speaking students and the role that bilingual education could play in overcoming them. Policy makers were encouraged to enact such bills, and the special interest groups were encouraged to build mass support for their enactment by hosting other state conferences.[31]

Several months after the Tucson conference, Ralph Yarborough, a US senator from Texas, introduced the first Bilingual Education Act in the United States. Two members of his staff, Alan Mandel and Gene Godley, worked with Monroe Sweetland, Guadalupe Anguiano, and Armando Rodriguez to draft this bill.[32] Sweetland and Anguiano had worked on the NEA report and on the Tucson conference, Rodriguez was the first Mexican American appointed by President Lyndon Johnson to the US Office of Education.[33] In order to appeal to other legislators outside of the Southwest, the bill was expanded to include all Spanish-speakers in the United States. During the negotiating process, legislators expanded the definition of those to be served further to include not only Spanish-speaking students but also all non-English-speaking students in the country. Despite its expansion, the emphasis of this policy was on Mexican origin schoolchildren.

In early January 1967, Senator Ralph Yarborough introduced the Bilingual American Education Act into the US Senate. "Mr. President, the time for action is upon us," he said upon introducing this bill. Mexican Americans have not achieved equality of opportunity in this country, he noted, and they have been the victims of "the cruelest form of discrimination" in the schools. He further added, "English only policies, no-Spanish-speaking rules, and cultural degradation have caused great psychological harm to these children and contributed to their poor performance in school and high dropout rates. Bilingual education can overcome many of these problems and improve their academic achievement."[34]

Although this bill suggested many activities, the most important were those involving the use of the Spanish language. "Among Spanish-Americans," Yarborough stated, "the teaching of the Spanish language and culture to pupils who speak but do not read the language may provide a basis for motivation and an opportunity for achievement not previously accorded the group."[35]

During the next eleven months support for bilingual education came from a variety of community organizations, civil rights groups, minority activists, and Spanish-speaking individuals such as Mexican Americans and Puerto Ricans. President Lyndon Baines Johnson, the Commissioner of Education, and a few politicians including Henry B. Gonzalez, Democratic congressperson from San Antonio, and John B. Connally, Democratic governor of Texas, did not support the enactment of the Bilingual Education Act. They were political enemies of Yarborough or else felt that the types of activities the bilingual bill proposed could be developed under Title I of the Elementary and Secondary Education Act.[36]

External support for bilingual education came from the NEA, Mexican American and Puerto Rican activists, and a few state departments of education. These groups or agencies, at the urging of the NEA or in cooperation with this organization, held a variety of conferences throughout the Southwest in support of finding solutions to the education of Mexican American students. Four follow-up conferences were held in April 1967. Three of these were in California (Fresno, Bakersfield, and Los Angeles) and one was in San Antonio, Texas. The final conference was held in Pueblo, Colorado, in the fall of 1967. In all of these conferences, the participants passed strong resolutions in support of bilingual education legislation.[37]

Legislators within the US Congress provided internal support for bilingual education. Key legislators held hearings in three states with significant numbers of Spanish-speaking children—Texas, California, and New York—and encouraged supporters to speak on behalf of this bill. Congressional allies also ensured that the bill passed both houses without serious modifications. In order to ward off potential opposition to the bill, the Senate Committee on Labor and Public Welfare adopted it as an amendment to the Elementary and Secondary Education Act of 1965. While this assured its passage in Congress, it also linked it up to poverty legislation and to its association with the War on Poverty.[38]

Individuals and groups supported this legislation for different reasons. Educators, as noted above, thought that this was the best instrument for improving achievement among these children. Bilingual education, especially the use of the child's native language, would help eliminate obstacles to achievement and promote cultural pride and self-worth. Others felt that bilingual education could be an instrument of comprehensive educational change and reinforce home-school relations. Others still, especially the emerging Chicana/o movement advocates and language specialists, viewed bilingual education as an instrument of cultural and linguistic preservation.[39]

The Bilingual Education Act was enacted by Congress in December 1967 and signed into law one month later by President Lyndon Baines Johnson.[40]

In its final version, the bill targeted all children who were limited in their ability to speak English. The purpose of the Bilingual Education Act of 1968 was twofold: (1) to encourage the recognition of the special educational needs of limited-English-speaking children and (2) to provide financial assistance to local educational agencies to develop and carry out new and imaginative public school programs designed to meet these special educational needs. The bill authorized a total of $85 million for a three-year period. These funds could be used for a variety of purposes, including planning, developing, and establishing "programs designed to meet the special educational needs of children of limited English-speaking ability in high poverty areas." Some funds could also be used to provide pre-service and in-service training for teachers, miscellaneous professional staff, and paraprofessionals involved in these programs. The bill likewise mandated the Commissioner of Education to establish in the Office of Education an Advisory Committee on the Education of Bilingual Children to provide advice on the implementation of this policy.[41]

EXPANSION: CHANGED CHARACTER

Although activists desired comprehensive reforms to improve the education of Mexican American and all other language minority children, they managed to enact only a minor piece of federal legislation. The bill—the Bilingual Education Act of 1968—was programmatically small, categorical in nature, compensatory in intent, and unclear or vague in its purposes and goals.[42]

During the next decade, however, activists strengthened and helped transform this minor piece of legislation aimed at low-income, limited-English-speaking students into a major reform aimed at all children. Activists made several significant changes to federal bilingual policy. They expanded the scope of federal legislation, sought to eliminate its compensatory features, expanded its goals to include bilingualism and biculturalism, and made the policy mandatory.

Expand Scope of Federal Legislation

In 1968 the Bilingual Education Act was categorical in nature. In keeping with federal legislative tradition, funding under the new bill was to be used by local educational agencies (LEAs) to develop innovative educational programs for specific categories of children, that is, poor schoolchildren with limited-English-speaking abilities. By the time it was reauthorized in 1974, the scope of bilingual education legislation expanded to include more wide-ranging activities. In this year, the emphasis of legislation shifted from providing financial assistance for the development of innovative educational programs to improving the "capacity" of local school officials to provide bilingual education. This meant that bilingual education legislation would now provide funds for several types of activities. In addition to funding the development of educational programs, it would also provide funds for professional and teacher-training development, curriculum development, research and data collection, and federal administration of bilingual education.[43] With respect to the latter, for instance, the bill led to the establishment of a national office of bilingual education, a national advisory group of bilingual education, and a national clearinghouse on bilingual education.[44] Congress strengthened these types of "capacity-building" activities in 1978.[45]

The expanding scope of bilingual education legislation was also reflected in funding patterns. Funding for bilingual education increased appreciably from $7.5 million to over $138 million between fiscal year 1969 and fiscal year 1978. (The fiscal year ran from October 1 to September 30).[46]

This increase in funds was a gradual and contested process. Although there was no overt opposition to the passage of this bill, the White House created obstacles. Under pressure from the White House, Congress failed to fund it during the fiscal year of its enactment.[47]

Despite White House opposition, Joshua Fishman argued that the major reason for no funding was due to lack of follow-up by the proponents of bilingual education. According to him, the proponents, new to national politics, had not realized that legislation was a never-ending process. Although Congress authorized a new program, no funds had been appropriated. In order to receive funds the proponents also had to lobby the appropriations committee. Instead, most of them left Washington after the bill was enacted and none remained to lobby for an appropriation for this piece of legislation.[48]

Fishman not only criticized the proponents of bilingual education for leaving town, he also called for the establishment of a bilingual education lobby and for closer ties with a variety of ethnic and educational groups that might serve as allies for bilingual education.[49] His suggestions were soon implemented in the struggle to strengthen this policy.

Pressures from different interests groups, especially Mexican American federal officials and community organizations, eventually led to the funding of this bill. Between 1968 and 1969, for instance, funding for bilingual education programs increased from zero level funding to $7.5 million. Four years later it increased to $75 million. By 1978, funding for bilingual education was at $138 million.[50] Although funding levels were still relatively small in contrast to that of Title I and other federal programs, they increased appreciably during the 1970s.

Modify Program: From Compensatory to Enrichment

The proponents of bilingual education also changed the compensatory character of this policy. They turned it into an enrichment program serving not only low income, limited-English-speaking children but also all children regardless of language ability, ethnicity, or social class.

Bilingual education was enacted into law as part of the War on Poverty programs. Poverty programs, in general, were based on the theory of cultural deprivation, that is, the idea that the cultural values, languages, and dialects minority children spoke accounted for their poor school performance.

With respect to Mexican Americans, the Spanish language and cultural values they shared were viewed as a deficit or as obstacles to learning. In order to succeed these children had to abandon them and acquire English. Compensatory programs such as bilingual education were aimed at overcoming these types of deficits.[51]

Because most legislators and educators viewed it as a compensatory program, bilingual education targeted only those children who were low income and limited in their ability to speak English. "The Congress hereby finds that one of the most acute educational problems in the United States is that which involves millions of children of limited-English-speaking ability because they come from environments where the dominant language is other than English," noted Congress in the first section of the Bilingual Education Act. "The urgent need," it further elaborated, "is for comprehensive and cooperative action now on the local, State, and Federal levels to develop forward-looking approaches to meet the serious learning difficulties faced by this substantial segment of the Nation's school-age population."[52]

Soon after its enactment, the advocates began to eliminate the compensatory features of this policy so that all children in the United States, regardless of socioeconomic status or language ability, could enroll in these programs. Their first success came with the publication of the regulations for implementing bilingual education in 1969. In these guidelines supporters of bilingual education deleted the poverty criteria for participation so that all limited-English-proficient children could be eligible, not simply those who were low income. They also developed a new regulation allowing English speakers to participate. "In an area eligible for a Title VII project," the regulations stated, "children from environments where the dominant language is English are eligible to participate when their participation is such as to enhance the effectiveness of the program."[53]

In 1974 the bilingual education bill incorporated the regulatory changes eliminating poverty as a requirement for participation in this program and allowing English speakers to enroll as well.[54] Four years later, the reauthorized bill set a limit as to the percentage of English-speaking students eligible for participation in these programs. In this year, it stipulated that up to 40 percent of children in bilingual education could be English speakers.[55]

The 1974 and 1978 bilingual education bills also added Native American children as an eligible population. In earlier years, the emphasis had focused primarily on children who spoke European languages and had not made provisions for children who spoke Indian languages and dialects.[56]

These new provisions helped to transform bilingual education from a compensatory to an enrichment program. Whereas before only low-income, limited-English-proficient children were eligible for bilingual instruction, by 1978 English-speaking children as well as language minority children, regardless of socioeconomic status or language ability, could enroll in these types of programs.

Despite these policy and regulatory changes, most educators, legislators, and laypersons continued to view bilingual education as a compensatory program and as part of the War on Poverty. Much of this had to do with the attitude they had toward the targeted population. Most individuals still viewed language minority children in deficit terms, as lacking in their ability to speak English.[57] The failure to speak English, in turn, was viewed as an obstacle to academic performance. Although the label used to target these individuals gradually expanded and changed from limited-English-speaking ability to limited-English-proficiency the idea of "deficiency" continued to permeate bilingual policy and practice.[58]

From Teaching English to Bilingualism and Biculturalism

The 1968 bilingual bill acknowledged the existence of "serious learning difficulties" faced by children who were limited in their ability to speak English and who came from poverty backgrounds. It also provided funds to local school districts "to develop and carry out new and imaginative elementary and secondary school programs" designed to meet the special educational needs of these children.[59] This bill, however, did not specify any goals, nor did it recommend a particular program, approach, or methodology. It merely stipulated that among the approved activities were: bilingual education, teaching the history and culture of the targeted population, improving school-community relations, early childhood education, adult education, vocational education, dropout programs, or "other activities which meet the purposes of this title."[60] Although bilingual education was mentioned as an approved activity, the legislation did not define what this was, neither did it specify the role of native language instruction in this program.

Lack of clarity on policy goals led to a public debate about what the purposes of this policy should be.[61] Although the initial framers of this policy sought to use bilingual education primarily as a means for improving academic achievement, during the 1970s the debate shifted to other concerns. Bilingual education, some argued, was an instrument for learning English.

Others argued that it was an approach for maintaining the child's native language and his/her cultural heritage.

In 1974 legislators attempted to clarify the goal of federal policy and provided a definition of bilingual education. The policy goal became one of providing equal educational opportunity for all children through the establishment and operation of bilingual education programs. Few, if any, individuals or organizations raised concerns about this policy goal. Most, if not all, actors involved in policy formation were in agreement with this broad goal. Despite this consensus, disagreements, misinterpretations, and conflicts emerged over the goals implied in the definition of bilingual education. The reauthorized bill, for instance, defined bilingual education as "instruction given in, and study of, English and, to the extent necessary to allow a child to progress effectively through the educational system, the native language of the children of limited-English-speaking ability." Additionally, it stipulated that "such instruction is given with appreciation for the cultural heritage of such children."[62] An additional provision of the bill likewise allowed English-speaking children to enroll in this program in order "that they may acquire an understanding of the cultural heritage of the children of limited-English-speaking ability for whom the particular programs of bilingual education is designed."[63]

The inclusion of native language instruction and cultural appreciation in the definition of bilingual education led to the origins of a contentious public debate over the goals of this policy. Should bilingual education use the children's native language only until they could speak English, or should it maintain their native language even after they learned English? The former model was called transitional bilingual education, the latter maintenance bilingual education.[64] Also, should the government promote assimilation or should it promote the preservation of ethnic minority cultures?

Most proponents of this policy interpreted this definition to mean that bilingual education had two major goals—the promotion of bilingualism and of cultural pluralism. For years, language specialists, educators, Latina/o activists, and others had supported using federal legislation to preserve the distinct languages and cultures of ethnic minority groups.[65] Their inclusion in the 1974 bill suggested that they had succeeded in reaching this objective.[66] The children enrolled in this program now would learn English and maintain their native language, they argued. They also would receive instruction in their "native" culture as they learned English.

Political leaders within the Office of Education vehemently disagreed with this interpretation and argued that bilingual education legislation was consistently clear—the purpose of bilingual education during the 1970s was "to achieve competence in the English language."[67] Although the bill allowed for the use of the native language and of the "native" culture, they were merely means to an end, not ends in themselves. The undersecretary for education, Frank Carlucci, best stated the Department of Health, Education and Welfare's position on bilingual education in early December 1974. He stated:

> A frequent misunderstanding which seems to have provoked unnecessary and fruitless debate over bilingual policy is the failure to distinguish the goals of bilingual/bicultural programs from the means of achieving them. P.L. 93–380 (the Bilingual Education Act of 1974) emphasizes strongly that "a primary *means* by which a child learns is through the use of such child's language and cultural heritage . . . and that children of limited English-speaking ability benefit through the fullest utilization of multiple language and cultural resources." But the law makes it equally clear that the ultimate goal of Federal bilingual education programs is "to demonstrate effective ways of providing for children of limited English-speaking ability, instruction designed to enable them, while using their native language, *to achieve competence in the English language.*"[68] (emphasis in original)

Carlucci's comments in many ways were more accurate than the interpretations offered by the proponents of bilingual education. Although the bilingual bill acknowledged the role that the native language could play while targeted children learned English, it did not promote bilingual education as an enrichment program where the native language was maintained.[69] Neither did it help to preserve the minority cultures. The primary goals of bilingual education, in other words, were English fluency and cultural assimilation.

The primacy of English learning, in fact, continued to be reflected in policy and program development for the next several years. In 1978 greater emphasis was placed on the goal of English learning in the new bilingual education bill. Unlike four years earlier when Congress encouraged the use of native languages in order to allow a child to progress through the educational system, in 1978 it stipulated that the reason for its use was "to allow a child to achieve competence in the English language." Congress also reaffirmed the importance of English learning as a goal in its reference to the participation of English speakers in bilingual education programs. According to the new bill the objective of their participation was "to assist children of limited English proficiency to improve their English language skills."[70]

Research and evaluation studies, likewise, indicated that the vast majority of bilingual programs during the 1970s were aimed at discouraging the use of the child's native language and at facilitating language shift among these children.[71]

From Voluntary to Mandatory

The proponents of bilingual education also strengthened this program through the courts, federal agencies, and the legislature. Initially, bilingual program participation was voluntary. In the enactment of this bill in 1968, Congress continued the principle of local control by allowing local school districts the option of participating in this federal program. By 1978 the option to participate had disappeared. All local educational agencies had to establish a bilingual education program if they had significant numbers of limited-English-speaking students. Failure to establish bilingual education would lead to a lawsuit or to a withdrawal of all federal school funds.

Civil rights policies became instrumental in the trend away from voluntary to mandatory policies and toward a federal preference for bilingual education approaches. In certain respects, then, bilingual education involved more than meeting the educational needs of these students; it also became a tool for ensuring their civil rights, that is, for ensuring that language minority group children were not discriminated against on the basis of their language or cultural heritage.

Four specific policies and actions—the *Lau v. Nichols* decision of 1974, the Equal Educational Opportunity Act of 1974 (EEOA), the Lau Remedies of 1975, and the Lau compliance reviews—added a mandatory aspect to federal bilingual education policy.[72] These policies mandated the participation of all school districts with significant numbers of language minority group children in bilingual education program development. They also narrowed the choices available to local school districts by discounting the use of English as a Second Language (ESL) methods and by mandating only methods that utilized the child's native languages and cultures.

The *Lau v. Nichols* decision was the result of local school officials in San Francisco that did not take advantage of the bilingual bill to establish programs aimed at improving the schooling of non-English-speaking children in the school district.[73] In this case the non-English students were Chinese.

In *Lau*, the Supreme Court ruled that it was unconstitutional for local school officials to deny non-English-speaking Chinese students instructional services in a language they understood. It also ruled that local school districts had to take affirmative steps to overcome the language "deficiency" these children experienced in order to open its instructional program to them. Although it did not mandate bilingual education, the decision did increase the local school's responsibility in ensuring that non-English-speaking children received an appropriate instruction in the schools.[74]

The decision was based not on the constitutional denial of equal protection but on the statutory and regulatory decisions pertaining to equal educational opportunity. More specifically, it reaffirmed the importance of the May 25 memo drafted by the Office for Civil Rights in 1970.[75] Prior to this year, all existing antidiscrimination laws applied to African Americans. None made reference to children who were culturally and linguistically different. To remedy the absence of Mexican Americans in federal programs, the federal government, in 1970, developed a wide-ranging policy known as the Memorandum of May 25, 1970 that stipulated the responsibilities of local school districts to non-English-speaking students. In general, it stipulated that discrimination on the basis of national origin in general and language in particular was prohibited in any agency receiving federal funds.[76]

The *Lau* decision had a significant impact on federal legislation.[77] Seven months after the ruling Congress enacted a new law that incorporated the Supreme Court findings. This new piece of federal legislation—the Equal Educational Opportunity Act of 1974 (EEOA)—prohibited discrimination against faculty, staff, and students and racial segregation of students. It also required school districts to take action to overcome barriers to students' equal participation. This law, in effect, as noted two legal scholars, "extended Lau to all public school districts, not just those receiving federal financial assistance."[78]

The following year, the Office for Civil Rights issued a document that came to be known as the Lau Remedies. This document was issued in response to many local school officials who did not know how to interpret the *Lau* decision. It specified the remedies available to school districts for eliminating those educational practices ruled unlawful under the *Lau* decision.

The Lau Remedies unfortunately created more problems for school officials and increased their opposition to bilingual education as well as to the federal government's involvement in it. This document discredited English language approaches to educating language minority children and declared that bilingualism was the only appropriate approach for improving educational access to the curriculum and school performance.[79] Acceptable programs for complying with the Lau Decision of 1974 included any one or a combination of the following: transitional, bilingual/bicultural, and multilingual/multicultural programs. None of these programs were clarified, but they all stipulated the use of non-English languages and cultures in instruction.[80] This document, in summary, established a federal preference for bilingual education.

In addition to these procedures the federal government also developed an elaborate civil rights enforcement mechanism and pressured local school districts to develop bilingual education programs. Although there were programmatic and interpretational problems and even opposition to the Lau Remedies, the Office for Civil Rights used it to negotiate compliance plans with over five hundred local school districts in the late 1970s. Coercion or the threat of coercion and the withdrawal of federal school funds served as the basis for the development of bilingual education programs.[81]

The various court rulings, especially the *Lau v. Nichols* Supreme Court ruling of 1974, the passage of the Equal Educational Opportunities Act of 1974, the Lau Remedies of 1975, and the civil rights enforcement effort by the Office of Civil Rights during the mid-1970s, led to mandates forcing all local school districts with significant numbers of non-English-speaking children to establish federal bilingual education programs. Local school districts by the late 1970s had no choice but to develop these programs. Participation in these programs was no longer a matter of choice but a legal mandate.

Despite the growth of bilingual education policies and programs during the 1970s, the majority of them tended to be assimilationist or "subtractive" in nature. These policies and programs, in other words, did not maintain or promote non-English languages in the schools, they tended to accelerate and facilitate the learning of English among language minority children at the expense of the first language.[82] Their subtractive nature, however, was overlooked by many individuals who saw the growth of non-English-language usage in public life as a threat to the political stability and cultural uniformity of this country.

DESEGREGATION V. BILINGUAL EDUCATION IN THE 1970s

Although successful in transforming bilingual education, the proponents of this curricular policy experienced challenges beyond political opposition or program misunderstanding. One of the most important challenges during the 1970s was another federal mandate—desegregation policy. This policy, embodied in judicial mandates, federal legislation, and executive actions issued between the mid-1950s and the 1970s, required the dispersal of minority students, including Mexican Americans. Bilingual education, on the other hand, often required the concentration of non-English-speaking minority students in order to bring together a critical mass of teaching resources.

Different Supreme Court decisions and policy statements supported both of these potentially clashing positions. The judicial basis for desegregation was the *Brown v. Board of Education* ruling in 1954, which prohibited racial segregation in education. The judicial support for bilingual education was the *Lau v. Nichols* decision of 1974, which ruled that local school districts had to take affirmative steps to overcome the language "deficiency" language minority students experienced.[83]

Mexican American activists and their allies did not perceive the requirement to provide special language programs to non-English language students as clashing with the requirement to desegregate the public schools. They believed that bilingual education could be effectively incorporated into desegregated settings.[84] However, a federal court in the Denver desegregation case in 1975 (*Keyes v. School District Number One*) shattered this illusion. It found that bilingual education was not a substitute for desegregation and had to be subordinate to a plan of school desegregation.[85] Gradually, unimpressive results led to diminished support for desegregation among Mexican origin activists and support for bilingual education flagged in the face of organized opposition to the concept. Fragile coalitions that had fought together for both programs weakened once there was no longer a common programmatic goal.

EMERGENCE OF OPPOSITION

Although bilingual education suffered setbacks during this period, they were not always obvious to the casual observer. The prevalence and growth of bilingual education, in addition to other social, economic, and political factors, created fears and anxieties among Americans of all colors, classes, and genders. These developments, especially the mandatory aspects of this policy and its alleged promotion of non-English languages and cultures, also sparked a vigorous opposition to bilingual education among federal policy makers, local school officials, administrators, and laypersons. In the latter part of the 1970s, this opposition was highly disorganized and limited primarily to journalists and researchers. This changed in the 1980s and 1990s.

During these decades, opposition to bilingual education became highly organized and was led by Republican officeholders in the executive and legislative branches of the federal government. Special interest groups, especially English-only organizations, conservative educators, and parent groups, soon joined the battle against bilingual education. Mexican American activists and their allies vigorously fought back every step of the way.

Although contested, the opponents pursued two major strategies—an ideological one aimed at attacking the empirical basis of bilingual education and a political one of repealing or modifying federal bilingual education policy.

Attacking Bilingual Education

The first major strategy attacked the empirical basis of federal bilingual education. In the early 1980s executive opponents within the Reagan administration developed arguments that questioned four major aspects of federal policy. First, they raised questions about the number of children needing bilingual education. They argued that the size of the bilingual student population eligible for federal services was smaller than had been estimated in prior years, and that most of them were already being served by these programs.[86] Second, they raised questions about the role of language in underachievement and argued that bilingual education was misdirected because the primary factors responsible for poor school performance were nonlinguistic in nature. Third, they attacked bilingual education because it failed to consider the severe financial, personnel, and assessment constraints local school districts faced in providing bilingual services to non-English-speaking (NES) students. Finally, they questioned the appropriateness of bilingual education. Bilingual education, the opponents noted, was not effective in improving the academic achievement of NES students or in teaching them English.[87] More importantly, they argued, alternatives to bilingual education existed. Among the ones most commonly mentioned were English immersion and English as a Second Language approaches.[88]

Other types of arguments were made in the late 1980s and 1990s. Some opponents, for instance, argued that bilingual education was not assimilating immigrant children as fast as it could or that it was promoting Hispanic separatism, cultural apartheid, and social fragmentation in general. A few even argued that bilingual education was not an educational program for children but an affirmative action program for Latinas/os.[89]

Others still argued, among other things, that the federal government was "dictating" the curriculum at the local level by mandating one single ap-

proach to educating NES children, that there was no federal legal requirement for schools to provide bilingual or bicultural education, that public
opinion was against this program, that language minority parents did not
support bilingual education because they felt it was more important for their
children to learn English than to maintain the native language, that English
was losing ground to other languages in the United States, or that newcomers to the United States were learning English more slowly now than in previous generations.[90]

The proponents of bilingual education at different points in time countered all of these charges. Most of them concentrated on the issue of effectiveness. They criticized the methodological flaws and conclusions of studies
indicating that bilingual education programs were not effectively teaching
these students.[91] Some noted that findings showing the success of well-
designed bilingual programs were distorted or suppressed.[92] A few of them
also argued that no significant research showing the success of English-only
methods existed.[93] Others still noted that the attack against this policy was
ideologically inspired or that the arguments against bilingual education were
"bogus." Racism and anti-Mexican sentiment, they noted, were at the core
of this opposition.[94]

Undermining and Modifying Policy and Practice

In addition to attacking various aspects of bilingual education policy, the
opposition also sought changes in federal policy, in its funding, and in the
federal role.

Opposition within the federal government came primarily from elected
officials in the executive and legislative branches of government. The former
I refer to as executive opponents, the latter as congressional opponents.

Executive opponents, led by two Republican presidents, sought to weaken
federal support for bilingual education. President Ronald Reagan initiated the campaign against this program in 1980.[95] He initially tried to halt
its growth by seeking rescissions and decreased funding.[96] In the 1986–87
fiscal year, however, the funding level for the Bilingual Education Act increased to $143 million. The need for Latina/o votes in the presidential elec-
tions and the wooing of these voters by the Republican Party led to this
increase.[97]

During his second term and with the support of some conservative La-
tinas/os, President Reagan developed a new initiative to undermine bilin-

gual education policy. He appointed William J. Bennett, an avid opponent, to head the Department of Education and to lead this initiative. Once in office, Bennett developed and implemented a coherent plan of attack.[98]

First, he eliminated the mandatory provisions of bilingual education by dismantling its civil rights component. More specifically, he withdrew the proposed and actual federal guidelines for ensuring compliance with nondiscrimination policies. He also persuaded the Department of Education to develop new regulations aimed at eliminating the use of non-English-language instruction in these programs and at promoting "local flexibility" in bilingual program designs.[99]

Second, he downgraded the primary instrument for enforcing the *Lau* decision—the Office for Civil Rights—by drastically reducing its budget and staff.[100]

Finally, he weakened the administration of bilingual education and tried to undo existing *Lau* agreements.[101]

Proponents of bilingual education, especially the National Association for Bilingual Education, the California Association for Bilingual Education, and the Texas Association for Bilingual Education, opposed all of these changes and criticized Bennett for his shortsightedness and the negative implications his strategy could have on language minority children.[102] Their opposition had no significant impact on his drive to undermine bilingual education.

Congressional opponents also took a variety of actions against this policy. Between 1980 and 2001 they introduced countless pieces of legislation aimed at repealing the federal bilingual education bill. In many cases, they also introduced English-only bills in an effort to eliminate bilingual education policies. None of them became law.

Unable to repeal bilingual education, congressional opponents sought changes in the policy. Two key changes were made in the 1980s.

One of these placed limits on the number of years ELLs could participate in bilingual programs (two to three years), on the number of English-speaking children eligible to participate (from 40 percent of total to none), and on the amount of non-English languages one could use in bilingual education (less than half a day; less than one hour per day).[103]

The other major change focused on redefining bilingual education policy to allow for the inclusion of English only language approaches. In 1984, for instance, the Bilingual Education Act was modified to include the development of an English-only instructional program known as Special Alternative Instructional Programs (SAIP).[104] Funding was guaranteed for SAIP but not for the others. During the next decade, guaranteed funding for SAIP increased from 10 to 25 percent of total bilingual education funds. Despite this gradual increase, the opponents of bilingual education were dissatisfied. They sought increased funding for English-only approaches and more drastic changes to bilingual education policy.[105]

In the first half of the 1990s, the election of President Bill Clinton to the White House, a Democrat and a strong supporter of bilingual education, temporarily halted the opposition's efforts at the executive level. Opposition to bilingual education, however, continued in muted forms throughout the country. Opponents continued to make the argument that bilingual education was not effective, that it was not teaching English, and that English-only language alternatives were available. They also argued that bilingual education was fostering linguistic segregation and contributing to the fragmentation or "disuniting of America" into competing ethnic groups. Proponents countered that none of these arguments had merit and that the most successful program for teaching English and for promoting assimilation was bilingual education.[106]

THE TRIUMPH OF ENGLISH ONLY

During the second half of the decade, and as a result of the control by Republicans of both chambers of Congress in 1996 and the election of Republican George W. Bush to the White House in 2000, opponents renewed their attempts to change bilingual education policy. In 2001 they succeeded in enacting a new bill with most of the provisions that they had wanted for a decade. This legislation, the No Child Left Behind Act, amended and reauthorized both the Elementary and Secondary Education Act and the Bilingual Education Act for the next six years.[107]

This bill authorized $26.5 billion in federal spending for the 2002 fiscal year that began October 1, a roughly $7 billion increase over 2001. It set up a comprehensive testing system to identify failing schools and needy students and stipulated that failing schools would get resources to get them back on track.[108]

This bill also reauthorized the Bilingual Education Act of 1994. It became Title III of the overall bill.[109] This title, a major overhaul of federal programs for the education of ELLS and recent immigrant students, provided more funds for their education, but it also officially repealed bilingual education and replaced it with an English-only piece of legislation.[110]

The bill had a short authorization section and three major subparts. Parts A and B were different components of the education act and the core of the bill. Part C focused on definitions of key terms mentioned in the bill.

TABLE 4.1. GOALS IN PARTS A AND B OF TITLE III (FORMALLY THE BILINGUAL
EDUCATION ACT), 2001

PART A	PART B
TITLE—English Language Acquisition, Language Enhancement, and Academic Achievement Act	TITLE—Improving Language Instruction Educational Programs for Academic Achievement Act
PURPOSES	PURPOSES
Establishes a program for both LEP & Immigrant children	Maintains distinct programs for LEP and Immigrant Children
Promotes English only instructional programs	Maintains bilingual instructional programs
Promotes monolingualism and monoculturalism	Promotes multi-lingual proficiency and multi-cultural understanding
Helps LEP/immigrant children meet high levels of academic achievement in English only	Helps LEP children meet rigorous academic achievement standards in English plus
Holds SEAs, LEAs & schools accountable for increases in English proficiency and in core academic content knowledge of LEP children by requiring demonstrated improvement in English	Promote systemic improvement and reform of educational programs servicing LEP children
Provide SEAs & LEAs with flexibility in implementing LIEP based on scientifically based research on teaching LEP children English	Develop data collection and dissemination, research materials, and technical assistance that are focused on school improvement for LEP children

Part A was quite distinct from Part B. The goals of both Parts A and B shared some similarities. Both, for instance, promoted English fluency among English language learners (ELLs), the new term for those the bill targeted, and encouraged meeting the challenging academic and achievement standards throughout the country. Despite these surface similarities, major differences existed between them. Part A promoted only English fluency whereas Part B promoted multilingual fluency and multicultural understandings. Part A also promoted academic achievement in English only whereas Part B emphasized academic achievement in English plus another language.

The specific provisions of each part likewise differed substantially. Part A established a formula grant program for developing English-only instructional programs, whereas Part B maintained a competitive grant program for the establishment and enhancement of bilingual programs. Both held state educational and local educational agencies accountable for increases in English proficiency and in core academic content and encouraged the funding of professional development activities. Part B, however, authorized the Secretary of Education to conduct data collection, dissemination, and research on ELLS and on bilingual education and to encourage the development and dissemination of instructional materials for bilingual programs. Part A did not.

In summary, Part A promoted a formula-based block grant to the states for establishing English-only programs, whereas Part B maintained a competitive grant program for the establishment and strengthening of bilingual education.

According to the bill, only one of these parts could be in effect at any particular time. Part A would become operational if the amount Congress appropriated equaled or exceeded $650 million dollars. Part B would be in effect only if Part A was not. Which part became operational then depended on the amount of money Congress appropriated.[111]

In January 2002, Congress appropriated $665 million dollars for FY2002.[112] Based on this appropriation, only Part A would be in effect. This meant that for all intents and purposes bilingual education was repealed and replaced by an English-only bill for ELLS and immigrant children.

Title III, in essence, reversed the language policy enacted in 1994. This earlier policy promoted academic achievement, multilingual proficiency, and multicultural understanding. It also encouraged capacity building and provided substantial funds for teacher training, research, and support services. This new policy—Title III—now stressed academic achievement and the learning of English only. The rapid teaching of English, noted James Crawford, would take precedence over everything else. "Accountability provisions, such as judging schools by the percentage of English Language Learners reclassified as fluent in English each year, are expected to discourage the use of native-language instruction," he stated. "Annual English assessments will be mandated, 'measurable achievement objectives' will be established, and failure to show academic progress in English will be punished," he further noted.[113]

Title III, unlike the 1994 bill, limited funding for capacity-building activities and restricted it to 6.5 percent of the total budget, or about $43 million

TABLE 4.2. PROVISIONS OF PARTS A AND B OF TITLE III (FORMALLY THE BILINGUAL
EDUCATION ACT), 2001

PART A OTHER PROVISIONS	PART B OTHER PROVISIONS
Establishes a formula grant program for establishing English only instructional programs	Maintains a competitive grant program for the establishment and enhancement of bilingual programs
Establishes an accountability system based on two-year evaluations focusing on teaching English and meeting academic and achievement standards.	Establishes an accountability system based on two-year evaluations of bilingual programs and on professional development activities.
Is silent on the need to support data collection, dissemination, and research on LEP children and on instructional programs for them.	Authorizes Secretary to conduct data collection, dissemination, and research on LEP children and on bilingual education.
Ignores the development and dissemination of instructional materials for bilingual programs	Encourages the development and dissemination of Instructional Materials for bilingual programs
Encourages the funding of professional development activities (SUBPART 3)	Encourages the funding of professional development activities
No special funding is provided for immigrant children.	Provides funds for establishing special programs and services to educate immigrant children
The Secretary shall neither mandate nor preclude the use of a particular curricular or pedagogical approach to educating LEP children.	The Secretary shall coordinate and ensure close cooperation with all entities serving LEP children.

for fiscal year 2002. The year before, funding for these types of activities amounted to $100 million. James Crawford noted that the limited funding in Title III would do little to address the critical shortage of teachers qualified to meet the needs of ELLS.[114]

Strangely enough, the radical change in policy occurred without any major opposition from Mexican American organizations or other proponents of bilingual education, including liberal Democrats and members of the Congressional Hispanic Caucus. Prominent members of Congress and former allies of Title VII, such as Edward Kennedy, likewise failed to defend native-language programs and willingly accepted the changes Republicans demanded in order to pass Bush's education bill.

More significantly, traditional allies of Title VII failed to provide an honest assessment of this new bill. No major statements were issued by groups such as NABE, MALDEF, or LULAC on this bill. The only exceptions to this "silence" by the supporters of bilingual education were James Crawford, the noted journalist, and Raul Izaguirre, director of the National Council de la Raza.

Crawford, in an obituary for the Bilingual Education Act, argued that Title VII "expired" quietly on January 8. The death of the thirty-four-year-old law, he noted "was not unexpected, following years of attacks by enemies and recent desertions by allies in Congress." He further added that while federal funds would continue to support the education of ELLS, the money would be spent to support programs aimed at developing English only. The repeal of bilingual education in general and the expunging of the word *bilingual* and the goal of proficiency in two languages, in particular, he added, "happened with barely a peep from the traditional political allies of bilingual education.[115]

Izaguirre, on the other hand, wrote more favorably of Title III and of the larger ESEA. Although silent on the elimination of native language instruction in Title III and on the replacement of the Bilingual Education Act with an English-only measure, he made several points in his analysis of this bill. First, Izaguirre commended the conference committee considering the reauthorization of the ESEA for completing work on this bill and for engaging in "a careful, deliberative process." During this process, he stated, "members of Congress displayed a degree of statesmanship that, compared to the demagoguery that has characterized the debate over bilingual education in California, Arizona, and Massachusetts, eschewed political rhetoric and maintained a focus on truly helping ELL students achieve academically while mastering English."[116] No mention was made of the exclusion of Latinas/os from the conference committee or of the role Kennedy and other Democrats played in abandoning the interests of bilingual education advocates. Second, he praised some key provisions and failed to criticize them or only provided moderate criticism of their potential negative impact on Latina/o students. He, for instance, praised the provisions to improve teachers' skills, provide parents with the information and options they needed to choose the right instructional program for children, and hold schools more accountable for helping ELLS acquire English and meet challenging academic benchmarks. But he failed to point out that, at least with respect to Title III, the new legislation significantly cut back funds for professional development and for supportive services aimed at helping ELLs acquire English and meet challenging academic content. Izaguirre also supported the block grant awards and the increases in federal funds to all states that had ELL students, not just the school districts that applied for grants through a competitive process. This support, however, was not without reservations. He wrote:

> Given that state governments are likely to experience budget deficits over the next several years while the number of ELLs continues to grow we approach this shift in policy with caution. Unless the schools receive increased resources to serve these additional ELLs, then the funds could end up being spread too thinly among schools to be effective. Thus, we believe that proper implementation of this legislation means that the Congress and the Bush Administration must close the loop by providing states the resources and technical assistance they need to provide ELLs with a quality education. In addition, they must more effectively monitor implementation of the program to ensure that the states are able to meet the ambitious goal.[117]

The passage of this bill meant that after several decades of attacking and undermining this policy the opponents finally succeeded in repealing bilingual education and in replacing it with an English-only one. The forces of conservatism, assimilation, and ignorance, in other words, triumphed over pluralism and over enlightened pedagogy.

Despite this setback many activists did not view this as the end for bilingualism in the United States. Josué M. González, one of the most important and influential advocates of bilingual education in the nation, exemplified this view. In reflecting on the demise of federal bilingual education policy and on the federal government's support for this policy, he noted that this temporary setback would not have a dampening effect on bilingualism. In the wake of this demise, González stated, bilingual educators throughout the country were building new and more exciting programs for all children. He added:

> Better and more potent forms of bilingual teaching have begun to emerge. Most of these are no longer transitional, remedial, or compensatory. The new bilingual education programs of the 21st century will have new dreams and new keywords that reflect the new and more powerful dreams of a diverse nation: biliteracy, enrichment, two-way, language for global understanding, and heritage language preservation.[118]

González's optimism was warranted given the historical trajectory of bilingual education in this country and the tremendous growth of the Latina/o population in the twenty-first century. Despite official neglect or governmental efforts to stamp out the use of non-English languages in American education, the bilingual education tradition has been kept alive over the centuries by language minority groups who have been denied power, prestige, and status in this country.[119] The continued increase of immigrants from Spanish-speaking countries of the Americas who refuse to abandon their languages and cultures will only contribute to the future growth of the bilingual tradition in the local schools. So while the battle for federal bilingual education policy has ended with the passage of the No Child Left Behind Act, the larger war for bilingualism will continue unabated.

CONCLUSION

The struggle for bilingual education as noted above has been long, contentious, and complex. Mexican Americans have played a key role in its establishment and in its development over the decades. This struggle, unlike most of the others Mexican American activists waged, was quite distinct in several ways. First, no one single organization or individual dominated this struggle. A host of Mexican American educators and organizations participated in enacting and implementing federal bilingual education policies from the 1960s to the early twenty-first century. Second, Mexican American activists did not engage in these battles by themselves. They joined forces with other language minority groups throughout the country and with a range of political, social, and educational organizations interested in improving the schooling of ELLs. This was truly a multiracial project aimed at developing complex and shifting coalitions and alliances across different regions in America and at different points in time. Third, these struggles indicated the depth of commitment by activists who truly believed that bilingual education was the most effective way for educating ELLs in this country. Individuals such as Josué M. González and Jose A. Cardenas devoted their entire professional lives to this cause and continue to do so as they approach their retirement years. Through the contentious debates, constant opposition, and political setbacks over the decades, these individuals and the organizations they supported never gave up. They held on to their faith that this was the right program for ELLs and for the future of this country.

FIVE

Beyond Public Education

Most people assume that the quest for education focused solely on public schools, but this is historically incorrect. Mexican Americans also sought instruction from religious authorities and private organizations or else they established their own schools. This long-standing tradition of seeking religious and alternative forms of education continued in the post-1960 years. Although a variety of private schools have been supported or established by Mexican Americans since the 1960s, little if any research has been conducted on them. The following thus is based on the limited writings on some of these schools. It is hoped that others will continue to collect archival data, conduct interviews with the founders, teachers, and students of these schools, and write additional historical articles and books on them. For now, I will only try to provide a sketch of their origins, evolution, and significance during the past half-century.

RELIGIOUS SCHOOLS

Mexican American parents and community activists have a long history of seeking religious instruction for their children. They have sought learning opportunities from a variety of religious entities, especially Catholic and Protestant ones, for a variety of reasons—to maintain religious and cultural values, to undermine discriminatory or exclusionary policies, to challenge Americanization, and to seek excellence in education.[1]

The tradition of enrolling in Catholic schools goes back to the Spanish colonial period. This tradition expanded during the nineteenth and early twentieth century. Over the centuries they attended a variety of Catholic institutions, such as boarding schools, academies, or parochial schools and colleges.[2]

Mexican Americans also enrolled in schools established by different Protestant denominations. Protestant school attendance is a more recent development and originated in the 1850s. It began in Texas and soon expanded to other parts of the Southwest. The greatest number of schools was established in New Mexico because of the lack of public and Catholic school facilities, the vast distances between villages, and Protestants' strong desire to convert Mexican and Hispanic children.[3]

Mexican origin parents continued to enroll their children in both Catholic and Protestant schools during the latter part of the twentieth and early twenty-first century but in smaller numbers. The following briefly documents how Catholic and Protestant schooling for Mexican children evolved during these years.

Although ethnic Mexicans sought Protestant schooling, religious denominations experienced difficulties in maintaining enrollment and in keeping schools open during the post-1960 years. Some key institutions with a strong record of academic excellence closed their doors during the 1970s and 1980s after providing instruction to Mexican Americans and immigrants from Mexico, Puerto Rico, and other Spanish-speaking countries for many decades. One of the best examples of a school that closed its doors in the 1970s is the Spanish American Institute located in Gardena, California. This school was established in 1913 with three purposes in mind—to develop a Christian character among Mexican boys, to promote industrial education, and to produce leaders "who will be a credit to their own race and become outstanding citizens."[4] Others such as the Presbyterian Menaul School in Albuquerque, New Mexico, the Lydia Patterson Institute in El Paso, Texas, and the Presbyterian Pan American School in Kingsville, Texas, continue to provide excellent instruction for Mexican Americans, Mexican immigrants, and other Spanish-speaking students into the twenty-first century. Their histories of academic excellence, Christian instruction, and leadership training have yet to be written.[5]

While Mexican origin students enrolled in a variety of Protestant schools during the late twentieth and early twenty-first century, the majority attended Catholic institutions. Many parents sent their children to Catholic schools because of their spiritually and intellectually demanding curriculum and because of their tolerant policies toward the Spanish language and the Mexican cultural heritage. Catholic schools took the lead in celebrating a variety of practices that originated in Mexico. One of the most important Mexican-based celebrations was the annual Feast of Our Lady of Guadalupe. This event celebrates the sixteenth-century appearance of the Mexicanized Virgin Mary to the peasant Juan Diego near Mexico City.[6]

Notwithstanding the community's support for Catholic instruction, over time fewer numbers of Mexican children enrolled in Catholic schools because of the increasing poverty among the population and increased costs for attending them. Their decreasing enrollment reflected larger trends in Catholic education.

During the latter part of the twentieth century, the Catholic Church experienced a significant decline in parochial school enrollment caused by a variety of factors, including deteriorating facilities, a shortage of nuns and priests who once ran the schools at no extra cost, the decreased ability to fund these schools, the growth of quality academic programs in the public schools, the church's relaxation of religious obligations, which included sending one's children to the parish school, and the demographic shifts by which relatively well-paid working-class parishioners of earlier decades were replaced by impoverished Latinos and other immigrants.[7] The problem of declining enrollment worsened in the early twenty-first century, and the Church began to close large numbers of schools in various cities. Between 1990 and 2009, the Catholic Church closed over two thousand parochial schools throughout the country. These closures had a significant impact on ethnic Mexican and other Latinas/os and led to decreasing opportunities for their children. In 2005, for instance, Cardinal Francis George closed twenty-three Catholic elementary schools in the Archdiocese of Chicago. Most of these schools were in the African American and Latina/o community. Many of them had long histories of being alternatives to public education for immigrant families.[8]

In response to this enrollment crisis, Catholic Church leaders in the early twenty-first century converted a few parochial schools to charter schools, merged schools, enrolled non-Catholics, and broadened the base of financial support to encourage more community involvement. Some church leaders added tithing (Archdiocese of Wichita) while others turned to private donors and philanthropic foundations to support its schools (Memphis). These creative actions led to the elimination of tuition, increased enrollment, and the reaffirmation of the importance of a Catholic identity for schoolchildren. They also led to the strengthening of a long-cherished tradition in the Chicana/o and Latina/o community of enrolling in schools aimed at providing a faith-based education comprised of excellence in instruction, validation of cultural and linguistic differences, and character development.[9] Despite these valiant efforts, Catholic enrollment, the number of Catholic schools, and Catholic instruction for ethnic Mexican students decreased over time.

NATIONALISM AND THE RISE OF CHICANA/O
ALTERNATIVE SCHOOLS

In many cases, Mexican Americans established their own schools. This tradition was long standing in the community, as indicated by the establishment of
different types of community-based "escuelitas" along the US-Mexico border
in the late nineteenth and early twentieth century.[10] These institutions, as several scholars have noted, were quite diverse with respect to clientele, length of
service, content, and governance structures. These included not only private
schools aimed at teaching the basic skills but also nationalist ones aimed at
contesting Americanization and segregation and at promoting Spanish language instruction, Mexican cultural knowledge, and ethnic Mexican history.[11]
This tradition continued in the post-1960s era, but it was strongly influenced
by nationalism in the 1960s and 1970s and conservatism in later years.

   In the 1960s and 1970s, Mexican Americans established schools influenced
by the Brown Power movement, the free school or alternative school movement in the United States, and the enactment of federal legislation promoting
innovations in higher education. The Brown Power movement provided the
ideological and political basis for the establishment of these schools. The free
school movement and federal legislation on educational reform provided the
spaces and limited funds to experiment with the development of unique institutions aimed at providing alternative ways of educating ethnic Mexican children in these years. These developments, in other words, contributed to the
idea of experimenting with educational structures, philosophies, operations,
and content in the days of nationalism. They also provided Chicanas/os
with educational spaces to discuss what these alternative ideas about schooling meant for a community on the move.[12]

   Youth activists referred to the schools established during the late 1960s
and 1970s as "Chicano alternative schools." Although no consensus existed
on what was meant by alternative, members of the community organized
these schools and they were both operated and conducted differently than
public or parochial schools.

Origins and Growth

Nationalist alternative schools originated in the summer of 1968 when the
Denver-based Crusade for Justice, one of the most influential organizations
of the emerging Chicana/o movement, opened a school to instill ethnic pride

15. Children in front of school. Courtesy MALDEF Special Collections, Stanford University, Stanford, California.

16. Huelga school, with children and teacher. Courtesy MALDEF Special Collections, Stanford University, Stanford, California.

in young Mexican Americans. In this school, youth were taught rudimentary history, culture, and politics. The initial ideas of pride and assertiveness led to calls for changes in the Denver public schools and to further protests over language, culture, and mistreatment in the schools. Additional consciousness raising, mobilizing, and failure to change the public schools led to the idea of establishing a school with the intent of teaching ethnic pride and promoting social change. It led to the founding of the Escuela Tlatelolco, a school controlled by the activist community for the benefit of Chicana/o students.[13]

During the next decade activists established more than twenty-five schools for Chicanas/os throughout the country.[14] Some of these were elementary and secondary schools. Among the most well documented, in addition to La Escuela Tlatelolco, were La Casa de la Raza in Berkeley, California, and La Escuela de la Raza Unida in Blythe, California.[15] Others were postsec-

17. Children at Huelga school. Courtesy MALDEF *Special Collections, Stanford University, Stanford, California.*

18. Children at Huelga school, around table. Courtesy MALDEF *Special Collections, Stanford University, Stanford, California.*

ondary educational institutions, including Colegio Cesar Chavez in Oregon; Colegio Jacinto Trevino, Juárez-Lincoln University, and Hispanic International University in Texas; and D-QU (Deganawidah-Quetzalcoatl), a Native American–Chicano institution, in Davis, California.[16]

A few urban areas had several alternative schools. One of these areas was Houston. In this city the community established a Mexican American university in 1970, an alternative junior and senior high school in 1972, and a half-day nonaccredited alternative education center in 1973. The university was known as the Hispanic International University. Its purpose was to offer an academic program "that would relate to the personal, cultural, and professional needs of the Mexican American community." Its name was changed in the mid-1980s and it soon closed its doors.[17] The junior and senior high school and the half-day nonaccredited alternative education center, especially the alternative school, known as the George I. Sánchez Junior and

Senior High School, were aimed at reducing the dropout rate of Mexican American students residing in the barrios of the East End in that city.[18]

Reasons for Establishing Schools

Alternative schools were established because public schools were not serving the academic needs of Mexican origin children, not training enough professional educators, or they were hostile toward the linguistic and cultural heritage of these students. The hostility was reflected in two major features of public education: the devaluation, denigration, or suppression of the Spanish language and the exclusion or distortion of the children's cultural heritage and historical experiences from the curriculum.[19]

Students, teachers, and community groups involved in the establishment of alternative schools commonly noted concern with deplorable educational conditions.[20] Casa de la Raza in Berkeley, California, emerged, noted its director Francisco Hernandez, because parents and community activists "were concerned about the lack of responsiveness on the part of the schools to the culture and language of Raza children in Berkeley."[21] Students involved in the Crusade for Justice's summer Freedom School, the origins of Escuela Tlatelolco in Denver, Colorado, expressed dissatisfaction with public and parochial education "for not relating curricula and teaching methods to their needs." "They also experienced frustration with instructors' inability, unpreparedness, and unwillingness to correlate their educational methods and material with the increased social, historical, and cultural awareness of the students."[22] Chicanos in Blythe, California, also noted the reason for the establishment of La Escuela de la Raza Unida: "to remedy the ingrained irrelevancy and insensitivity of the local public schools toward their children."[23] Lack of commitment on the part of the public schools in Houston regarding the teaching of any aspect of the ethnic Mexican experience—"historical, cultural, sociological, or political"—became one of the primary reasons for the establishment of George I. Sánchez School in Houston, Texas.[24]

Colegio Jacinto Trevino emerged in order to meet the need for bilingual teachers in South Texas. Narciso Alemán, one of the Mexican American Youth Organization (MAYO) activists involved in protests and school walkouts in the Rio Grande Valley, recalled that when activists demanded the hiring of Chicana/o teachers and administrators one of the superintendents told him that there were none with a college degree. He and other MAYO members, realizing the need for such a college, then made concrete plans to establish one at their statewide conference in December 1969. Two issues discussed at this conference, held in Mission, Texas, were the need for bilingual educators and for political unity. At the end of the conference the attendees unanimously agreed to found a college for the training of Chicana/o teachers. The proposed goal of the *colegio* was "to develop a Chicano with conscience and skills, [to give] the barrios a global view, [and] to provide positive answers to racism, exploitation, and oppression." Its objective was to develop a bilingual, bicultural program to train teachers of Chicana/o children. Those participating in the establishment of this college named it Jacinto Trevino, in honor of a local border hero.[25]

Common Features of Alternative Schools

Chicana/o alternative schools, for the most part, were quite diverse with respect to funding, philosophies, governance structures, curricula, teaching styles, and grade levels. A few of these were preschool programs, others encompassed grades from kindergarten to high school, while still others were postsecondary institutions. In some cases, these schools were public, in others private. If the latter, they peacefully coexisted with public school systems.

Despite this diversity, they had some features in common. These schools were controlled by Chicanas/os, infused with nationalism, and committed to encouraging social change. Let me elaborate on each of these features.

1. NATIONALISM AND COMMUNITY CONTROL OF SCHOOLS

One common feature of Chicana/o alternative schools was community control. Unlike public schools, which were controlled and staffed by Anglos, alternative schools were controlled by Chicanas/os. The idea of community control of the schools emerged in several plans developed during the Chicana/o movement.[26] Two of the most important were El Plan del Barrio (1968) and El Plan Espiritual de Aztlán (1969). According to these documents Chicanas/os, in order to gain liberation from an oppressive society, needed to control all of those institutions and agencies operating in and affecting them. Corky Gonzáles, one of the movement's most well known leaders, best stated this idea when he said, "we have to understand that liberation comes from self-determination." Gonzáles further interpreted self-determination as taking over "the institutions within our community."[27] When applied to education, self-determination meant that Chicanas/os had "the right to select for themselves their own form of education; to decide independently of national, state, or local agency what, when and how to teach Chicanos."[28]

The right to self-determination in education then stipulated that Chicanas/os would be responsible for the establishment of these institutions and for determining their structure, content, and procedures. In practical terms, this usually meant that the most activist members of the community would make these decisions. In a few cases, parents, staff, and on occasion some students participated in decision making. Ironically, increased democracy in decision making led to chaos, political infighting, and frustration in at least two schools. The limited histories of Chicanas/os' alternative schools suggests that one of the major reasons for the decline of both Colegio Cesar Chavez in Oregon and Jacinto Trevino in South Texas was the intense infighting and polarization that occurred in these decision-making structures.[29]

2. NATIONALISM AND ACADEMIC INSTRUCTION

A second common feature of these alternative schools pertained to language and culture. Public schools in general taught all of their courses in English and suppressed or repressed the language and culture of Chicana/o children. Many activists felt that one of the reasons for low academic achievement was the suppression and devaluation of their linguistic and cultural heritage. The reintroduction or incorporation of the Spanish language and Mexican culture, in conjunction with other changes in the context and content of the school, would improve their academic performance. Academic success, in other words, could be attained if the schools taught in a "culturally relevant" context.[30] For this reason then, alternative schools taught basic (K-12) or advanced skills (Institutions of Higher Learning [IHL]) and diverse forms of knowledge by using the children's language and culture and by providing positive reinforcement.

The incorporation of language and culture was a complex process that varied between and within alternative schools.[31] With respect to the Spanish language, for instance, it was allowed as a language of communication in the school, as a language of instruction in the classroom, or as a subject matter. Every institution incorporated and valued Spanish in its own unique way. Tlatelolco, for example, taught Spanish as a subject and La Escuela de la Raza Unida used it interchangeably with English in instruction throughout grades K-12.[32]

Alternative schools taught Mexican cultural values and beliefs in various ways. Some promoted culture through required courses in Chicana/o Studies or through electives such as art, dance, and choir. Tlatelolco, for instance, taught Mexican history, Chicano music, folkloric dancing, choir in Spanish, and contemporary affairs dealing with the Southwest, Mexico, and

Latin America, among other things.[33] It also organized the different grades
on the basis of indigenous groups. Kindergarten classes, for instance, were
Olmecas, first graders were Mayas, second graders Toltecas, third graders
Teotihuacanos, and such. This culturally based form of organizing instruction instilled pride whenever teachers, students, and parents talked about
their children in the school.

"At Tlatelolco one never hears children, parents or staff refer to students
as first graders, second graders, etc. Rather, reference is made to students
being of a particular tribe." When parents speak of their child's class it
is common to hear them say, "My son is an Olmeca," or "My daughter
is a Chichimeca." Similarly, one hears the children, when referring to
themselves, stating, "I am a Mayan," or "I am a Teotihuacano."[34]

In some cases, no formal cultural classes were taught. Still, the schools reflected the cultural heritage in various ways. One of these was to honor and
celebrate patriotic or religious events such as Cinco de Mayo (May 5) and 16 de
Septiembre (September 16), two of Mexico's most important holidays. The
former celebrates the day in which Mexican troops defeated French forces invading Mexico; the latter is its independence day. La Escuela de la Raza Unida
celebrated el Cinco de Mayo and el 16 de Septiembre every year. Escuela Tlatelolco added other days, such as Emiliano Zapata's birthdate (April 10), the
initiation of the Mexican Revolution day (November 20), and the anniversary
of the Tlatelolco Massacre in Mexico City (October 2). Other schools showed
respect and support for Mexican culture by displaying it throughout the school
grounds. In La Escuela de la Raza Unida, for instance, the walls had murals
and paintings related to Mexican culture, including a picture of La Virgen de
Guadalupe (The Virgin of Guadalupe), Mexico's patron saint.[35]

In some of these schools culture was taught indirectly. George I. Sánchez
exemplified this approach. At this school, the teachers made a constant effort
to relate the subject matter to Chicana/o culture, history, or politics. "For
example, English as a second language has built into its overall learning ex-
ercises thirty reading modules on Chicano heroes and personalities. History
focuses on World, US and Texas historical events, adding an analysis from
the perspective of the Chicano people."[36]

In a few cases, activists sought to use the schools as a means to preserve
the ethnic and cultural identity of the community, not as a way to improve
academic achievement. "Chicano history and culture have been denied,"

declared the Colegio Cesar Chavez Student Handbook. "Thus, Colegio offers a bilingual/bicultural program through which Chicanos may maintain their culture, [and] resurrect their history."[37] La Casa de la Raza, noted Francisco Hernandez, its director, was an effort to preserve the ethnic identity of the Chicana/o students. The Casa activists responsible for establishing the school believed that because of strong assimilationist sentiments in the United States and negative attitudes toward Chicanas/os, Mexican children were losing their language and culture. They wanted to use the school to maintain this ethnic identity by conducting the instruction bilingually, that is, in Spanish and English, using the Mexican culture throughout the curriculum, instructing the students through the complete K-12 sequence, and having a governance structure dominated by members of the Mexican origin community.[38]

3. COMMITMENT TO SOCIAL CHANGE

Finally, most of the alternative schools sought to develop an awareness of social and political problems within the community through dialogue or study and to encourage action to resolve them. Some schools sought to develop awareness through action rather than through study and dialogue. Regardless, these schools then promoted not only basic or advanced academic skills and knowledge but also political education and social activism. Colegio Cesar Chavez "recognizes the value and importance of a broad-based education . . . by which students may acquire the skills with which to address the social dilemmas [of] poverty, racism, [and such]."[39] Universidad de Aztlán had many programs aimed at promoting social change. One of the programs, for instance, addressed itself to the need for studying and advocating for social change in social services, especially the welfare department. The school's program established a welfare rights committee composed of students from the university as well as students from City College and Fresno State University in Fresno, California. "Their work is to help any people who have complaints against the welfare department and getting them to the department and getting them something, helping in translating, helping at fair hearings, and so forth. That's their thing in terms of students who want to be social workers."[40] Tlatelolco best expressed the philosophy embraced by many alternative schools: "Tlatelolco's philosophical objective goes beyond effecting academic competency. We perceive education not only as the intellectual development of the individual for his benefit but as a social orientation and development process for social change which will benefit a collective group."[41]

Other schools did not focus on training leaders but on training community-based researchers who would conduct investigations on issues benefiting the community. Universidad de Aztlán, for instance, mandated that university students engage in high school–oriented projects aimed at providing educational services to students. One of these provided counseling to high school students, another was a reading tutorial program, and the final one was called "Yo Soy Chicano" and was geared toward providing assistance to junior high school students.[42]

DIVERSITY OF CHICANA/O ALTERNATIVE SCHOOLS

Chicana/o alternative schools reflected a vast diversity of structures, philosophies, goals, curricula, sources of funding, and clientele. This diversity is reflected in the following description of several schools—Farmworkers Community School (summer school), La Escuela Tlatelolco (K-12), Casa de la Raza (K-12), Colegio Jacinto Trevino (grades 13–14), and Deganawidah-Quetzalcoatl University (D-QU).[43]

Farmworkers Community School

Unlike other schools, the Farmworkers Huelga School was not an alternative but a supplement to the public schools. Farmworker children between the ages of five and fifteen attended two sessions a week after school ended. The school began in September 1969 when it was funded by the National Council of Churches' National Farm Worker Ministry, California. It supplemented public education by training children to carry on the work begun by César Chávez and those belonging to the farm worker's Union, and it offered basic instruction in reading, math, science, singing, crafts, painting, and Spanish. The school stressed reading improvement and utilized Freirean approaches to teaching it.

Although Spanish and Mexican American culture was promoted in the school it emphasized the union and its activities. This school involved students in union activities and made an effort to involve families in the operation of the school.[44]

Escuela Tlatelolco

This school began in 1968 when the Crusade for Justice founded an all-Chicana/o summer school, but it officially opened year round in October

1970 as a fully accredited private school (K–college) with 250 students. Chicanismo, or ethnic pride, permeated all levels of education at Tlatelolco. Students spoke Spanish or Indian dialects, took pride in their cultural heritage, and learned values associated with Chicana/o culture. The school opposed competition, a value associated with Anglo capitalist culture, and promoted cooperation, familial relationships, and political unity. Students took regular and elective classes at the primary, junior, and senior levels, but the school had a more flexible schedule than the Denver public schools. Students devoted one day of the week to independent study or to class excursions at the senior level. Students also could take nine months of "block study." Each level of education was devoted to the study of a Mexican indigenous group.

The *colegio*, comprised of thirty-five students in the early years, was associated with Goddard College in Plainfield, Vermont. College students at the *colegio* took formal classes and taught at Tlatelolco. This kept student-teacher ratio at school low (5:1) and gave rise to intimate relationships between students and teachers. The *colegio* part of the school closed down in 1973 but the grade school continued in various forms to the present.[45]

Casa de la Raza

This high school began in 1970 as part of the Berkeley School District's experimentation with racial integration. The board initiated Casa de la Raza and Black House, a separate school for blacks, in response to a 1970 boycott of Martin Luther King Junior High. The school, which remained open for two years, from 1970 to 1972, offered a bilingual-bicultural curriculum for 150 Chicana/o children from grades 1 to 12. In addition to teaching a variety of required courses and electives and providing internships the school also utilized the Spanish language and Mexican culture in the curriculum. It promoted cooperation among students, shared learning, and community projects. Likewise, it hired Chicana/o teachers and professionals to provide the instruction. It had a low student-teacher ratio of 6:1 at the elementary level, but it lacked adequate resources and facilities.[46]

Deganawidah-Quetzalcoatl University (D-QU)

The university was established by a coalition of Chicana/o and Indian activists who took over 643 acres of farmland at the site of an abandoned army communications station six miles west of Davis, California. This land was declared surplus federal property in July 1970 and six months later was given to the Indian-Chicana/o coalition to establish the university. It opened its doors on July 6, 1971, after winning several million dollars in federal contracts. It had a thirty-two-member board of trustees comprised of Indians and Chicanas/os. Its plans were to develop four colleges with a total enrollment of 1,500. During its first year, only one college, called Tiburcio Vasquez, actually enrolled students. The college offered a variety of community college courses but they all had a "distinct ethnic orientation." For example, a natural science class could study tribal mind-altering techniques while a history class could trace the development of California's farm labor movement. Tiburcio Vasquez also gave students credit for attending workshops and seminars, for participating in tribal dances and political campaigns, and for planting corn and squash. It graded exclusively on a pass-superior basis. It did not believe in failing students. It offered a BA degree, a two-year AA degree, and high school equivalency certificates. Students, in many cases, designed their own courses. The school was a community-based, community-controlled institution of higher education.[47]

Colegio Jacinto Trevino

Colegio Jacinto Trevino was founded by Mexican American Youth Organization activists in Mission, Texas. Many of these activists knew that traditional schools could not help them in their struggle for survival and social justice. They blamed the public schools for the misery confronting their community and desired to train a socially committed corps of teachers to reeducate the community so that it could determine its own destiny. The *colegio* began in the fall of 1970 as the nation's first all-Chicana/o graduate program. A year later the *colegio* added an undergraduate program. Students received credit from Antioch College. All first year graduate students taught undergraduates.

Jacinto Trevino formed loose relationships with several other *colegios*, especially Tlatelolco. It accepted grants from a variety of public and private sources. In 1971 it moved into a twelve-room, two-story mansion in Mercedes, Texas. The old monastery where it originated could not accommodate its rapid growth.

Similar to other institutions, those in charge of *el colegio* infused the curriculum and instruction with Chicana/o culture. Emphasis was placed on rejecting negative views of this culture and of accepting pride in being Mexicana/o. In addition to innovations in instruction, the *colegio* had a governing council comprised of community representatives. As mentioned before, while this allowed for increased activity on the part of community groups, it led to conflicts within the governing council. *El colegio* closed its doors in the late 1970s.[48]

Latina/o Alternative Schools and Free Schools

The above institutions were all different in many ways, as indicated in the various approaches to the incorporation of language and culture, curriculum development, community participation, and instructional methods. In many ways, however, Chicana/o alternatives to conventional schooling resembled, in some respects, the educational actions found in the free school movement popular in the 1960s and 1970s. Most of these institutions encompassed more educational levels than the average institution, maintained remarkably low student-teacher ratios, and modified the teaching-learning relationship. Chicana/o alternative schools, however, deviated from those in the free school movement in several significant ways. Unlike free schools, Chicana/o alternative schools tried to meet the needs of poor people, established rapport with the surrounding community, taught basic and advanced intellectual skills, used Spanish in the instructional process, and incorporated elements of Mexican culture into the curriculum. More importantly, they promoted the idea of developing social change agents, individuals who could take action against the debilitating and oppressive structures and practices impacting their own education and their communities.[49] Those in the free school movement, as Jonathan Kozol pointed out in his book, *Free Schools*, failed to promote these goals.[50]

CHICANO ALTERNATIVE SCHOOLS IN TRANSITION DURING THE 1980S

Many of the alternative schools experienced a short life span because of lack of funds, an increasingly hostile political environment, or political infighting. By the late 1970s, only a handful of them remained. Among these were Tlatelolco in Denver, Colegio Cesar Chavez in Oregon, George I. Sánchez School in Houston, and La Escuela de la Raza Unida in Blythe, California. By this time, the United States was undergoing an economic recession and the political climate was becoming less hospitable to nationalist-based alternative schools in particular or alternative schools in general.

During the 1980s, a few alternative schools continued to hang on but with significant modifications.[51] Among the most important loss was el Colegio Cesar Chavez, which closed its doors in 1983. Of particular importance also was the establishment of the National Hispanic University (NHU) in 1981. This university signaled the types of changes necessary for an institution to survive in the 1980s. The NHU lost some of its nationalist and working-class orientation, it shared power with non-Chicanos and corporate America, it appealed to non-Chicanos, and it became more focused with respect to its mission as it emphasized academic achievement and occupational training in a multicultural context.

Although influenced by nationalism, NHU was a hybrid institution supported and controlled by prominent Anglos and Chicanas/os.[52] This institution, unlike most of those established in the 1970s, was based on bilingual education research in the precollege grades and on educational models available for African American children. The founders of NHU, especially the visionary and late Dr. Bob Cruz, believed that a small, private independent college geared toward meeting the needs of diverse groups of individuals, especially Latinas/os, was necessary. "NHU recognized in its origins that Hispanic learners needed something different," declared the NHU website. "They needed an educational system that acknowledged their learning needs. This was the starting point for the NHU," it added. The promotion of advanced skills and careers in business, education, or technology, however, had to be done within a multicultural educational experience, which NHU embraced. "The purpose of providing the opportunity for multicultural education to qualified individuals is expressed in all phases of the University's operations, from the selection of professors to the design of the curriculum." Thus while offering academically rigorous programs and professional development the school practiced and advocated "cultural pluralism that respects and appreciates diversity as a model for interaction in the classroom, university and society."[53] This culturally respectful framework coupled with the research conducted on historically black colleges and universities led to a model for educating Latina/o learners, a model built on appreciation for cultural diversity, high expectations, positive role models, and academic support systems.[54]

TRANSFORMATIONS: FROM CHICANA/O TO CHARTER SCHOOLS IN THE 1990S

In the latter part of the 1990s, Chicanas/os continued their alternative educational tradition, but they moved away from nationalist-based institutions and toward charter schools. These institutions, unlike those in the 1970s, did not

emphasize teaching cultural pride, nor did they promote cultural and linguistic maintenance or "culturally relevant" instruction for Chicana/o students.
Rather, they focused strictly on improving academic achievement among
"high-risk" students residing in economically deprived urban school districts.[55] These types of schools emerged as part of the rise of conservatism in
the United States and as a response by school officials to greater demands by
business interests for market solutions to educational problems.[56]

Charter schools operated with public funds but were independent of local school boards and most government rules. Between 1991 and 2009 more
than 4,600 charter schools were established. In 2009 charter schools served over
1.4 million students in forty states, Puerto Rico, and the District of Columbia.[57]

Charter schools were established for a variety of reasons. Some of the most
common were dissatisfaction with educational quality and school district bu-
reaucracies, increased autonomy by the sponsoring organization or agency,
the desire of a school to "realize an educational vision," promoting parental
and community involvement in education, and serving special populations.[58]

Less than 5 percent of the student population attended charter schools,
but these institutions created choices for parents of all colors and classes and
competition for traditional public schools. Ethnic Mexican communities, similar to many other groups, were dissatisfied with the type of education their
children had been getting for decades. They also did not feel that the public
schools were interested in changing the ways in which they instructed their
children.[59] In the 1990s, many of these parents and community groups joined
the charter school movement.

The ethnic Mexican community supported two types of charter schools,
those established by non-Chicanos and those founded by Chicana/o individuals and organizations. The former emphasized academic achievement for
Mexican origin and other Latina/o children but did not specifically address
their linguistic and cultural concerns. They also did not involve the Mexican
origin community in the governance and administration of the schools. The
latter emphasized academic achievement for Chicana/o children but within
the context of community involvement and a culturally sensitive environment.

Support for Non-Latino Charter Schools

For close to two centuries, Mexican American parents have supported a
wide range of community-based schools sponsored and controlled by non-
Chicanos.[60] This type of support continued in the post-1960s.

An example of community support for non-Chicano schools can be found in Houston, Texas. In this city, ethnic Mexican parents and activists supported the establishment of several charter schools, including Knowledge Is Power Program (KIPP) and YES Prep.[61] Both of these institutions developed innovative and successful strategies to improve the academic achievement of Chicana/o students from poverty backgrounds, but neither one of them included the community or its culture in the schools. Let me elaborate on the history of YES to show how this charter school addressed Chicana/o school performance, community decision making, and culture.

YES Prep, originally known as Project Youth Engaged in Service (YES), began as a small charter school project in Houston's East End, a mostly Chicana/o community, and has become the city's most successful charter school. Chris Barbic started Project YES in 1995 while teaching at Rusk Elementary School. He wanted to offer elementary school students an alternative to the low-performing middle schools that they would eventually attend.

Barbic, similar to many of the young people who became involved in the creation of exciting and innovative school reforms in the United States during the 1990s, was a Teach for America Corps member. Teach for America (TFA) is a nonprofit organization whose mission is to build a movement aimed at eliminating educational inequity by enlisting the nation's most promising future leaders in this effort. In this case, this meant recruiting recent graduates from some of the country's elite colleges willing to commit several years of their lives to educating low-income minority students. Barbic was one of these idealistic individuals who became a Teach for America member. The two-year commitment soon, however, turned into a life-long venture.[62]

The first class at YES enrolled fifty-eight low-income Mexican American students at Rusk Elementary School. In 1998 the staff of the program applied for a state charter, moved to a new site in the East End, and enlarged the program to include high school. With this move Project YES, an elementary-based program, became YES College Preparatory School, an open-enrollment state charter school for middle and high school students. In 2001 YES received a generous gift from the Brown Foundation. This allowed it to move to a permanent site in southeast Houston. Within a decade, the staff opened up four more schools—North Central (2003), Southwest (2004), East End (2006), and Lee (2007) (see table 5.1). By the end of the decade YES Prep announced a plan to open eight additional schools.[63]

YES's goal is to "increase the number of low-income Houstonians who graduate from a four-year college prepared to compete in the global market-

TABLE 5.1. GROWTH OF YES PREP CAMPUSES, 1998–2007

Name of School	Date founded	Grades served	No. of students
South East	1998	6–12	720
North Central	2003	6–11	650
Southwest	2004	6–10	502
Eastend	2006	6–9	460
Lee	2007	6–7	140

place and committed to improving disadvantaged communities." Its emphasis is on developing an academically enriching curriculum for economically disadvantaged Latina/o or African American students who historically have been denied higher educational opportunities in the larger society. YES Prep maintains extremely high standards for success, including parental and student commitment to excellence, community service projects, constant communication with teachers especially during evenings and weekends, extended school instruction, summer school, and college research trips.[64]

YES Prep has an excellent track record of providing quality and innovative instruction. "Since its first year of operation," notes one of its newsletters, "YES College Prep has received an 'Exemplary rating' from the Texas Education Agency."[65] Also, since its first graduating class in 2001, all of YES Prep's seniors have been accepted into four-year colleges, including Harvard, Yale, Rice, Stanford, and the University of Texas at Austin. Over 90 percent of YES graduates are first-generation college bound. In nearly a decade, YES students have earned nearly $23 million in scholarships and financial aid. YES is the only charter school system that has earned the top Texas Education Agency ratings of Exemplary and Recognized at each campus every year. Other top honors include the following:[66]

1. Top 100 High Schools in America
   Newsweek 2006, 2007
2. Top 100 High Schools in America
   US News & World Report, 2007, 2008
3. Best Houston High School
   Houston Chronicle, 2008
4. Houston's Best Public School
   Houston Press, 2006, 2007

5. Texas honor roll
   Texas Business & Education Coalition, 2006, 2007
6. All YES Schools Rated Exemplary & Recognized
   Texas Education Agency, 10th Consecutive Year
7. Dispelling the Myth Award for Educational Excellence
   in Low-Income Communities
   Education Trust, 2003

Although the school emphasizes excellence in instruction, it excludes the ethnic Mexican community from any significant involvement in its governance and administration. It also ignores the language and culture of the children in the school. Both the Spanish language and the Mexican American cultural heritage officially play no significant role in this school. Likewise, the Chicana/o community is excluded from participating in the shaping of the content, structure, and direction of YES schools. The board of directors, the advisory board, and even the leadership team responsible for YES Prep's policies, administration, and development, for example, are exclusively Anglo. Despite their exclusion, Mexican American and Mexican immigrant parents actively support YES schools and teachers because of their strong desire for quality educational opportunities. More specifically, they support YES because of their innovations in instruction, the high expectations of its teaching staff, and the exciting learning opportunities it provides for low-income minority students.[67]

Ethnic Mexican Charter Schools

Chicanas/os have not only supported institutions sponsored by non-Chicanos, they have also established their own charter schools. Prior to the rise of the charter school movement in the early 1990s, they had been involved in the creation of a host of community-based institutions. Even before the brown power movement and the rise of nationalist-based Chicana/o alternative schools, Mexican Americans had been involved in the establishment of community schools. The League of United Latin American Citizens (LULAC), for example, originated the idea of the Little Schools of the 400 as early as 1957. Felix Tijerina, a prominent Mexican American businessman from Houston and national president of LULAC from 1956 to 1960, was the brainchild behind the Little Schools. The primary objective of the Little Schools was to teach Mexican American preschool children four hundred essential English words that would provide them with a better opportunity for succeeding in the first grade. While the learning of English was the primary objective of the Little Schools curriculum, emphasis was also placed on respecting the children's cultural background, on encouraging the parents to participate in school activities, and on preparing the children to adjust to a school environment. Hundreds of Little Schools were established between 1957 and 1962, and thousands of Mexican Americans were successfully educated in them.[68] The growth of the Little Schools of the 400 in the 1950s and 1960 and of Chicana/o alternative schools the following two decades indicated the presence of a strong school tradition in the community.

Once the charter school movement emerged, Mexican American activists transformed existing community schools into charter schools or else they established new ones. Although they did not officially promote the teaching of cultural pride, charter school advocates encouraged improved academic achievement within a culturally sensitive environment. The experience of Chicanas/os in Houston demonstrates how some activists took advantage of the opening in education to create charter schools that were academically enriching yet continued to be inclusive of the community and its cultural heritage.

In Houston, Mexican Americans began to establish their own charter schools in the mid-1990s. Three of the earliest were founded in 1996. In this year the state legislature passed a law allowing the establishment of six experimental charter schools in Houston. Three of these were aimed at developing innovative approaches to educating ethnic Mexican or Latina/o children: the SER-Niños charter school, the Raul Yzaquirre School for Success, and the George I. Sánchez (GIS) Charter School.

SER-Niños charter school, sponsored by a nonprofit group known as SER-Jobs for Progress of the Texas Gulf Coast Inc., was designed for the largely immigrant population of Gulfton, an impoverished neighborhood located in southwest Houston. This school stressed learning for parents as well as students, high academic standards, and dual language instruction. The message being sent out, noted its first director, Diane Mancus, was that speaking several languages was an asset, not an embarrassment.

The second charter school, the Raul Yzaguirre School for Success, offered East End middle school students a supportive school environment in "self-contained" classrooms. This innovation allowed students to spend the day with one teacher instead of migrating from class to class as is typical of most middle school students in the regular public schools.

The final school, the GIS Charter School, also in the East End, had similar goals to Yzaguirre but for high school students. The GIS school was originally established in the early 1970s as an alternative school for students who had dropped out of school. The charter school, however, focused not on the returning dropout but on those who were at risk of dropping out. Richard Farias, a well-known community educator and activist, was the chief operating officer for the Raul Yzaguirre School for Success and used to direct the GIS school years earlier.[69] Both the Raul Yzaguirre School for Success and the GIS Charter School focus on improving the academic achievement of Mexican American students but in a culturally sensitive context.[70]

The tremendous support for charter schools by Mexican Americans during the 1990s encouraged the National Council de La Raza, one of the nation's largest Latina/o organizations, to launch an ambitious initiative in 2001 to develop fifty new charter schools throughout the country. This initiative, NCLR officials noted, was "a direct response to the increasingly alarming educational outcomes of Latino students and to the growing involvement of NCLR affiliates in offering educational services and programs to students in their communities." The purpose of these schools was to "significantly increase educational opportunities and high school graduation rates for Latinos," it noted. More specifically, NCLR and the community-based organizations (CBOs) affiliated with it, hoped to create a network of schools that were more conducive to the success of students by paying special attention to the linguistic needs of English language learners. Its affiliates, NCLR noted,

> provide critical academic and social services to children and adults not served, or poorly served, by mainstream schools and government agencies. They offer low cost pre-school programs, after-school services for youth, and an array of adult literacy, ESL, and job training opportunities. NCLR believes that this holistic approach to education can best meet the unique and varied academic and non-academic needs of Latino students, including those related to language and culture.[71]

The consistent and active support by Mexican American and other Latina/os for charter schools is another phase in the community's drive to improve the educational opportunities for its children. It is a tradition going back centuries and it will probably continue in the decades to come.

TABLE 5.2. PARTIAL LIST OF CHICANA/O ALTERNATIVE SCHOOLS, 1968–1978

Name	Year est.	No. of students	Grades	City
La Academia de la Nueva Raza	unknown		n.a.	Dixon, NM
Escuela y Colegio Tonantzín	1973		unknown	Santa Fe, NM[72]
Escuela Antonio José Martínez	1973		unknown	Las Vegas, NM[73]
Colegio Genaro Vasquez, Centro	unknown		unknown	LA, CA
Joaquin Murieta de Aztlan Escuela del Barrio	unknown		unknown	San Diego, CA
Escuela del Barrio, summer	1972/73	30+	7–12	San Jose, CA[74]
Centro Infantil	1973		pre-K	Oakland, CA
La Escuelita	1975		K-3	Oakland, CA[75]
Oakland Street Academy	1973		unknown	Oakland, CA
Casa de la Raza	1971–73		K-12	Berkeley, CA
Escuela Tiburcio Vasquez	1969–1980s		pre-K	SB, CA[76]
Huelga/Farmworker Community School	1969 Sum		6–12	Delano, CA
La Escuela de la Raza Unida	1972–79?	50	K-12	Blythe, CA[77]
Emiliano Zapata	1978		K-12	San Jose, CA[78]
Universidad de Aztlán	unknown		IHL	Del Rey CA
Colegio de la Mision	unknown		IHL	SF, CA
D-Q University	1971		IHL	Davis, CA
El Colegio de Ninos	1972		Pre-K	unknown, TX[79]
George I. Sanchez	1973–present		9–12	Houston, TX
Colegio Jacinto Trevino	1970		IHL-MA	Mercedes, TX[80]
Colegio Jacinto Trevino	1970–73		IHL	SA, TX
Juárez-Lincoln Center	1971		IHL	Austin, TX
Hispanic International	1971		IHL	Houston, TX
Escuela y Colegio Tlatelolco	1968–present	30–90	K-12	Denver CO[81]
Colegio Cesar Chavez	1973–83		IHL	Mt. Angel, OR

Sources: Educacion Alternativa, prepared by Reynaldo Flores Macias et al. (Hayward, CA: Southwest Network, 1975), 78; *Chicano Alternative Education* (Hayward, CA: Southwest Network, 1973), 21; Joan Kalvelage, "Cinco Exemplos," *Edcentric*, double issue (October–November, n.d) 5–7, 28–42; Franciso Javier Hernandez, "Schools for Mexicans: A Case Study of a Chicano School" (PhD diss., Stanford University, 1982), 57–67.

CONCLUSION

The continuation of the community's long tradition of support for religious and alternative schooling illustrates the diversity of the Mexican American struggle for educational opportunity in the contemporary period. Community activists and educators did not simply seek to eliminate all forms of discrimination in the public schools or to advocate for significant reforms in public education. Their strategies for increased and improved educational opportunities went beyond public schools. They also included strong support for religious instruction during all these years, for alternative schools in the 1960s and 1970s, and for charter schools in the more recent period. The quest for quality education and for recognition of linguistic and cultural diversity thus was a multifaceted and fascinating one that expanded significantly during the latter part of the twentieth and the early twenty-first century. A tradition that continues to this date.

Conclusion

In this concluding section I will summarize my arguments and then briefly discuss a few lessons learned from this study.

This study examined the Mexican American quest for education in the years from 1960 to the present. It asked several important questions about those involved in school reform efforts and the factors impacting their decisions. Who were the individuals and organizations that led these struggles for education in this period and what motivated them to get involved? What were their specific goals and what specific strategies did they utilize to achieve them? Why did they choose these strategies and how successful were they in these efforts?

I argued that in the post-1960 years an increasing number of ethnic Mexican activists—both individuals and members of organizations—participated in the struggles for education. These activists continually rejected substandard forms of schooling for their children and fought for improved educational opportunities. They pursued three major strategies to reach their goals— contestation, advocacy, and alternative forms of education. Each of these strategies included a host of parallel or complementary measures aimed at obtaining or improving their children's schooling in this country.

Activists, for instance, contested a variety of exclusionary and discriminatory school policies and practices viewed as detrimental to their children's cultural and academic interests. They also advocated and struggled for reforms that reflected their community, that valued and respected their cultural and linguistic heritage, and that met their academic needs. These ambitions were reflected in the struggles for positions of power in education, for access to all levels of education, for quality instructional programs, and for pluralism. Ethnic Mexican activists likewise looked beyond public education for learning opportunities. They enrolled their children in religious and private institutions controlled by Anglos or established their own schools to educate their children. Private, nonsectarian education was significantly influenced by contextual factors such as nationalism in the 1960s and 1970s and conservatism after 1980.

These diverse strategies were not relatively new, nor were they significantly different from those earlier activists used. Mexican American activists in the decades before the 1960s used similar strategies to improve access to educational opportunities in both public and private schools.

Despite their similarities there were differences. Those in the post-1960 period were broader in scope and more diverse in nature. Discrimination struggles, for instance, were limited primarily to segregation in the past. In the post-1960 years, they were expanded to include other areas of public education, including unequal funding of schools, various forms of testing, especially high-stakes testing, curriculum, preschool and higher education access, and both governance and administration.

A novel development during this period was the significant participation of Mexican American high school and college students in school reform efforts. Unlike the adult members of the ethnic Mexican community who focused on litigation, students turned to mass mobilization and direct action tactics to challenge various forms of discrimination in the local schools. The school walkouts represented this approach.

Advocacy struggles also expanded during this period. In the past, these efforts were not as common. In the post-1960 years Mexican Americans advocated for a variety of reforms in more communities for longer periods of time. Their advocacy struggles were more extensive and intensive than in prior decades. Activists also developed a greater number of nationalist and private schools that met their diverse desires and needs than those of the past.

Mexican American struggles for education differentially impacted school policies and practices. In some cases, it was significant, in others less so.

Their efforts, for instance, eliminated the pattern of structural exclusion and the linguistically subtractive curriculum. Prior to 1960, ethnic Mexicans were excluded from important positions of influence in the public schools. The children's language also was repressed and devalued in the administration of the schools. These patterns were significantly modified in the post-1960 years. The former was disrupted and replaced with one of differentiated inclusion; the latter was replaced with one more sensitive to the Spanish language of the Mexican child. The elimination of no-Spanish-speaking rules at the local school level, the repeal of English-only laws throughout the country, and the passage of state policies that sanctioned, encouraged, or mandated the use of non-English languages in the schools reflected this development.

Mexican American activism also moderately impacted the pattern of student access to education and the culturally subtractive curriculum. Prior to the 1960s, students were provided limited access to the elementary, secondary, and postsecondary grades. Students also were provided with a curriculum that sought to subtract or divest them of their cultural heritage. Both of these patterns underwent some minor modifications during the years after 1960 because of activism. Access to the preschool grades and to postsecondary education increased gradually after 1960. The culturally subtractive curriculum also became more tolerant after 1960. Unlike the pre-1960 years, it did not seek to divest Mexican origin children of their heritage. Instead, it sought to reaffirm their heritage by valuing and incorporating Mexican cultures and histories into the schools.

Despite these successes, educational activism failed to reverse or halt the basic trends of school segregation, unequal funding of the public schools, access to quality educational programs, and the pattern of low achievement. These patterns continued to be immune to change and actually strengthened during the post-1960s largely because of rapidly changing demographic developments, especially the tremendous growth of Mexican and Latina/o immigration and opposition from political leaders, school officials, and conservative organizations.

The actions by Mexican American activists, in essence, expanded, extended, and diversified the historic struggle for educational opportunity activists waged in the first half of the twentieth century.

LESSONS LEARNED

What have we learned from this study of community activism in education in the contemporary period?

First, the struggle for education is much broader than historians have led us to believe. Historians of education have framed this effort largely as a struggle for educational equality.[1] While the struggle for education has included efforts aimed at eliminating discrimination in the schools, this study has shown that it also sought other goals. In addition to seeking social justice in the schools, it sought to improve the academic achievement of Latina/o students, maintain their ethnic identity, and increase the community's political power in the schools. The struggle for education then was not one monolithic, unified movement focused only on eliminating discrimination in the schools. Rather, it was a series of overlapping and staggered movements aimed at accomplishing a variety of goals.

Another lesson learned from this history is that activism did not die down during these decades. It ebbed and flowed over the decades based on a variety of social, economic, political, and cultural factors at the local, state, national, and international levels.

The continuity of activism is reflected in the evolution of these struggles. Some, like the struggle against segregated schools, originated in the late 1960s but soon dissipated from the public arena. By the late 1970s, for example, few activists filed lawsuits against school segregation or worked to actively eliminate this educational practice. The efforts to oppose school segregation, however, were quickly replaced by attempts aimed at promoting bilingual education. Other reforms such as the struggle for Chicana/o Studies emerged in the late 1960s and continued into the present. The recent protests by high school and university students in opposition to cutbacks in Chicana/o Studies programs in California and Arizona indicate that these types of struggles are still being waged by courageous and committed individuals but not well publicized.[2] Chicana/o educational activism then did not end. It underwent a significant transformation and continues to this day. The mainstream media, however, has ignored or marginalized it.

Another lesson this history teaches us is the importance of language and culture to the community. These two elements of the Mexican heritage are important for maintaining the community's ethnic identity as advocated by cultural nationalists during the 1960s and 1970s. They are also important for improving the academic achievement of ethnic Mexican children as advocated by educators throughout all of the decades under consideration. This suggests that continued efforts by public school officials to stamp out, ignore, or demean language and culture in education will only serve to mobilize activists against them. The community's desire to maintain its identity also indicates that activists will continue to support and promote reforms aimed at preserving the Spanish language and the Mexican culture in the schooling of their children.

Finally, this history teaches us that those involved in these struggles were ordinary people who came from all walks of life. Few if any major leaders of the ethnic Mexican civil rights movement, for instance, participated in these reform efforts. These struggles also were not dominated by any one organization or individual. They involved countless organizations and individuals of different ages, occupations, genders, and ideological perspectives. Some of these activists and organizations such as LULAC and the American GI Forum were part of the old guard. Others were new and emerged in the 1960s or later. Included in this group were students, women, parents, and a host of grassroots and community organizations such as MALDEF, IDRA, and MAYO. This mix of old and new actors engaged in a multifaceted and complex series of actions designed to achieve a variety of purposes. Although diverse, these activists shared a common passion. They would no longer tolerate segregated and substandard schools, pervasive underachievement, cultural neglect, or political exclusion.

Notes

Introduction

1. In the text the terms *Chicana/o, Mexican origin, Mexican American,* and *ethnic Mexican* will be used interchangeably. I will use the term *Latina/o* whenever both Mexican origin and other Spanish origin individuals are included in the discussion or whenever the data fail to make distinctions among the various subgroups.

2. See, for instance, Charles Wollenberg, *"Mendez v. Westminster," California Historical Quarterly* 55 (Winter 1974): 317–32; Arnoldo De León, "Blowout 1910 Style: A Chicano School Boycott in West Texas," *Texana* 12 (1974): 124–40; and Carl Allsup, "Education Is Our Freedom: The American G.I. Forum and the Mexican American School Segregation in Texas, 1948–1957," *Aztlán* 8 (Spring 1977): 27–50.

3. For an overview of this literature see Guadalupe San Miguel Jr., "Status of the Historiography of Mexican American Education: A Preliminary Analysis," *History of Education Quarterly* 26 (1986): 523–36, and Victoria-María MacDonald, "Hispanic, Latino, Chicano, or 'Other'?: Deconstructing the Relationship between Historians and Hispanic American Educational History," *History of Education Quarterly* 41, no. 3 (2001): 365–413.

4. Tom Carter did one of the first monographs on the education of Mexican Americans in 1970. Despite its title, this book was not a historical study of Mexican Americans in the school but a sociological one. Unlike most sociological studies of that period, Carter's contained an important amount of historical information. See Tomas P. Carter, *Mexican Americans in School: A History of Educational Neglect* (Princeton, NJ: College Entrance Examination Board, 1970).

5. See Guadalupe San Miguel Jr., *Let All of Them Take Heed* (College Station: Texas A&M University Press, 2001; originally published in 1987); Rubén Donato, *The Other Struggle for Equal Schools* (Albany: State University of New York Press, 1997); Lynne Marie Getz, *Schools of Their Own* (Albuquerque: University of New Mexico Press, 1997); Guadalupe San Miguel Jr., *Brown, Not White* (College Station: Texas A&M University Press, 2002); Richard Valencia, *Mexican Americans and the Courts* (Albany: State University of New York Press, 2009); Philippa Strum, *Mendez v. Westminster: School Desegregation and Mexican American Rights* (Lawrence:

University Press of Kansas, 2010); Paul A. Sracic, *San Antonio v. Rodriguez and the Pursuit of Equal Education: The Debate over Discrimination and School Funding* (Lawrence: University Press of Kansas, 2006), Mario T. Garcia and Sal Castro, *Blowout! Sal Castro and the Chicano Struggle for Educational Justice* (Chapel Hill: University of North Carolina Press, 2011).

6. Although emphasis is placed on activism in this study, readers should note that another tradition of scholarship exists within the field of Mexican American educational history. This other tradition emphasizes institutional developments in education and examines what schools have done to or for Mexican American students and how these students have fared in them. For a better understanding of these two scholarly traditions in the history of Mexican origin education in the United States, see San Miguel, "Status of the Historiography of Mexican American Education: A Preliminary Analysis," 523–36. For a brief historical study utilizing these two approaches, see Guadalupe San Miguel Jr. and Richard R. Valencia, "From the Treaty of Guadalupe Hidalgo to Hopwood: The Educational Plight and Struggle of Mexican Americans in the Southwest," *Harvard Educational Review* 68, no. 3 (1998): 353–412.

7. In addition to those listed in note 1 see Meyer Weinberg, *A Chance to Learn* (New York: Cambridge University Press, 1976); Charles Wollenberg, *All Deliberate Speed* (Berkeley: University of California Press, 1976); Guadalupe San Miguel Jr., "Mexican American Organizations and the Changing Politics of School Desegregation in Texas, 1945–1980," *Social Science Quarterly* 63 (December 1982): 701–15; Guadalupe San Miguel Jr., "The Struggle against Separate and Unequal Schools: Middle Class Mexican Americans and the Desegregation Campaign in Texas, 1929–1957," *History of Education Quarterly* 23 (Fall 1983): 343–59; Roberto Alvarez Jr., "The Lemon Grove Incident: The Nation's First Successful Desegregation Court Case," *Journal of San Diego History* 32 (Spring 1986): 116–35; Francisco E. Balderrama, "The Battle against School Segregation," in *The Los Angeles Mexican Consulate and the Mexican Community in Los Angeles, 1929–1936* (Tucson: University of Arizona Press, 1982): 55–72; Gilbert G. Gonzalez, "The Rise and Fall of De Jure Segregation in the Southwest," in *Chicano Education in the Era of Segregation* (Philadelphia: Balch Institute Press, 1990), 147–56; Christopher Arriola, "Knocking on the Schoolhouse Door: Mendez v. Westminster—Equal Protection, Public Education, and Mexican Americans in the 1940s," *La Raza Law Journal* 8 (1995): 166–207; Vicki L. Ruiz, "We Always Tell Our Children They Are Americans": *Mendez v. Westminster* and the California Road to *Brown v. Board of Education*," *College Board Review* 200 (Fall 2003): 21–27; Vicki L. Ruiz, "South by Southwest: Mexican Americans and Segregated Schooling, 1900–1950," *OAH Magazine of History* (Winter 2001): 23–27; Richard R. Valencia, "The Mexican American Struggle for Equal Educational Opportunity in *Mendez v. Westminster:* Helping to Pave the Way for *Brown v. Board of Education*," *Teachers College Record* 107, no. 3 (2005): 389–423; Jennifer McCormick and César Ayala, "Felícita 'La prieta' Méndez and the end of Latino Segregation in California," *Centro: Journal of the Center for Puerto Rican Studies* 19 (2007): 13–35; Philippa Strum, *Mendez v. Westminster: School Desegregation and Mexican American Rights* (Lawrence: University Press of Kansas, 2010); Mary Melcher, "'This Is Not Right': Rural Arizona Women Challenge Segregation and Ethnic Division, 1925–1950,"*Frontiers* 20, no. 2 (1999): 190–214; Laura K. Muñoz, "Separate but Equal? A Case Study of *Romo v. Laird* and Mexican American Education," *Organization of American Historians Magazine of History*, 15, no. 2 (2001): 28–35; Jeanne M. Powers and Lirio Patton, "Between *Mendez* and *Brown: Gonzales v. Sheely* (1951) and the Legal Campaign against Segregation," *Law and Social Inquiry* 33, no. 1 (2008): 127–71.

8. See, for instance, Mario Garcia, "Education and the Mexican American: Eleuterio Escobar and the School Improvement League of San Antonio," in *Mexican Americans* (New Haven, CT: Yale University Press, 1989), 62–83; Lynne Marie Getz, "George I. Sánchez in New Mexico," in *Schools of Their Own* (Albuquerque: University of New Mexico Press, 1997), 48–65; and E. C. Condon, J. Y. Peters, and C. Suiero-Ross, "Educational Testing and Spanish-Speaking Exceptional Children," in *Special Education and the Hispanic Child: Cultural Perspectives* (Reston, VA: Council for Exceptional Children, 1979): 16–32.

9. Richard R. Valencia, *Chicano Students and the Courts* (Albany: State University of New York Press, 2008), xv.

10. Guadalupe San Miguel Jr., *Let All of Them Take Heed* (College Station: Texas A&M University Press, 1987); Mario Garcia, *Mexican Americans* (New Haven, CT: Yale University Press, 1989); Arnold Leibowitz, *Educational Policy and Political Acceptance: The Imposition of English as the Language of Instruction in American Schools* (Washington, DC: Center for Applied Linguistics, 1971); Erlinda Gonzales-Berry, "Which Language Will Our Children Speak? The Spanish Language and Public Education Policy in New Mexico, 1890–1930," in *The Contested Homeland: A Chicano History of New Mexico*, ed. Erlinda Gonzales-Berry and David R. Maciel (Albuquerque: University of New Mexico Press, 2000), 169–90; Gilbert G. Gonzalez, "Culture, Language, and the Americanization of Mexican Children," in *Chicano Education in the Era of Segregation* (Philadelphia: Balch Institute Press, 1990), 30–45; and T. Simmons, "The Citizen Factories: The Americanization of Mexican Students in the Texas Public Schools, 1920–1945" (PhD diss., Texas A&M University, 1976).

11. Despite his commitment to improving the academic achievement of Hispano children through comprehensive school reforms, several scholars have noted that Tireman was well intentioned but misguided in his efforts. See Getz, *Schools of Their Own*, 92–95, and David Bachelor, *Educational Reform in New Mexico: Tireman, San José, and Nambé* (Albuquerque: University of New Mexico Press, 1991).

12. For a sampling of these curricular and instructional reforms see Elma A. Neal, "Adapting the Curriculum to Non-English-Speaking Children," *Elementary English Review 6–7* (September 1929): 183–85; Clara Peterson Ebel, "Developing an Experience Curriculum in a Mexican First Grade" (master's thesis, Arizona State Teachers College, 1940); Getz, *Schools of Their Own*, 66–103; Gonzalez, *Chicano Education in the Era of Segregation*, 113–35; Matthew D. Davis, *Exposing a Culture of Neglect: Herschel T. Manuel and Mexican American Schooling* (Greenwich, CT: Information Age Publishing, 2005); and San Miguel, *Let All of Them Take Heed*, 114–45.

13. Quoted in Carlos Muñoz Jr. *Youth, Identity, Power: The Chicano Movement* (New York: Verso, 2002), 31.

14. F. Campbell, "Missiology in New Mexico, 1850–1900: The Success and Failure of Catholic Education," in *Religion and Society in the American West*, ed. C. Guarneri and D. Alvarez (Lanham, MD: University Press of America, 1987): 59–78; Victoria-María MacDonald and Teresa García, "Historical Perspectives on Latino Access to Higher Education, 1848–1990," in *The Majority in the Minority: Expanding the Representation of Latina/o Faculty, Administrators and Students in Higher Education*, ed. Jeanette Castellanos and Lee Jones (Sterling, VA: Stylus

Publishing, 2003); and Gerald McKevitt, "Hispanic Californians and Catholic Higher Education: The Diary of Jesús María Estudillo, 1857–1864," *California History* 69, no. 4 (1990): 322.

15. Edith J. Agnew and Ruth K. Barber, "The Unique Presbyterian School System of New Mexico," *Journal of Presbyterian History* 49, no. 3 (1971): 197–221; Susan M. Yohn, *A Contest of Faiths: Missionary Women and Pluralism in the American Southwest* (Ithaca, NY: Cornell University Press, 1995), 167–211; Carolyn Atkins, "Menaul School: 1881–1930 . . . Not Leaders, Merely, but Christian Leaders," *Journal of Presbyterian History* 58, no. 4 (1980): 279–98.

16. Yohn, *A Contest of Faiths,* 167–211.

17. Ibid.

18. San Miguel, *Let All of Them Take Heed;* James William Cameron, "The History of Mexican Public Education in Los Angeles, 1910–1930" (PhD diss., University of Southern California, 1976).

19. Jovita Gonzalez, "Social Life in Cameron, Starr, and Zapata Counties" (master's thesis, University of Texas, 1930), 75; Francisco Hernandez, "Mexican Schools in the Southwest," unpublished paper, n.d. (in author's possession). James Cameron, "Schools for Mexicans," in Cameron, "The History of Mexican Public Education," 169–83.

Chapter 1

1. One major exception to this general pattern of exclusion occurred in the San Felipe school district located in Del Rio, Texas. See Steven W. Prewitt, "We Didn't Ask to Come to This Party": Self-Determination Collides with the Federal Government in the Public Schools of Del Rio, Texas, 1890–1971" (PhD diss., University of Houston, 2000); and Jesse J. Esparza, "Schools of Their Own: The San Felipe Independent School District and Mexican American Educational Autonomy, Del Rio, Texas, 1928–1972" (PhD diss., University of Houston, 2008).

2. For an overview of these patterns see Guadalupe San Miguel Jr. and Richard R. Valencia, "From the Treaty of Guadalupe Hidalgo to Hopwood: The Educational Plight and Struggle of Mexican Americans in the Southwest," *Harvard Educational Review* 68, no. 3 (1998): 363–77.

3. Craig A. Kaplowitz, *LULAC: Mexican Americans and National Policy* (College Station: Texas A&M University Press, 2005).

4. HoustonISD.org; LAusd.k2.ca.us/laud/board/secretary; cps.edu/About_CPS/the _Board_of_Education/BoardBios/Pages/Boardbios.aspx (all accessed March 30, 2009).

5. Nationally, Latinas/os experienced a pattern of token representation in school board positions. National data for 2004 showed that in the early twenty-first century they comprised only 3.8 percent of local school board members throughout the country. Whites and African Americans, on the other hand, represented 85.5 percent and 7.8 percent, respectively. Fredrick M. Hess, *School Boards at the Dawn of the 21st Century,* 25. Cited in Joel Spring, *American Education* (Boston, MA: McGraw Hill, 2006), 158.

6. The call for increased representation came in the early 1990s. See Jessica Hernandez, "More Hispanics Are Needed on HISD Board," *Houston Chronicle,* April 12, 1991, 15.

7. Arnoldo De León, *Ethnicity in the Sunbelt* (Houston: Center for Mexican American Studies Program, University of Houston, 1989); *District and School Profiles* (Houston: Houston Independent School District, 2002).

8. Roberto Haro, "The Dearth of Latinos in Campus Administration," in *The Status of Hispanics in Higher Education*, Tuesday, reported in *The Chronicle of Higher Education*, December 11, 2001. Report sent by e-mail to author by Baltazar A. Acevedo Jr., December 12, 2001; Roberto Haro, "Choosing Trustees Who Care about Things That Matter," *Chronicle of Higher Education*, December 8, 1995, B1–B2; Roberto Haro, "Latinos and Academic Leadership in American Higher Education," in *Latinos in Higher Education*, ed. David J. León (New York: JAI, 2003), 155–91.

9. Texas A&M appointed a Latina to head its campus in 2009, but she was removed several months later. For an article on Dr. Elsa A. Murano, the twenty-third president of Texas A&M University and the first Latina in its history, see "Office of the President: President Murano's biography," www.tamu.edu/president/biography.html (accessed April 6, 2009).

10. For an example of this, see *Crisis in the Ranks: The Under-Representation of Hispanic Faculty and Administrators in Texas Public Institutions of Higher Education*, report prepared by Ed C. Apodaca for the Texas Association of Chicanos in Higher Education, 1974 (report in author's possession), and Adalberto Aguirre Jr. and Ruben O. Martinez, *Chicanos in Higher Education: Issues and Dilemmas for the 21st Century*, ASHE-ERIC Higher Education Report No. 3 (Washington, DC: George Washington University, School of Education and Human Development, 1993), especially 53–68.

11. Guadalupe San Miguel Jr., *Contested Policy: The Rise and Fall of Federal Bilingual Education in the United States, 1960–2001* (Denton: University of North Texas Press, 2002).

12. See, for instance, Susana Flores and Enrique G. Murillo Jr., "Power, Language, and Ideology: Historical and Contemporary Notes on the Dismantling of Bilingual Education," *Urban Review* 33, no. 3 (2001): 183–206.

13. San Miguel, *Contested Policy*, and "Language Legislation in the USA," James Crawford Website and Emporium, http://ourworld.compuserve.com/homepages/JWCrawford/langleg.htm.

14. For an example of how one local community responded, see Lourdes Diaz Soto, *Language, Culture, and Power: Bilingual Families and the Struggle for Quality Education* (Albany: State University of New York Press, 1997).

15. San Miguel and Valencia, "From the Treaty of Guadalupe Hidalgo to Hopwood," 363–77.

16. "News Release: NCLR Applauds Introduction of Congresswoman Solis' Preschool Bill," September 16, 2004. E-mail sent to author by the National Council de La Raza (NCLR), September 17, 2004.

17. In early May 2007, at the writing of this essay, Congress passed federal legislation to expand access to early childhood and education programs for Latina/o children. Whether this

will significantly increase access is difficult to foretell at this point. See "News Release: NCLR Applauds Passage of the Improving Head Start Act of 2007," May 3, 2007. E-mail sent to the author on May 3, 2007.

18. Weinberg, *A Chance to Learn*, 140–52, and MacDonald and García, "Historical Perspectives on Latino Access to Higher Education, 1848–1990," 15–43.

19. Christine I. Bennett, "Research on Racial Issues in American Higher Education," in *Handbook of Research on Multicultural Education*, ed. James Banks and Cherry McGee Banks (San Francisco: Jossey-Bass, 2004), 852; Harriett Romo and Joanne Salas, "Successful Transition of Latino Students from High School to College," in *Latinos in Higher Education*, ed. David J. León (New York: JAI, 2003), 108.

20. Robert Bernstein, "Hispanics Become More Prevalent on College Campuses," www .census.gov/population/www/socdemo/school.html (accessed March 4, 2009).

21. León, *Latinos in Higher Education*, 3; also see William B. Harvey and Eugene L. Anderson, *Minorities in Higher Education: Twenty-First Annual Status Report* (Washington, DC: American Council on Education, 2005), 11.

22. Patricia Gandara, "Forward," in *Latinos in Higher Education*, ed. León, xi.

23. Romo and Salas, "Successful Transition of Latino Students from High School to College," 108.

24. Michal Kurlaender and Stella M. Flores, "The Racial Transformation of Higher Education," in *Higher Education and the Color Line: College Access, Racial Equity, and Social Change*, ed. Gary Orfield, Patricia Marin, and Catherine L. Horn (Cambridge, MA: Harvard Education Press, 2005), 21.

25. Kurlaender and Flores, "The Racial Transformation," 24.

26. Gilbert G. Gonzalez, "Culture, Language, and the Americanization of Mexican Children," in *Chicano Education in the Era of Segregation* (Philadelphia: Balch Institute Press, 1990), 30–45; Timothy Simmons, "The Citizen Factories: The Americanization of Mexican Students in the Texas Public Schools, 1920–1945" (PhD diss., Texas A&M University, 1976).

27. Lloyd Marcus, *The Treatment of Minorities in Secondary School Textbooks* (New York: Anti-Defamation League of B'nai B'rith, 1961).

28. Michael Kane, *Minorities in Textbooks: A Study of Their Treatment in Social Studies Texts* (Chicago: Quadrangle Books, 1970), 130.

29. Carlos E. Cortés, "A Bicultural Process for Developing Mexican American Heritage Curriculum," in *Multilingual Assessment Project: Riverside Component, 1971–1972 Annual Report*, ed. Alfredo Castaneda, Manuel Ramirez, and Leslie Herold (Riverside, CA: Systems and Evaluations in Education, 1972), 5.

30. Linda K. Salvucci, "Mexico, Mexicans, and Mexican Americans in Secondary-School United States History Textbooks," *History Teacher* 24, no. 2 (1991): 203–22.

31. The book she mentioned was written by Ernes May and Winthrop Jordan. See Salvucci, "Mexico, Mexicans, and Mexican Americans," 207.

32. Salvucci, "Mexico, Mexicans, and Mexican Americans, 209.

33. Ibid., 210.

34. Linda K. Salvucci, "Getting the Facts Straight: New Views of Mexico and Its Peoples in Recently Adopted US History Textbooks in Texas," *Public Historian* 14, no. 4 (1992): 57–69.

35. Joseph A. Rodríguez and Vicki L. Ruiz, "At Loose Ends: Twentieth-Century Latinos in Current United States History Textbooks," *Journal of American History* 86, no. 4 (2000): 1689.

36. Gary Orfield, "Schools More Separate: Consequences of a Decade of Resegregation," Harvard Civil Rights Project, Cambridge, MA, 2001, 33, table 9; see also Gary Orfield, "The Growth of Segregation: African Americans, Latinos, and Unequal Education," in *Dismantling Desegregation: The Quiet Reversal of Brown v. Board of Education*, ed. Gary Orfield, Susan E. Eaton, and the Harvard Project on School Desegregation (New York: New Press, 1996), 53–72.; Richard R. Valencia, Martha Menchaca, and Rubén Donato, "Segregation, Desegregation, and Integration of Chicano Students: Old and New Realities," in *Chicano School Failure and Success,* ed. Richard R. Valencia (New York: Routledge, 2002), 73.

37. Valencia, *Chicano School Failure and Success,* 95.

38. For examples of unequal education and the efforts made to reform the school finance system in one state, see Gregory C. Rocha and Robert H. Webking, *Politics and Public Education: Edgewood v. Kirby and the Reform of Public School Financing in Texas* (Minneapolis: West Publishers, 1992).

39. For historical explanations of underachievement, see E. H. Edson, "Risking the Nation: Historical Dimensions on Survival and Educational Reform," *Issues in Education* 1, nos. 2 and 3 (1983): 171–84; and Guadalupe San Miguel Jr. "Cycles of Concern: A Historical Perspective on the Dropout Problem," *California Public Schools Forum* 1 (Fall 1986): 20–31.

40. Much of this data has been presented in national studies on Latina/o students in the schools since the 1970s. For representative studies, see *Make Something Happen: Hispanics and Urban High School Reform*, vols. 1 and 2 (Washington, DC: Hispanic Policy Development Project, 1984); Gary Orfield, "Hispanic Education: Challenges, Research, and Policies," *American Journal of Education* 95, no. 1 (1986): 1–25; and *From Risk to Opportunity: Fulfilling the Educational Needs of Hispanic Americans in the 21st Century* (Washington, DC: The President's Advisory Commission on Educational Excellence for Hispanic Americans, 2003).

41. A recent article has referred to the schools having significant percentages of Latina/o and racial minority dropout rates as "dropout factories." See Gary Scharrer, Jenny Caputo, Zeke MacCormack, and Jennifer Radcliffe, "Report Points to 'Dropout Factories'/Study Highlights 185 Texas Schools Losing Students Quickly, Including 42 in Houston Area," *Houston Chronicle*, October 31, 2007, 2, www.Houstonchronicle.com (accessed November 7, 2007).

42. Nick Vaca referred to this as the biological determinist perspective. In the early decades of the twentieth century he argued that it provided a racial reason for immigration restriction

and for explaining low IQ test scores. Some soon used this theory as an explanatory framework for interpreting school success by the second quarter of the century. See Nick Vaca, "The Mexican American in the Social Sciences, 1912–1970, Part 2 [1936–1970]," *El Grito* 16 (Fall 1971): 17–51.

43. For overviews of these different deficit models see Vaca, "The Mexican American in the Social Sciences," 17–51; Allan C. Ornstein, "Recent Historical Perspectives for Educating the Disadvantaged," in *Educating the Disadvantaged,* ed. Russell C. Doll and Maxine Hawkins (New York: AMS Press, 1971), 147–67; and Richard R. Valencia, ed., *The Evolution of Deficit Thinking: Educational Thought and Practice* (Washington, DC: Falmer Press, 1997).

44. Vaca, "The Mexican American in the Social Sciences," 17–51.

45. For one of the first studies to document the role that schools played in the pattern of low achievement, see Thomas P. Carter, *Mexican Americans in School: A History of Educational Neglect* (Princeton, NJ: College Entrance Examination Board, 1970). See also Tomás A. Arciniega, "The Myth of the Compensatory Education Model Education of Chicanos," in *Chicanos and Native Americans: The Territorial Minorities,* ed. Rudolph O. de la Garza, Z. Anthony Druszewski, and Tomás A. Arciniega (Englewood Cliffs, NJ: Prentice-Hall, 1971), 173–83. For several recent studies pointing to institutional structures, policies, and practices as responsible for school failure, see Angela Valenzuela, *Subtractive Schooling: US-Mexican Youth and the Politics of Caring* (Albany: State University of New York Press, 1999), 5, and Michelle Fine, *Framing Dropouts: Notes on the Politics of an Urban High School* (Albany: State University of New York Press, 1991). For more general studies of the impact of schools on academic achievement, see W. Brookover, ed., *School Social Systems and Student Achievement: Schools Can Make a Difference* (Brooklyn: F. F. Bergin, 1979).

46. For two examples of these macro approaches to explaining low academic performance, see Samuel Bowles and Herbert Gintis, *Schooling in Capitalist America* (New York: Basic Books, 1976), and John U. Ogbu, "Variability in Minority School Performance: A Problem in Search of an Explanation," *Anthropology and Education Quarterly* 18 (1987): 312–34.

47. Constance Walker, "Hispanic Underachievement: Old Views and New Perspectives," in *Success or Failure?: Learning and the Language Minority Student,* ed. Henry Trueba (Cambridge, MA: Newbury House Publishers, 1987), 15–32.

48. For a good example of this type of study, see Laurence Steinberg, Patricia Lin Blinde, and Kenyon S. Chan, "Dropping Out among Language Minority Youth," *Review of Educational Research* 54, no. 1 (1984): 113–32. They argue that the combination of socioeconomic disadvantages and early academic failure contributes to the higher dropout rate of language minority youth. For another example, see Russell W. Rumberger, "Chicano Dropouts: A Review of Research and Policy Issues," in *Chicano School Failure and Success: Research and Policy Agendas for the 1990s,* ed. Richard R. Valencia (New York: Falmer Press, 1991), 64–90.

49. See especially John Ogbu, *The Next Generation: An Ethnography of Education in an Urban Neighborhood* (New York: Academic Press, 1974), and *Minority Education and Caste: The American System in Cross-Cultural Perspective* (New York: Academic Press, 1978).

50. See Maria Eugenia Matute-Bianchi, "Ethnic Identities and Patterns of School Success and Failure among Mexican-Descent and Japanese-American Students in a California High School: An Ethnographic Analysis," *American Journal of Education* 95, no. 1 (1986): 233–55; and Henry T. Trueba, *Success or Failure? Learning and Language Minority Students* (New York: Newbury House Publishers, 1987). For continuing critiques of Ogbu's thesis in the 1990s, see Douglas E. Foley, "Reconsidering Anthropological Explanations of Ethnic School Failure," *Anthropology and Education Quarterly* 22, no. 1 (1991): 60–94; and Hugh Mehan, Lea Hubbard, and Irene Villanueva, "Forging Academic Identities: Accommodation without Assimilation among Involuntary Minorities," *Anthropology and Education Quarterly* 25, no. 2 (1994): 91–117.

51. Ogbu continued to be an influential scholar in this area. See, for instance, John U. Ogbu, "Variability in Minority School Performance: A Problem in Search of an Explanation," *Anthropology and Education Quarterly* 18, no. 4 (1987): 312–34. For an exemplary study on school success and failure, see Harriett D. Romo and Toni Falbo, *Latino High School Graduation: Defying the Odds* (Austin: University of Texas Press, 1996). For a more recent study, see Mariella Espinoza-Herold, *Issues in Latino Education: Race, School Culture, and the Politics of Academic Success* (Boston: Pearson Education Group, 2003).

52. For several examples of student school success, see Marcelo Suárez-Orozco, "Immigrant Adaptation of Schooling: A Hispanic Case," in *Minority Status and Schooling: A Comparative Study of Immigrant and Involuntary Minorities*, ed. Margaret A. Gibson and John U. Ogbu (New York: Garland Publishing, 1991), 37–61; Lourdes D. Soto, "Success Stories," in *Research and Multicultural Education: From the Margins to the Mainstream*, ed. Carl A. Grant (London: Falmer Press, 1992), 153–64; Gisela Ernst, Elsa L. Statzner, and H. T. Trueba, eds., "Alternative Visions of Schooling: Success Stories in Minority Settings," *Anthropology and Education Quarterly* 25, no. 3 (1994): 317–35. For the way in which parents assist students in forging school success, see Concha Delgado-Gaitan, "School Matters in the Mexican American Home: Socializing Children to Education," *American Educational Research Journal* 29, no. 3 (1992): 495–513; "Involving Parents in the Schools: A Process of Empowerment," *American Journal of Education* 100, no. 1 (1991): 20–46; and "Consejos: The Power of Cultural Narratives," *Anthropology and Education Quarterly* 25, no. 3 (1994): 298–316.

53. Gisela Ernst and Elsa L. Statzner, "Alternative Visions of Schooling: An Introduction," *Anthropology and Education Quarterly* 25, no. 3 (1994): 200–207. Quote is from p. 201.

54. These studies were reacting to one of Ogbu's arguments that minorities failed to achieve academically because they tended to equate schooling with assimilation into the dominant group. These counterstudies showed that caste-like minorities such as African Americans, Mexican Americans, or Puerto Ricans could succeed at school and maintain their own identity. See, for instance, Nilda Flores-González, "Puerto Rican High Achievers: An Example of Ethnic and Academic Identity Compatibility," *Anthropology and Education Quarterly* 30, no. 3 (1999): 343–62; and Hugh Mehan, Lea Hubbard, and Irene Villnueva, "Forming Academic Identities: Accommodation without Assimilation among Involuntary Minorities," *Anthropology and Education Quarterly* 25, no. 2 (1994): 91–117.

55. Frederick Erickson, "Transformation and School Success: The Politics and Culture of Educational Achievement," *Anthropology and Education Quarterly* 18, no. 4 (1987): 335–56; Hugh

Mehan, Irene Villanueva, Lea Hubbard, and Angela Lintz, *Constructing School Success: The Consequences of Untracking Low-Achieving Students* (New York: Cambridge University Press, 1996); Pedro Reyes, Jay D. Scribner, and Alicia Paredes Scribner, eds., *Lessons from High-Performing Hispanic Schools: Creating Learning Communities* (New York: Teachers College Press, 1999).

56. The educational psychologist Richard P. Valencia took a leading role in promoting the idea of investigating both Latino school failure and success. See Richard R. Valencia, ed., *Chicano School Failure and Success: Research and Policy Agendas for the 1990s* (New York: Falmer Press, 1991). For a historical treatment of school success in one state—Colorado—see Rubén Donato, "Hispano Education and the Implications of Autonomy: Four School Systems in Southern Colorado, 1920–1963," *Harvard Educational Review* 69 (Summer 1999): 117–49.

57. See, for instance, Brookover, *School Social Systems and Student Achievement*.

58. See, for instance, Carlos Arce, "Chicano Participation in Academe: A Case of Academic Colonialism," *Grito del Sol: A Chicano Quarterly* 3 (1978): 75–104. See also Michael A. Olivas, ed., *Latino College Students* (New York: Teachers College Press, 1986).

59. One of the earliest studies to use the metaphor of the pipeline was published in 1988. See Laura Rendón and A. Nora, "Hispanic Students: Stopping the Leaks in the Pipeline," *Educational Record* 68, no. 4 (1988): 79–85. A few scholars have recently used the metaphor of the highway instead of the pipeline. For an elaboration of Latina/o education as an educational highway on the road to the university and beyond, see the preface in *The Latina/o Pathway to the Ph.D.: Abriendo Caminos*, ed. Jeanett Castellanos, Alberta M. Gloria, and Mark Kamimura (Sterling, VA: Stylus Publishing, 2006), xxiii–xxxv.

60. For a recent look at the status of Chicana/o education by way of the educational pipeline, see Tara J. Yasso and Daniel G. Solórzano, "Leaks in the Chicana and Chicano Educational Pipeline," *Latino Policy and Issues Brief* 13 (March 2006) (UCLA Chicano Studies Research Center).

61. These types of studies began in the 1970s and continued to be published during the 1970s and 1980s. See, for examples, the following: Richard I. Ferrín, Richard W. Jonsen, and Cesar M. Trimble, *Access to College for Mexican Americans in the Southwest*, Higher Education Surveys Report No. 6 (Princeton, NJ: College Entrance Examination Board, July 1972); Samuel Betances, "Puerto Ricans and Mexican Americans in Higher Education," *The Rican* 1, no. 4 (1974): 27–36; Corinne Sánchez, "Higher Education y La Chicana?" *Encuentro Femenil* 1, no. 1 (1973): 27–33; Ronald W. López, Arturo Madrid-Barela, and Reynaldo Flores Macías, *Chicanos in Higher Education: Status and Issues*, Monograph no. 7 (Los Angeles: Chicano Studies Center Publications, UCLA, 1976); and Michael A. Olivas, "Hispanics in Higher Education: Status and Issues," *Educational Evaluation and Policy Analysis* 4 (1982): 301–10. For a more recent study, see Adalberto Aguirre Jr. and Ruben O. Martinez, *Chicanos in Higher Education: Issues and Dilemmas for the 21st Century*, ASHE-ERIC Higher Education Report No. 3 (Washington, DC: George Washington University, School of Education and Human Development, 1993).

62. For several studies pointing to the historical aspects of the experiences of Chicanas/os and Latinas/os in higher education, see Carlos Muñoz Jr., *Youth, Identity, and Power* (New York:

Verso, 1989); Weinberg, *A Chance to Learn;* and Victoria-María MacDonald, *Latino Education* (New York: Palgrave Macmillan, 2004).

63. Aguirre and Martinez, *Chicanos in Higher Education;* León, *Latinos in Higher Education.*

64. Michael A. Olivas, *The Dilemma of Access* (Washington, DC: Howard University Press, 1979); E. Padrón, "Hispanics and Community Colleges in *A Handbook on the Community College in America,* ed. G. Baker (Westport, CT: Greenwood Press, 1994); and Laura Rendón, R. Jalomo, and K. Garcia, "The University and Community College Paradox: Why Latinos Do Not Transfer," in *The Educational Achievement of Latinos: Barriers and Success,* ed. A. Hurtado and E. Garcia (Santa Cruz: Regents of the University of California, 1994), 227–58.

65. Alna M. Zambone and Margarita Alicea-Sáez, "Latino Students in Pursuit of Higher Education: What Helps or Hinders Their Success?" in *Latino Students in American Schools: Historical and Contemporary Views,* ed. Valentina I. Kloosterman (Westport, CT: Praeger, 2003), 63–78.

66. For one of the earliest studies to address gender in Chicana/o higher education, see Corinne Sánchez, "Higher Education y La Chicana?" *Encuentro Femenil* 1, no. 1 (1973): 27–33.

67. Carlos Muñoz Jr., "The Quest for Paradigm: The Development of Chicano Studies and Intellectuals," in *History Culture, and Society: Chicano Studies in the 1980s* (Ypsilanti, MI: Bilingual Press 1983), 19–36.

68. For an overview of this issue, see especially Roberto Haro, "Latinos and Academic Leadership in American Higher Education," in *Latinos in Higher Education,* ed. David J. León (New York: JAI, 2003), 155–92.

69. See, for instance, Michael A. Olivas, ed., *Latino College Students* (New York: Teachers College Press, 1986); Aguirre and Martinez, *Chicanos in Higher Education;* and León, *Latinos in Higher Education.*

70. Alana M. Zambone and Margarita Alicea-Sáez, "Latino Students in Pursuit of Higher Education: What Helps or Hinders Their Success?," in *Latino Students in American Schools: Historical and Contemporary Views,* ed. Valentina I. Kloosterman (Westport, CT: Praeger, 2003), 63–78. See also Patricia Gándara, *Over the Ivy Walls: The Educational Mobility of Low-Income Chicanos* (Albany: State University of New York Press, 1995).

71. S. Ting, "First-Year Grades and Academic Progress of College Students of First-Generation and Low-Income Families," *Journal of College Admissions* (Winter 1998): 15–23; Zambone and Alicea-Sáez, "Latino Students in Pursuit of Higher Education."

72. Zambone and Alicea-Sáez, "Latino Students in Pursuit of Higher Education"; León, *Latinos in Higher Education.*

Chapter 2

1. For histories of the struggle against educational discrimination by the Mexican American community during the first half of the twentieth century, see San Miguel and Valencia, "From

the Treaty of Guadalupe Hidalgo to Hopwood," 353–77; and San Miguel, *Let All of Them Take Heed.*

2. For an overview of the literature on the LA walkouts, see Francisco A. Rosales, "The Fight for Educational Reform," in *Chicano: The History of the Mexican American Civil Rights Movement* (Houston: Arte Público Press, 1997), 175–95; Dolores Delgado Bernal, "Chicana School Resistance and Grassroots Leadership: Providing an Alternative History of the 1968 East Los Angeles Blowouts" (PhD diss., University of California, Los Angeles, 1997); Kaye Briegel, "Chicano Student Militancy: The Los Angeles High School Strike of 1968," in *An Awakened Minority: The Mexican Americans,* ed. Manuel P. Servin (New York: Macmillan, 1974), 215–25; Carlos Muñoz Jr., "The Politics of Protest and Chicano Liberation: A Case Study of Repression and Cooperation," *Aztlán* 5, nos. 1 and 2 (1974): 119–41; and Carlos Muñoz Jr., "The Politics of Educational Change in East Los Angeles," in *Mexican Americans and Educational Change,* ed. Alfredo Castañeda, Manuel Ramírez III, Carlos E. Cortés, and Mario Barrera (New York: Arno Press, 1974), 83–104.

3. Mario T. Garcia and Sal Castro, *Blowout: Sal Castro and the Chicano Struggle for Educational Justice* (Chapel Hill: University of North Carolina Press, 2011).

4. Muñoz, "The Politics of Educational Change in East Los Angeles," 86.

5. On the walkouts in Denver, see for instance Ernesto B. Vigil, *The Crusade for Justice: Chicano Militancy and the Government's War on Dissent* (Madison: University of Wisconsin Press, 1999), 81–87. On Chicago protests, see Carmen Maria Torres Sanchez, "An Historical Inquiry into the Role of Community Activist Organizations in Dealing with the Problem of Overcrowded Elementary Schools in the Hispanic Community of Chicago, 1970–1990" (EdD diss., Northern Illinois University, 1993).

6. For studies on student protests in Texas, see Armando Navarro, "MAYO: Protagonists for Educational Change," in *MAYO: Avante Garde of the Chicano Movement* (Austin: University of Texas Press, 1995), 115–48; and Baldemar James Barrera, "'We Want Better Education!': The Chicano Student Movement for Educational Reform in South Texas, 1968–1970 (PhD diss., University of New Mexico, 2007). For information on walkouts in different cities, see Juan O. Sanchez, "Walkout Cabrones: The Uvalde School Walkout of 1970," *West Texas Historical Association Year Book* 68 (1992): 122–33; Juan O. Sanchez, "Encina: The Uvalde School Walkout" (master's thesis, Sul Ross State University, 1992); Guadalupe San Miguel Jr., "The Community Is Beginning to Rumble: The Origins of Chicano Educational Protest in Houston, 1965–1970," *Houston Review* 13 (1991): 127–47; Miguel A. Guajardo and Francisco J. Guajardo, "The Impact of Brown on the Brown of South Texas: A Micropolitical Perspective on the Education of Mexican Americans in a South Texas Community," *American Educational Research Journal* 41, no. 3 (2004): 501–26; Baldemar James Barrera, "Edcouch Elsa High School Walkout: Chicano Student Activism in a South Texas Community" (master's thesis, University of Texas, El Paso, 2001); and B. James Barrera, "The 1968 San Antonio School Walkouts: The Beginning of the Chicano Student Movement in South Texas," *Journal of South Texas* 21, no. 1 (2008), 39–61.

7. Rosales, "The Fight for Educational Reform," 175–95.

8. Navarro, "MAYO: Protagonists for Educational Change," 115–48.

9. See Muñoz, "The Politics of Educational Change," and Muñoz, "The Politics of Protest and Chicano Liberation," 119–41.

10. On Cucamonga, California, see Armando Navarro, "Educational Change through Political Action," in *Mexican Americans and Educational Change*, ed. Alfredo Castañeda, Manuel Ramírez III, Carlos E. Cortés, and Mario Barrera (New York: Arno Press, 1974), 105–39. On Crystal City, see Navarro, "MAYO: Protagonists for Educational Change," 115–48, and Armando Navarro, *The Cristal Experiment: A Chicano Struggle for Community Control* (Madison: University of Wisconsin Press, 1998). On Houston, see Guadalupe San Miguel Jr., *Brown, Not White: School Integration and the Chicano Movement* (College Station: Texas A&M University Press, 2001). On Uvalde, see Sanchez, "Walkout Cabrones," 122–33; Sanchez, "Encina," 1992. On Edcouch Elsa, see Barrera, "Edcouch Elsa High School Walkout."

11. Javier Rodriguez, "Blackboard Bungle: Part I," *Houston Press*, April 19, 1990, 8–20; Javier Rodriguez, "Blackboard Bungle: Part II," *Houston Press*, April 26, 1990, 1, 8–15.

12. On the school closure issue, see Richard R. Valencia, "The School Closure Issue and the Chicano Community," *Urban Review* 12 (1980): 5–21, at 10.

13. Puerto Ricans in New York City also participated in similar efforts but several years earlier. Unlike Mexican Americans, Puerto Rican activists collaborated with and joined a black-initiated effort to support comprehensive integration plans in the New York City schools. Planning and growing support among Puerto Ricans for a boycott to support integration in that city began in the fall of 1963 and continued into the early months of the following year. On February 3, 1964, over one hundred thousand Puerto Rican students joined several hundred thousand black students in boycotting the New York City public schools to protest the lack of significant integration. Although Puerto Ricans supported the struggle for integration they also argued that Spanish-speaking kids had special needs that local officials had failed to address. They thus supported not only integration but also improvement in the quality of schools found in their communities. See "Boycott Cripples City Schools; Absences 360,000 above Normal; Negroes and Puerto Ricans Unite," *New York Times*, February 4, 1964; ProQuest Historical Newspapers The New York Times (1851–2005), 1; and Peter Kihss, "Puerto Ricans Gain," *New York Times*, February 6, 1964; ProQuest Historical Newspapers The New York Times (1851–2005), 1.

14. San Miguel, *Brown, Not White*.

15. Juan Gómez-Quiñones, *Mexican Students por La Raza: The Chicano Student Movement in Southern California, 1967–1977* (Santa Barbara, CA: Editorial La Causa, 1978), 16–19.

16. Most scholars acknowledge that the student movement was largely a youth movement. While youth in the universities organized to deal with issues of institutional discrimination, young people in the community also organized to deal with problems confronting Mexican Americans in their neighborhoods. In a few cases, community-based organizations were comprised of both college and noncollege youth. The most prominent of these community-based youth organizations were the Brown Berets in California and the Mexican American Youth Organization (MAYO) in Texas. See Gómez-Quiñones, *Mexican Students por La Raza*, and

Navarro, "*MAYO:* Protagonists for Educational Change." See also David Montejano, *Quixote's Soldiers: A Local History of the Chicano Movement, 1966–1981* (Austin: University of Texas Press, 2011).

17. Gómez-Quiñones, *Mexican Students por La Raza*, 21.

18. Marisol Moreno, "'Of the Community, for the Community': The Chicana/o Student Movement in California's Public Higher Education, 1967–1973" (PhD diss., University of California, Santa Barbara, 2009); George Mariscal, *Brown-Eyed Children of the Sun: Lessons from the Chicano Movement, 1965–1975* (Albuquerque: University of New Mexico Press, 2005), 210–46.

19. Jose B. Cuellar, "A History of SFSU's La Raza Studies," paper presented at "Taking Control of Our Destinies: El Desarrollo de Chicana and Chicano Studies: A Symposium on Standards, Processes, and Assessment for Developing and Maintaining Chicana and Chicano Studies in California," San Diego State University, October 15, 1999; http://www.sfsu.edu~cecipp/a_history.htm (accessed April 16, 2003); Muñoz, *Youth, Identity, and Power*, 131; Mariscal, *Brown-Eyed Children of the Sun;* Moreno, "Of the Community, for the Community."

20. Although El Plan de Santa Bárbara called for the establishment of a department, a research center, and a Chicano Studies library, most institutions implemented only aspects of this plan. In some places, a department was established. In others, a research center, and in still others a specialized curricula within existing academic units. At UCLA, for instance, the administration established a Chicano Studies Research Center in 1969. At UC Santa Barbara, on the other hand, a Chicano Studies program more in keeping with the one proposed in El Plan de Santa Bárbara was established. The units established at UCSB in 1972 included an academic department, a research center, a community service center, and student support services. Carlos Muñoz Jr., *Youth, Identity, Power: The Chicano Movement* (New York: Verso, 1989), 133–34.

21. C. J. Sanchez, "Chicano Studies: A Challenge for Colleges and Universities," *Civil Rights Digest* 3, no. 4 (1970): 36–39; Alfred I. Zuniga and Barbara Rigby-Acosta, "A Study of the Nature of Chicano Studies Written between 1968 and 1974: A Tentative Description," in *Perspectives on Chicano Education*, ed. Tobias and Sandra Gonzalez (Stanford, CA: Chicano Fellows Program, 1975): 103–23.

22. Moreno, "Of the Community, for the Community."

23. Carlos Manuel Haro, ed., *The Bakke Decision: The Question of Chicano Access to Higher Education*, Chicano Studies Center Document no. 4 (Los Angeles: University of California at Los Angeles, 1976). See also William Trombley, "Court Rejects College Plans for Minorities," *Los Angeles Times*, September 17, 1976, and National Lawyers Guild and the National Congress of Black Lawyers, *Affirmative Action in Crisis: A Handbook for Activists* (Detroit, 1977). While the lower court and the state supreme court ruled against affirmative action, the US Supreme Court took a middle position. See *Regents of the University of California v. Bakke*, 1978.

24. Muñoz, *Youth, Identity, Power*, 174.

25. In the early 1990s, students mobilized against the failure by the UCSB administration to hire Rudy Acuña, the founding member of the Chicano Studies Department at California State University at Northridge and often called the "father of Chicano Studies." In 1990 he was invited

to apply for a professorship in the Chicano Studies Department at the University of California at Santa Barbara (UCSB). Although the department submitted his name as the sole candidate for the position, he was not offered the position. In 1992 Acuña filed suit against UCSB for racial, political, and age discrimination. A federal judge rejected the claims of ethnic and political bias but heard the case on the grounds of age discrimination. For the next three years, students at UCSB and in many campuses throughout the state and in other parts of the country organized a series of demonstrations against the university. On October 30, 1995, Acuña won the verdict in Los Angeles. For information on the causes and consequences of the University of California's failure to hire him, see Rudy Acuña, *Sometimes There Is No Other Side: Chicanos and the Myth of Equality* (Notre Dame, IN: University of Notre Dame Press, 1998).

26. For a recent study documenting community challenges to these discriminatory policies, see Richard R. Valencia, *Chicano Students and the Courts: The Mexican American Legal Struggle for Educational Equality* (New York: New York University Press, 2008).

27. For a history of these cases, see George A. Martinez, "Legal Indeterminacy, Judicial Discretion, and the Mexican American Litigation Experience: 1930–1980," *University of California at Davis Law Review* 27 (1994): 557–618; Steven H. Wilson, "Brown over 'Other White': Mexican Americans' Legal Arguments and Litigation Strategy in School Desegregation Lawsuits," *Law and History Review* 21, no. 1 (2003): 145–94; and Guadalupe San Miguel Jr. "The Impact of Brown on Mexican American Desegregation Litigation, 1950s to 1980s," *Journal of Latinos and Education* 4, no. 4 (2005): 221–36.

28. Wilson, "Brown over 'Other White,'" 145–94.

29. *Brown v. Board of Education of Topeka*, 347 US 483 (1954).

30. *Romero v. Weakly*, 131 F. Supp. 818 (S.D. Cal.), rev'd 226 F.2d 399 (9th Cir. 1955).

31. For a summary of these developments, see Martinez, "Legal Indeterminacy, Judicial Discretion, and the Mexican American Litigation Experience," 557–618.

32. Wilson, "Brown over 'Other White,'" 145–94.

33. Jorge C. Rangel and Carlos M. Alcala, "Project Report: De Jure Segregation of Chicanos in Texas Schools, *Harvard Civil Rights–Civil Liberties Law Review* 7 (1972): 331–49.

34. The first three cases filed by Mexican American parents in the late 1960s were: *Chapa v. Odem Ind. School Dist.*, Civil Action No. 66-C-92 (S.D. Tex., July 28, 1967) (unreported); *Perez v. Sonora Ind School District*, Civil Action No. 6-224 (N.D Tex., Nov. 5, 1970); *Cisneros v. Corpus Christi Independent School District*, 324 F. Supp. 599 (S.D. Tex. 1970), No. 71-2397 (5th Cir., July 16, 1971).

35. On California, see *Soria v. Oxnard School District Board of Trustees*, 328 F. Supp. 155 (1971). On Colorado, see *Keyes v. School District No. 1*, 313 F. Supp. 61 (D. Colo. 1970), rev'd, 445 F.2d 990 (10th Cir. 1971), cert. granted, 40 U.S.L.W. 3335 (US Jan. 18, 1972); 380 F. Supp. 673 (D. Col. 1973), 521 F. 2d 465 (10th Cir. 1975).

36. *Cisneros v. Corpus Christi Independent School District*, 324 F. Supp. 599 (S.D. Tex., June 4, 1970), 606.

37. *Ross v. Eckels*, 434 F.2d 1140 (5th Cir. 1970).

38. *Ross v. Eckels*, 434 F.2d 1140 (5th Cir. 1970), 1150.

39. *Houston Chronicle*, August 16, 1970, cited in San Miguel, *Let All of Them Take Heed*, 190.

40. San Miguel,, *Let All of them Take Heed*, 180.

41. *Keyes v. School District No. 1*, Denver, Colorado, 445 Fed Rep, 2d Series (10th Cir., June 11, 1971); 380 F. Supp. 673 (D. Col. 1973).

42. *Lau v. Nichols*, 414 US 563 (1974).

43. For a comprehensive history of bilingual education policy, see Guadalupe San Miguel Jr. *Contested Policy: The Rise and Fall of Federal Bilingual Education Policy in the United States, 1960–2001* (Denton: University of North Texas Press, 2004)

44. See, for instance, Josué M. González, *Towards Quality in Bilingual Education / Bilingual Education in the Integrated School* (Rosslyn, VA: National Clearinghouse for Bilingual Education, 1979).

45. *Keyes v. School District No. 1*, Denver, Colorado, 445 Fed Rep, 2d Series (10th Cir., June 11, 1971); 380 F. Supp. 673 (D. Col. 1973), 521 F.2d 465 (10th Cir. 1975).

46. In most of these cases, they sought intervention in order to argue that ethnic Mexican children had distinct needs that the court had to address in integrating the schools. See, for instance, M. Beatriz Arias, "Desegregation and the Rights of Hispanic Students: The Los Angeles Case," *Center for the Study of Evaluation*, UCLA, 6, no. 1 (1979): 14–18; Carlos Haro, *Mexican/Chicano Concerns and School Desegregation in Los Angeles*, Monograph no. 9 (Los Angeles: Chicano Studies Center Publications, UCLA, 1977). See also more generally, Gary Orfield, *Must We Bus? Segregated Schools and National Policy* (Washington, DC: Brookings Institution, 1978).

47. San Miguel, *Let All of Them Take Heed;* Wilson, "Brown over 'Other White,'" 145–94.

48. Gary Orfield, Susan E. Eaton, and the Harvard Project on School Desegregation, eds., *Dismantling Desegregation: The Quiet Reversal of Brown v. Board of Education* (New York: New Press, 1996), 53–56.

49. The Mexican American struggle against unequal funding of public education was part of a nationwide movement that eventually involved over thirty states. Between 1971 and 1973 fifty-two lawsuits were filed in federal and state courts in more than thirty states attacking local property taxes as the chief support for public schools because they resulted in unequal educational opportunities for children. But in the Southwest, Mexican Americans were in the forefront of this effort. For a detailed discussion of the school finance cases as well as the issues raised by school finance reform in general during the 1970s and 1980s, see Walter I. Garms, James W. Guthrie, and Lawrence C. Pierce, eds., *School Finance: The Economics and Politics of Public Education* (Englewood Cliffs, NJ: Prentice-Hall, 1978); Howard A. Glickstein, *Inequality in School Financing: The Role of the Law* (Washington, DC: US Commission on Civil Rights, 1972); Betsy Levin, "Recent Developments in the Law of Equal Educational Oppor-

tunity," *Journal of Law and Education* 4, no. 3 (1975): 411–47; and A. Thomas Stubbs, "After Rodriguez: Recent Developments in School Finance Reform," *Tax Lawyer* 44, no. 1 (1991): 313–41.

50. *Serrano v. Priest*, 5 Cal.3d 584, 96 Cal. Reptr. 601, 487 Pac.2d 1241 (1971); *Serrano v. Priest*, Civil No. 938,254 (Cal. Super. Ct., April 10, 1974), 102–103; *Rodriguez v. San Antonio Independent School District*, C.A. No. 68–175–5A (W.D. Tex 1971).

51. Garms, Guthrie, and Pierce, *School Finance*, 37.

52. John McDermott, "Serrano: What Does It Mean?," *Un Nuevo Dia* (newsletter published by the Chicano Education Project, Lakewood, Colorado), vol. 3 (Spring 1977): 5, 18–19. For the court's ruling, see *Serrano v. Priest*, Gen. Civil No. 938254 (Superior Court for L.A. County, Cal, January 8, 1969).

53. *Serrano v. Priest*, App., 89 Cal.Rptr 345 (Sept 1, 1970).

54. *Serrano v. Priest*, Sup., 96 Cal.Rptr. 601 (Aug 30, 1971).

55. For further elaboration of the principle of fiscal neutrality, see John Coons, William H. Clune III, and Stephen D. Sugarman, *Private Wealth and Public Education* (Cambridge, MA: Harvard University Press, 1971).

56. For a brief review of the legislative changes made to the school finance system in response to the 1971 ruling, see Garms, Guthrie, and Pierce, *School Finance*, 217–18, and McDermott, "Serrano: What Does it Mean?," 5, 18–19.

57. See *San Antonio ISD v. Rodriguez*, 411 US 1(1973).

58. *Serrano v. Priest*, Civil No. 938, 254 (Cal. Super.Ct., April 10, 1974).

59. *Serrano v. Priest*, 557 P.2d 929. (Dec 30, 1976).

60. Hanif S. Hirji, "Inequalities in California's Public School System: The Undermining of Serrano v. Priest and the Need for a Minimum Standards System of Education," *Loyola of Los Angeles Law Review*, 32, no. 583 (1999), llr.lls.edu/volumes/v32-isssue2/hirjipdf (accessed September 28, 2007); Arthur F. Coon, "Separate and Unequal: Serrano Played an Important Role in Development of School District Policy," library.findlaw.com/199/Dec/1/129939.

61. A three-judge court was impaneled in January 1969 to address the plaintiffs concerns. In December 1971 the court rendered its judgment. The trial was delayed for two years to permit extensive pretrial discovery and to allow completion of a pending Texas legislative investigation concerning the need for changes in its public school finance system. *San Antonio Indep. School Dist. v. Rodriguez*, 411 US 1 (1973), 1282.

62. *Rodriguez v. San Antonio*, ISD 337 F. Supp. 280 (W.D. Tex. 1971).

63. In early 1972, the state appealed directly to the US Supreme Court. The Supreme Court heard arguments on the case in October 12, 1972, and made a ruling on March 21, 1973. *San Antonio Indep. School Dist. v. Rodriguez*, 411 US 1 (1973).

64. It also ruled that this was not a proper case in which to examine a state's laws under standards of strict judicial scrutiny. See *San Antonio ISD v. Rodriguez*, 411 US 1 (1973).

65. William P. Hobby Jr. and Billy D. Walker, "Legislative Reforms of the Texas Public School Finance System, 1973–1991," *Harvard Journal on Legislation* 28 (1991): 379–94.

66. Many activists turned to promoting change in other aspects of Mexican American life, especially the electoral arena. For an excellent history of their increased political involvement during the 1970s and early 1980s, see Rodolfo Rosales, *The Illusion of Inclusion: The Untold Political Story of San Antonio* (Austin: University of Texas Press, 2000). Public interest and equity activists throughout the country also continued their efforts to reform school finance systems. For a discussion of these efforts, see A. Thomas Stubbs, "After Rodriguez: Recent Developments in School Finance Reform," *Tax Lawyer* 44, no. 1 (1990–91): 313–40.

67. For an overview of developments in Texas during the 1980s, see Gregory C. Rocha and Robert H. Webking, *Politics and Public Education: Edgewood v. Kirby and the Reform of Public School Financing in Texas* (Minneapolis: West Publishers, 1992).

68. For a discussion of these two approaches to challenging school financing schemes in the United States, see Stubbs, "After Rodriguez," 313–40.

69. Hobby and Walker, "Legislative Reform of the Texas Public School Finance System," 384.

70. *Edgewood Indep. School Dist. V. Kirby,* No. 362,516 (250th Dist. Ct., Travis Cty., Tex. June 1, 1987), rev'd, 761 S.W.2d 859 (Tex. Ct. App. 1988), rev'd, 777 S.W.2d 391 (Tex. 1989).

71. Act of June 7, 1990, 71st Leg., 6th C.S., ch.1, 1990 Tex. Gen. Laws 1.

72. *Edgewood Indep. School Dist. V. Kirby,* 777 S.W.2d 391 (Tex. 1989), 399.

73. Edgewood II, 804 S.W.2d 491 (Tex. 91).

74. Act of April 11, 1991, ch. 20, Secs. 16.001–21930, 1991 Tex. Sess. Law Serv. 20 (Vernon).

75. See Lt. Gov. Bill Ratliff, "Finding a Way to Equitably Fund Texas Schools Hasn't Been Easy," *Houston Chronicle*, October 28, 2001, editorial.

76. Connie Mabin, "Property-Rich Districts Claim Funding System Is Illegal Tax," *Houston Chronicle*, March 28, 2003, 1A, 43A.

77. During the 1980s it also led to the underrepresentation of Latinos in gifted and talented programs. For an overview of the issues involved in this area, see Arlene C. Dannenberg, *Meeting the Needs of Gifted and Talented Bilingual Students: An Introduction to Issues and Practices* (Quincy: Massachusetts Department of Education, Office for Gifted and Talented, 1984, reprint); M. Machado, "Gifted Hispanics Underidentified in Classrooms," *Hispanic Link Weekly Report*, February 1987, 1; and Linda M. Cohen, "Meeting the Needs of Gifted and Talented Minority Language Students: Issues and Practices," FOCUS: The National Clearinghouse for Bilingual Education," www.ncela.gwu.edu/pubs/classics/focus/08gifted.htm (accessed June 14, 2007).

78. *Diana v. California State Board of Education,* Complaint filed by Plaintiffs, C.A. No. C-70 37 RFP (N.D. Cal., Feb. 3, 1970), found in *Student Classification Materials* (Cambridge, MA: Center for Law and Education, 1973), 218–22, information is on 218.

79. In Arreola, the court ruled that plaintiffs had a right to participate in the decision to place La-tino students in these classes. An injunction was granted to prohibit the continuation of these classes unless a hearing was provided before placement. In 1972 blacks joined this lawsuit as intervenors because of the deleterious impact that testing was also having on these children. For a review of the evolution of this case, see Henry J. Casso, "A Descriptive Study of Three Legal Challenges for Dis-proportionate Placement of Mexican American and Other Linguistically and Culturally Different Children Into Educably Mentally Retarded Classes" (EdD diss., University of Massachusetts, 1973).

80. In the Diana case, a group of nine Latino students claimed that their placement in EMR classes had been based on tests that relied on verbal English skills and ignored their own native language skills. *Diana v. California State Board of Education*, Complaint filed by Plaintiffs, C.A. No. C-70 37 RFP (N.D. Cal., Feb. 3, 1970), found in *Student Classification Materials* (Cambridge, MA: Center for Law and Education, 1973), 218–22.

81. In Covarrubias a claim was filed on behalf of twelve black and five Mexican American pupils "erroneously assigned" to EMR classes. A preliminary injunction was entered enjoin-ing the state of California from using IQ tests to place such children in classes for the educable mentally retarded. For more information on this case see Casso, "A Descriptive Study of Three Legal Challenges."

82. In Guadalupe the plaintiffs challenged the uses of IQ tests for placement in EMR classes. The court ruled that they were discriminatory. See *Guadalupe v. Tempe Elementary School District*, No. 3, Civ. No. 71–435 (D. Ariz., 1972). See also R. W. Henderson and R. R. Valencia, "Nondiscriminatory School Psychological Services: Beyond Nonbiased Assessments," in *School Psychology in Contemporary Society*, ed. J. R. Bergan (Columbus, OH: Charles E. Merrill, 1985), 340–77; and Richard R. Valencia, *Chicano Students and the Courts* (New York: New York Univer-sity Press, 2008).

83. Despite this consent decree, the state failed to comply with it. A year later the Board of Education was held in contempt. Failure to comply continued for several more years. As late as 1979 MALDEF was still negotiating this case. For a copy of the contempt order, see *Diana v. Cali-fornia State Board of Education*, No. C-70–37-FRP (N.D. Cal., May 24, 1974), found in *Student Classification Materials*, supplement (Cambridge, MA: Center for Law and Education, 1976), 4. For a brief description of MALDEF's continuing efforts to negotiate with the board on compli-ance issues, see letter from Ronald T. Vera, MALDEF attorney, to author, December 5, 1979 (in author's possession).

84. Information on Arrellano and Ruiz can be found in *Student Classification Materials* (Cam-bridge, MA: Center for Law and Education, 1973), 289–96 (*Ruiz v. State Board of Education*), 385–92 (*Arellano v. Board of Education:* In this case, Mexican American parents went to court on April 20, 1972, and claimed that standardized tests discriminated against the culturally differ-ent and the poor, that such instruments were used to sort the culturally different and the poor disproportionately into low-ability tracks, and that schooling in such tracks deprived the students of equal educational opportunity).

85. *Lora v. Board of Education of the City of New York*, Complaint (E.D.N.Y., no date), located in *Student Classification Materials* (Cambridge, MA: Center for Law and Education, 1973), 85.

86. *Morales v. Shannon*, 516 F.2d 411 (C.A. 5, 1975).

87. *Hernandez v. Stockton Unified Sch. Dist.*, No. 101016 (Superior Ct. of San Joaquin County, 10/1/75) (Clearinghouse Review #7805), located in *Student Classification Materials* (Cambridge, MA: Center for Law and Education, 1973), 85.

88. In *Morales v. Shannon*, 516 F.2d 411 (C.A. 5, 1975), the district court found no segregative intent in the assignment of students to separate schools or no discrimination in their assignment to ability groups despite the disproportionate placement of Mexican American students in low-ability classes. For general discussion of tracking, see D. Kirp, "Schools as Sorters: The Constitutional and Policy Implications of Student Classification," *University of Pennsylvania Law Review* 121, no. 705 (1973); M. Sorgen, "Testing and Tracking in Public Schools," *Hastings Law Journal* 24 no. 1129 (1973).

89. Thomas P. Carter and Roberto D. Segura, *Mexican Americans in School: A Decade of Change* (New York: College Entrance Exam Board, 1979), 175–79.

90. Casso, "A Descriptive Study of Three Legal Challenges."

91. In 1990, Congress retitled this bill the Individuals with Disabilities Education Act (IDEA). San Miguel and Valencia, "From the Treaty of Guadalupe Hidalgo to Hopwood," 386. See also Blandina Cárdenas, "Defining Equal Access to Educational Opportunity for Mexican American Children: A Study of Three Civil Rights Actions Affecting Mexican American Students and the Development of a Conceptual Framework for Effecting Institutional Responsiveness to the Educational Needs of Mexican American Children" (EdD, University of Massachusetts, 1974).

92. See, for instance, Gilbert G. González, "The System of Public Education and Its Function within the Chicano Communities, 1910–1930" (PhD diss., University of California, Los Angeles, 1974); "Racism, Education, and the Mexican Community in Los Angeles, 1920–1930," *Societas* 4 (1974): 287–301; and *Chicano Education the Era of Segregation* (Philadelphia: Balch Institute Press, 1990). See also J. R. Rafferty, "Missing the Mark: Intelligence Testing in Los Angeles Public Schools," *History of Education Quarterly* 28 (1988): 73–93; "Educational Tests: How Important Is 'Opportunity to Learn?'" *Child Assessment News* 2 (1992): 8–11; R. R. Valencia and R. J. Rankin, "Evidence of Content Bias on the McCarthy Scales with Mexican American Children: Implications for Test Translation and Nonbiased Assessment," *Journal of Educational Psychology* 77 (1985): 197–207.

93. R. R. Valencia and S. Aburto, "The Uses and Abuses of Educational Testing: Chicanos as a Case in Point," in *Chicano School Failure and Success: Research and Policy Agendas for the 1990s*, ed. R. R. Valencia (London: Falmer Press, 1991), 203–51; R. R. Valencia, "Educational Testing and Mexican American Students: Problems and Prospects," in *The Elusive Quest for Equality: 150 Years of Chicano/Chicana Education*, ed. J. F. Moreno (Cambridge, MA: Harvard Educational Review, 1999), 123–40.

94. Nick C. Vaca, "The Mexican American in the Social Sciences, 1912–1970; Part I: 1912–1935," *El Grito* 3, no. 3 (1970); Nick C. Vaca, "The Mexican American in the Social Sciences, 1912–1970; Part II: 1936–1970," *El Grito* 4, no. 1 (1970).

95. R. R. Valencia and S. Aburto, "The Uses and Abuses of Educational Testing: Chicanos as a Case in Point," in *Chicano School Failure and Success: Research and Policy Agendas for the 1990s*, ed. R. R. Valencia (London: Falmer Press, 1991), 203–51; R. R. Valencia, "Educational Testing

and Mexican American Students: Problems and Prospects," in *The Elusive Quest for Equality: 150 Years of Chicano/Chicana Education*, ed. J. F. Moreno (Cambridge, MA: Harvard Educational Review, 1999), 123–40.

96. Dannenberg, *Meeting the Needs of Gifted and Talented Bilingual Students;* Machado, "Gifted Hispanics Underidentified in Classrooms," 1; and Cohen, "Meeting the Needs of Gifted and Talented."

97. J. R. Mercer, "In Defense of Racially and Culturally Non-Discriminatory Assessment," *School Psychology Digest* 8 (1979): 89–115; J. Mercer and J. Lewis, *System of Multicultural and Pluralistic Assessment: Technical Manual* (New York: Psychological Corporation, 1979); E. Pena, "Dynamic Assessment: The Model and Language Applications," in *Assessment of Communication and Language*, ed. K. Cole, P. Dales, and D. Thal (Baltimore: Brookes, 1996), 281–307.

98. Much of the criticism was directed at Texas because of its leadership role in the development of testing reforms negatively impacting the learning opportunities of Mexican Americans and other students of color. See Valencia, "Educational Testing and Mexican American Students," and Richard R. Valencia, Bruno J. Villarreal, and Moises F. Salinas, "Educational Testing and Chicano Students: Issues, Consequences, and Prospects for Reform," 289–292, in *Chicano School Failure and Success: Past, Present, and Future*, ed. Richard R. Valencia (London: Routledge Falmer, 2002), 253–309.

99. See *GI Forum et al v. Texas Education Agency et al*, 87 F. Supp.2d 667 (W.D. Tex. 2000). S. E. Phillips, ed., "Defending a High School Graduation Test: *GI Forum v. Texas Education Agency* [special issue]," *Applied Measurement in Education* 13, no. 4 (2000); Richard R. Valencia and E. M. Bernal, eds., "The Texas Assessment of Academic Skills (TAAS) Case: Perspectives of Plaintiffs' Experts [special issue]," *Hispanic Journal of Behavioral Sciences* 22, no. 4 (2000).

100. Phillips, "Defending a High School Graduation Test," 2000; Valencia, and Bernal, "The Texas Assessment of Academic Skills (TAAS) case."

101. For information on opposition to Senate Bill 4, see Valencia, Villarreal, and Salinas, "Educational Testing and Chicano Students," 253–309.

102. For information on one Texas organization's position (Austin-based Texas for Quality Assessment-TQA), see www.texastesting.org/TQABrief.htm. For its legislative agenda, see www.texastesting.org/LegislativeSummary.htm.

103. *Serna v. Portales Municipal Schools*, 351 F. Supp. 1279 (N.D. Mex. 1972), aff'd, 499 F.2d 1147 (10th Cir. 1974).

104. In 1972, Puerto Ricans in New York City also filed a lawsuit against local school officials for failure to provide appropriate instruction to Spanish-speaking children. They claimed that for close to a decade local school leaders had publicly endorsed and supported bilingual education for Puerto Rican children and for all immigrant children enrolling in the public schools. Failure to honor this decade-old commitment forced them to file a lawsuit aimed at compelling local school officials to establish this much-needed educational service. This case assumed the name of *Aspira of New York, Inc. v. Board of Education of the City of New York*. See *New York Times*, May 2, 1963, 37, col. 1 ("Calvin E. Gross Opposes 'Melting Potism' and Supports Bilingual Education for

Puerto Ricans and All New Arrivals"); "Statement of Policy of Board of Education of New York City," adopted April 18, 1965, issued April 28, 1965, 602 ("The Board Policy Encouraged Bilingualism and Biculturalism for All Children Especially 'Spanish-Speaking Ones"); and "Testimony Given by Dr. Bernard E. Donovan, Superintendent of Schools, New York City, before the House General Subcommittee on Education of the House Committee on Education and Labor on H.R. 9840 and H.R. 10224," press release #451–6667, New York City Board of Education, July 7, 1967 ("Donovan Supported a Bilingual Maintenance Approach"). All of these are cited in Herbert Teitelbaum and Richard J. Hiller, "Bilingual Education: the Legal Mandate," in *Bilingual Multicultural Education and the Professional: From Theory to Practice*, ed. Henry T. Trueba and Carol Barnett-Mizrahi (Rowley, MA: Newbury House Publishers, 1979), 20–53, note 50, p. 46.

105. The Federal District and the Ninth Circuit Court of Appeals rejected the plaintiffs' claims. The Supreme Court, however, ruled against them and argued that failure to provide Chinese-speaking children with meaningful instruction violated their rights under federal statutes. It thus avoided the constitutional issue and relied solely on Title VI. *Lau v. Nichols*, 488 f.2d 791 (9th Cir. 1973), 414 US 563 (1974).

106. Teitelbaum and Hiller, "Bilingual Education."

107. The Lau decision also influenced developments in New York City. It encouraged the local officials to accept a consent decree in 1974. This decree, negotiated by Aspira of New York, Inc., was quite extensive and more far-reaching than what Lau recommended. Despite its comprehensive nature, the decree did not reach all Latino students, only those classified as ELLS. Latinos and other children who were fluent in English and doing poorly in school were not affected. *Aspira of New York, Inc. v. Board of Education of the City of New York*, 72 Civ. 4002 (S.D.N.Y., August 29, 1974) (unreported consent decree).

108. *Serna v. Portales Municipal Schools*, 351 F. Supp. 1279 (N.D. Mex. 1972), aff'd, 499 F.2d 1147 (10th Cir. 1974).

109. *Rios v. Read*, 73 F.R.D. 589 (E.D.N.Y. 1977).

110. *Castaneda v. Pickard*, 648 F.2d 989 (5th Cir. 1981). See also *Cintron v. Brentwood Union Free School District Board of Education*, no. 75–8746 (Sup. Ct. August 14, 1975), where the court ruled that federal law dealing with bilingual education personnel took prominence over state tenure laws sanctioning the firing of bilingual teachers with less tenure than nonbilingual teachers.

111. *Otero v. Mesa County Valley School District No. 51*, 408 F. Supp. 162 (D. Colo, 1975). For a review of these cases, see Teitelbaum and Hiller, "Bilingual Education."

112. David Tyack, ed., *Turning Points in American Educational History* (Lexington, MA: Xerox College Publishing, 1967), 228.

113. *Analysis of the Seals Decision In Re: Alien Children Decision and Its Implications for US Immigration Law and Policy*, A Report Prepared by Mario Cantú and Francisco X. Garza for the National Council of La Raza (Washington, DC: National Council of La Raza, February 3, 1981), 7.

114. There was no debate on this issue. The law was amended by a voice vote of the legislators. See *Analysis of the Seals Decision*, 7.

115. Texas Education Code, Annotated Title 1, Section 21.031.

116. Nancy Manougian, "*Plyler v. Doe:* Equal Protection for Illegal Aliens," *Capital University Law Review* 12, no. 1 (1982): 144.

117. Peter Roos, the attorney arguing the case before the Supreme Court, noted at a conference celebrating the twenty-fifth anniversary of *Plyler* that they waited for several years because they were searching for the right case to pursue in the courts. Comments by Peter Roos, "Plyler: 25 Years Later," conference organized by MALDEF, St. Mary's University, September 14, 2007. Author moderated the panel where Roos presented.

118. *Hernandez v. Houston Independent School District*, 558 S.W.2d 123 (Tex.Civ. App. 1977), application for writ of error refused, id.

119. *Hernandez v. Houston Independent School District*, 558 S.W.2d 121 (Tex. Civ. App. 1977), application for writ of error refused, id.

120. For a brief discussion of his strategy, see Michael A. Olivas, "*Plyler v. Doe*, the Education of Undocumented Children, and the Polity," in *Immigration Stories*, ed. David A. Martin and Peter H. Schuck (New York: Foundation Press, 2005), 197–220, esp. 199–204.

121. *Doe v. Plyler*, 458 F. Supp. 569 (E.D. Tex. 1978). *Analysis of the Seals Decision*, 1981, incorrectly says that the case was filed in May 1977. For personal reflections by some of the major players in the *Plyler* case, including Judge William Wayne Justice, Jim Plyler (Superintendent), Michael McAndrew (an activist assisting in getting legal assistance for the lawsuit), and Jose Lopez (one of the parents listed as a plaintiff), see *Plyler v. Doe:* 25 Years Later, www.dallasnews.com/s/dws/photography/2007/plyler website (accessed September 11, 2007).

122. *Doe v. Plyler*, 458 F. Supp. 569 (E.D. Tex. 1978).

123. For all of the lawsuits filed during these years, see note 28 in Olivas, "*Plyler v. Doe*," 216.

124. The idea of consolidation came from Peter Schey. Peter Roos initially opposed consolidation because it would complicate the issues, encourage the state to use better-trained counsel, and it was not part of his carefully laid out long-term strategy. On his opposition to consolidation, see Olivas, "*Plyler v. Doe*," 204–207.

125. *In re Alien Children Educ. Litigation*, 501 F. Supp. 544 (S.D. Tex 1980).

126. Cited in *Analysis of the Seals Decision*, 19.

127. *Plyler v. Doe*, 457 US 202 (June 15, 1982), 6.

128. For a brief overview of these two cases, see Jose A. Medina, "Legal Overview," in *Conference on the Education of Undocumented Students: Status and Suggested Remedies* (San Antonio, TX: Intercultural Development Research Association, May 11, 1979), 10–14. See also *Doe v. Plyler*, 458 F. Supp. 573–574 (1978) for a summary of the Hernandez case.

129. It issued a "summary affirmance of the consolidated Houston cases." Olivas, "*Plyler v. Doe*," 207.

130. *Plyler v. Doe,* 457 US 202 (June 15, 1982), 6.

131. "Supreme Court Justice Orders That Undocumented Children in Texas May Attend Public School Free," *El Sol* (Houston, Texas), no. 36, vol. 15, September 10, 1982.

132. For an example of one scholar making this point, see Manougian, *"Plyler v. Doe,"* 143–59.

133. These provisions have been issued as a flyer by MALDEF and distributed by various organizations. See "School Opening Alert," Flyer, n.d. Distributed by MALDEF.

134. For further elaboration on these issues see the discussion in Olivas, *"Plyler v. Doe."*

135. H. H. Scott, "Desegregation in Nashville: Conflicts and Contradictions in Preserving Schools in Black Communities," *Education and Urban Society* 15 (1983): 235–44.

136. Richard R. Valencia, *Understanding School Closures: Discriminatory Impact on Chicano and Black Students,* Policy Monograph Series, no. 1 (Stanford, CA: Stanford University Stanford Center for Chicano Research, 1984); *School Closures and Policy Issues,* Policy Paper No. 84-C3 (Stanford, CA: Stanford University, Institute for Research on Educational Finance and Governance, 1984).

137. Quoted in Richard R. Valencia, "The School Closure Issue and the Chicano Community," *Urban Review* 12 (1980): 5–21, at 10.

138. The author was actively involved in the Santa Barbara community and was the chair of the Latino education caucus, a subcommittee of Latinos for Better Government, a community-based group involved in local affairs. As chair of this committee, the author helped parents and community groups oppose the local board's decision to close some of the Latino schools in that district. Author's note.

139. Valencia, "The School Closure Issue," 5–21; Richard R. Valencia, "The School Closure Issue and the Chicano Community: A Follow-Up Study of the Angeles Case," *Urban Review* 16 (1984): 145–63.

140. For an overview of the Santa Barbara, California, and the Phoenix, Arizona, cases, see Valencia, *Understanding School Closures.*

141. Valencia, "The School Closure Issue," 17.

142. Elizabeth Martinez, *500 Years of Chicano History* (Albuquerque, NM: SouthWest Organizing Project, 1991), 200

143. Ibid., 198.

144. Ibid., 201.

145. Ibid., 200.

146. Ibid., 194

147. "College Expels Fraternity," *Houston Chronicle,* October 30, 1997.

148. "Hispanics Upset by Sorority Garb: Baylor Students at Party Dressed as Gangsters, Pregnant Women," *Houston Chronicle,* April 29, 1998, 19A.

149. For the info on the lawsuit, *Williams v. State of California,* see http://www.decentschools.com/.

150. "Chicano Studies at UNM in Trouble," e-mail from D. Xavier Medina to G. San Miguel, February 10, 2003.

151. "Latino Roundtable Meeting with President Monday," e-mail from Roberto Calderon to G. San Miguel, September 26, 2003.

152. "UNM name change," e-mail from Jessica Torrez to NACCS Listserv and G. San Miguel, November 1, 2004.

153. "Statement from Ward Churchill," e-mail from Estevan Flores to G. San Miguel, February 1, 2005.

154. "Book burning of Bless Me Ultima," e-mail from Margo Gutierrez to G. San Miguel, February 4, 2005.

155. "Texas bill would repeal top 10% law," e-mail from Roberto Calderon to G. San Miguel, February 4, 2005.

156. "Heat, No Light," e-mail of article sent by Roberto Calderon to G. San Miguel, February 25, 2005.

157. "UT Austin University denies Chicana Professor Tenure," e-mail from Roberto Calderon to G. San Miguel, March 1, 2005.

158. "Protesters confront UT conservative group," e-mail from Angela Valenzuela to G. San Miguel, March 3, 2005.

159. "Students Arrested at UC Santa Cruz," e-mail from Roberto Calderon to G. San Miguel, May 4, 2005.

160. "Update on the Struggle to Save the BA Program in Chicano Studies at CSUCI," e-mail from Jose G. Moreno to G. San Miguel.

161. "New doctoral program at Michigan State Chicano/Latino Studies," e-mail from Angela Valenzuela to G. San Miguel, November 27, 2005.

162. "Ex-NACCS national Chair Faces Tenure Struggle," e-mail from Jose G. Moreno to G. San Miguel, February 20, 2006. He was given a memo of dismissal by chair Robert Cutter on October 18, 2005

163. "Surge in Latino Activism," Insidehighered.com news, April 10, 2006, www.insidehighered.com/news/2006/04/10/latino (accessed December 26, 2008).

164. John MacCormakc, "Racist Video Causes Uproar on A&M Campus," *San Antonio Express-News,* November 8, 2006 (e-mail sent to San Miguel).

165. "Defend the Honor Campaign: A Day of Remembrance and Honor," e-mail from Roberto Calderon to G. San Miguel, September 7, 2007.

166. "Imbalanced Hispanic Historical Exhibit at Texas A&M University Must Be Corrected," e-mail from Angelita Garcia Alonzo to G. San Miguel, June 2, 2006.

167. "City-wide call for November 10th Rally supporting the Columbia University Hunger Strikers," e-mail from Carlos Muñoz Jr. to naccs-tejas and G. San Miguel, November 10, 2007.

168. "TEKS," e-mail from Trinidad Gonzales to G. San Miguel, November 28, 2008.

169. "Mexican American Legislative Caucus," e-mail from Dan Arellano to G. San Miguel, February 21, 2008.

170. [1] Gary Scharrer, "Hispanic Input Urged on Curriculum," *Houston Chronicle*, March 15, 2008, B4; Gary Scharrer, "Critics Lambast Education Board on English Curriculum," *Houston Chronicle*, March 27, 2008, B4.

171. "TEKS," e-mail from Trinidad Gonzales to G. San Miguel, November 28, 2008.

172. "Save Chicano Studies at Ohlone College," e-mail from Roberto Calderon to G. San Miguel, April 11, 2008.

173. Howard Fischer, "Measure Backs 'American Values' in State Schools," April 16, 2008, e-mail article sent by Rudy Acuña to G. San Miguel.

174. "Freedom Riders on their way," Letter from Dr. Cintli Rodriguez to Historia Listserv via Roberto Calderon, sent May 12, 2010 (in author's possession).

175. "Students take over TUSD boardroom in faceoff over ethnic studies," http://www.kgun9.com/story/14520347/students-take-over-tusd-board-meeting-over-ethnic-studies (accessed April 27, 2011).

176. "Ethnic Studies: Support the strike and stand in solidarity," http://us.mg201.mail.yahoo.com/dc/lauch?.gx=0&.rand=cq2ugtq6bdkvj (accessed April 27, 2011).

Chapter 3

1. For an overview of the politics of appointing Mexican Americans to positions of influence at the federal level, see Julie Leininger Pycior, *LBJ and Mexican Americans: The Paradox of Power* (Austin: University of Texas Press, 1997), 185, 199–201. See also Rubén Donato, *The Other Struggle for Equal Schools* (Albany: State University of New York Press, 1997), 61; Clayton Brace, *Federal Programs to Improve Mexican-American Education* (Washington, DC: US Office of Education, Mexican-American Affairs Unit, 1967), ERIC Document No. ED014338; and Report by the National Advisory Committee on Mexican American Education, *The Mexican American: Quest for Equality* (Washington, DC: US Department of Health, Education and Welfare, 1968). ERIC No. ED049841.

2. John Staples Shockley, *Chicano Revolt in a Texas Town* (Notre Dame, IN: University of Notre Dame Press, 1974); and Armando Navarro, *The Cristal Experiment: A Chicano Struggle for Community Control* (Madison: University of Wisconsin Press, 1998), 17–51.

3. Armando Navarro, "Educational Change through Political Action," in *Mexican Americans and Educational Change*, ed. Alfredo Castañeda, Manuel Ramírez III, Carlos E. Cortés, and Mario Barrera (New York: Arno Press, 1974; originally printed in 1971), 105–39, at 117.

4. Navarro, "Educational Change through Political Action," 117.

5. Ibid., 118–25.

6. Navarro notes that in January 1970, a new MAPA chapter was organized. Known as the West End MAPA chapter, this group linked up two former chapters—the Ontario MAPA and the original Cucamonga-Upland chapter. This group was more militant than the original MAPA chapter. The MAPA militants organized several Chicano movement events and sought the creation of more jobs in the community. Navarro, "Educational Change through Political Action," 125–26.

7. Ibid., 129–32.

8. See ibid.

9. See Navarro, *The Cristal Experiment*, esp. 217–51; Shockley, *Chicano Revolt in a Texas Town*, 111–49; and Armando L. Trujillo, *Chicano Empowerment and Bilingual Education: Movimiento Politics in Crystal City* (New York: Garland Publishers, 1998).

10. Navarro, *The Cristal Experiment*, 317–43.

11. On the clash between Mexican Americans and blacks in search of a superintendent for the Houston schools, see Donald R. McAdams, *Fighting to Save Our Urban Schools—And Winning: Lessons from Houston* (New York: Teachers College Press, 2000). For information on Chicago, see Jorge Oclander, "Hispanics Condemn Lack of School Jobs," *Chicago Sun-Times*, December 12, 1994, 6.

12. For a recent view of the struggle for Latina/o power in education and the impact it has had on race relations in one Chicago community, see Abdon M. Pallasch, "Curie Principal Still Out: Hispanic Majority on LSC Refuses to Reverse Vote," *Chicago Sun-Times*, March 11, 2007, http://www.suntimes.com/news/education/292313,CST-NWS-curie11.article (accessed March 11, 2007). See also the insightful article on black-brown tensions in the Compton, California, schools by Emily E. Straus. She argues that this conflict began in the 1970s and continued into the early twenty-first century. See "Unequal Pieces of a Shrinking Pie: The Struggle between African Americans and Latinos over Education, Employment, and Empowerment in Compton, California," *History of Education Quarterly* 49, no. 4 (2009): 507–29.

13. Christine Phelan, "Youth Shut Out by Labor Market: Nearly 5.5 Million Youth Out-of-School and Jobless," http://www.clasp.org/CampaignForYouth/PolicyBrief/YouthShutOut ByLaborMarket.htm (accessed May 19, 2009).

14. For further information on this struggle see chapter 2.

15. Guadalupe San Miguel Jr. and Richard R. Valencia, "From the Treaty of Guadalupe Hidalgo to Hopwood: The Educational Plight and Struggle of Mexican Americans in the Southwest," *Harvard Educational Review* 68, no. 3 (1998): 353–412.

16. The struggle for compensatory education was not limited to Mexican Americans only. Puerto Ricans also fought for these programs. Aspira of New York, Inc., for instance, wanted Puerto Rican and other Latina/o students to get access to compensatory and remedial programs in the New York Public schools during the early 1970s. See Isaura Santiago Santiago, "*Aspira of New York, Inc. v. Board of Education* Revisited," *American Journal of Education* 95, no. 1 (1986): 149–99.

17. Guadalupe San Miguel Jr., *Contested Policy: The Rise and Fall of Federal Bilingual Education in the United States* (Denton: University of North Texas Press, 2004); Santiago Santiago, *"Aspira of New York, Inc. v. Board of Education* Revisited," 149–99.

18. Guadalupe San Miguel Jr., "Actors Not Victims: Chicanas/os and the Struggle for Educational Equality," in *Chicanas/Chicanos at the Crossroads: Social, Economic, and Political Change,* ed. David R. Maciel and Isidro Ortiz (Tucson: University of Arizona Press, 1996).

19. See "News release: NCLR Applauds Passage of the Improving Head Start Act of 2007," May 3, 2007. E-mail sent to G. San Miguel by NCLR, May 3, 2007.

20. For an example of opposition to magnet/vanguard programs in Houston during the mid-1970s, see "Minority Report: Making HISD Educational Policies and Programs More Responsive and Responsible to Needs of Educationally Deprived Students," February 24, 1975 (in author's possession.). On Latino support for gifted/talented and magnet programs, see Guadalupe San Miguel Jr., "Ignoring Ethnicity Is a Slap in the Face of All Colors by HISD," *Houston Chronicle,* September 28, 1997, C1, C5.

21. Carlos Muñoz Jr., "From Segregation to Melting Pot Democracy: The Mexican American Generation," in *Youth, Identity, Power: The Chicano Movement,* 19–46.

22. For an overview of the quest for a Chicano-black controlled college in the University of California at San Diego, see George Mariscal, "To Demand That the University Work for Our People," in *Brown-Eyed Children of the Sun: Lessons from the Chicano Movement, 1965–1975* (Albuquerque: University of New Mexico Press, 2005), 210–46. For an overview of the development of Chicana/o Studies, see Carlos Muñoz Jr., "The Development of Chicano Studies, 1968–1981," in *Chicano Studies: A Multidisciplinary Approach,* ed. Eugene E. García, Francisco A. Lomelí, and Isidro D. Ortiz (New York: Teachers College Press, 1984), 5–18.

23. For an excellent history of the origins and development of Chicano Studies in the United States, see Rodolfo F. Acuña, *The Making of Chicana/o Studies: In the Trenches of Academe* (New Brunswick: NJ: Rutgers University Press, 2011). See also Michael Soldatenko, *Chicano Studies: The Genesis of a Discipline* (Tucson: University of Arizona Press, 2009).

24. Muñoz, *Youth, Identity, Power: The Chicano Movement,* 84.

25. Dolores Delgado Bernal, "Chicana/o Education from the Civil Rights Era to the Present," in *The Elusive Quest for Equality: 150 Years of Chicana/o Education,* ed. José F. Moreno (Cambridge, MA: Harvard Educational Review, 1999), 77–110.

26. Victoria-María MacDonald, John M. Botti, and Lisa Hoffman Clark, "From Visibility to Autonomy: Latinos and Higher Education in the US, 1965–2005," *Harvard Educational Review* 77, no. 4 (2007): 474–504, esp. 483–86.

27. H. Homero Galicia and Clementina Almaguer, *Chicano Alternative Education* (Hayward, CA: Southwest Network, 1973), iii. For more information on these alternative institutions, see chapter 6.

28. MacDonald, Botti, and Clark, "From Visibility to Autonomy," 492.

29. San Miguel, "Actors Not Victims," 159–80. On the increase of racism on one campus, see S. McBay, *The Racial Climate on the MIT Campus: A Report of the Minority Student Issues Group* (Boston: MIT, Office of the Dean for Student Affairs, 1986).

30. Rodolfo F. Acuña, *Occupied America: A History of Chicanos*, 6th ed. (New York: Pearson Longman, 2007), 316–18.

31. For explanations of these incidents and proposals to improve racial climates on higher education campuses, see Sylvia Hurtado, Alma R. Clayton-Pedersen, Walter Recharde Allen, and Jeffrey F. Milem, "Enhancing Campus Climates for Racial/Ethnic Diversity: Educational Policy and Practice," *Review of Higher Education* 21, no. 3 (1998): 279–302.

32. MacDonald, Botti, and Clark, "From Visibility to Autonomy," 488.

33. For an overview of this case, see Ricard Valencia, *Chicano Students and the Courts* (Albany: State University of New York Press, 2008).

34. MacDonald, Botti, and Clark, "From Visibility to Autonomy," 484.

35. For some examples of these studies, see Michael A. Olivas, ed., *Latino College Students* (New York: Teachers College Press, 1986); Adalberto Aguirre and Ruben O. Martínez, *Chicanos in Higher Education: Issues and Dilemmas for the 21st Century*, ASHE-ERIC Higher Education Report no. 3 (Washington, DC: George Washington University, School of Education and Human Development, 1993); and Patricia P Gándara, "Passing through the Eye of the Needle: High-Achieving Chicanas," *Hispanic Journal of Behavioral Sciences* 4, no. 2 (1982): 167–79.

36. R. D. Goldman and B. N. Hewitt, "An Investigation of Test Bias for Mexican American College Students," *Journal of Educational Measurement* 12 (1975): 187–96; and Maria Pennock-Roman, "Fairness in the Use of Tests for Selective Admissions of Hispanics," in *Latino College Students*, ed. Michael A. Olivas (New York: Teachers College Press, 1986). On Bakke, see *Regents of the University of California v. Bakke*, 438 US 265 (1978).

37. Proposition 209 prohibited local and state agencies from granting "preferential treatment" to racial/ethnic minorities and/or women in the areas of state contracting, employment, and education. For an overview of these and several other measures, see San Miguel and Valencia, "From the Treaty of Guadalupe Hidalgo to Hopwood," 158.

38. Ibid., 160–61.

39. Ibid., 353–412.

40. Will Potter, "Texas Admissions Plan Has Not Increased Diversity at Flagship Campuses, Study Finds," *Chronicle of Higher Education*, http://chronicle.com/daily/2003/01/2030124011n.htm. January 24, 2003 (accessed October 30, 2007). For the role Mexican Americans played in the formulation of the plan, in its sponsorship, and in its impact on minority enrollment in Texas universities, see Melissa Watkins, "The Top 10 Percent Plan," www.utexas.edu/depts/cms/anniversary/toptenpercent.html (accessed October 30, 2007). For an excellent overview of the issues this plan has raised, see Rita Barr, "Should Texas Change the Top 10 Percent Law?," *Focus Report*, February 25, 2005 (Austin: House Research Organization, Texas House of Representatives, 2005).

41. For an example of a community struggle to establish a university that would benefit Mexican American students living in the inner city, see Louis Mendoza and Rodolfo Rosales, eds., *Bringing the University Home: The San Antonio Community's Struggle for Educational Access* (San Antonio: Hispanic Research Center, 1999).

42. Victoria-María MacDonald, John M. Botti, and Lisa Hoffman Clark, "From Visibility to Autonomy: Latinos and Higher Education in the US, 1965–2005," *Harvard Educational Review* 77, no. 4 (2007): 474–504.

43. HSIS had been placed under the generic category of "Strengthening Institutions" in Title A under Title III of the 1992 legislation. It got its own title—Title V—in the Higher Education Act of 1965 as amended in 1998. See MacDonald, Botti, and Clark, "From Visibility to Autonomy," 492.

44. See Ibid., 494–98.

45. For an overview of the fascinating and complex legal issues involved in college access for undocumented students, see Michael A. Olivas, "*Plyler v. Doe, Toll v. Moreno,* and Postsecondary Admissions: Undocumented Adults and 'Enduring Disability,'" *Journal of Law and Education* 15, no. 19 (1986); and Michael A. Olivas, "Storytelling Out of School: Undocumented College Residency, Race, and Reaction," *Hastings Constitutional Law Quarterly* 22, no. 1019 (1995).

46. Michael A. Olivas, "*Plyler v. Doe,* the Education of Undocumented Children, and the Polity," in *Immigration Stories,* ed. David Martin and Peter Schuck (New York: Foundation Press, 2005), 197–220. See also Olivas, "Storytelling Out of School,"

47. Olivas, "*Plyler v. Doe,* the Education of Undocumented Children, and the Polity." See also Michael A. Olivas, "IIRIRA, The DREAM Act, and Undocumented College Student Residency," *Journal of College and University Law* 30, no. 435 (2004).

48. The latest effort to pass this bill occurred on October 24, 2007. On this day the Senate killed the DREAM Act on a procedural vote. For further information on this issue, see Wendy Hess, "Congress Kills the American DREAM," *Al Día Newspaper,* November 3, 2007, www.pontealdia .com/press.php?article=26026&section=53&edition=390 (accessed November 3, 2007)

49. For two examples, see Frank Angel, "Program Content to Meet the Educational Needs of Mexican Americans," and Horacio Ulibarri, "Educational Needs of the Mexican-American." Both of these were prepared for the National Conference on Educational Opportunities for Mexican-Americans, April 25–26, 1968, Austin, Texas, and published by the ERIC Clearinghouse on Rural Education and Small Schools, New Mexico State University, in 1968. See also the following: Julian Nava, "Bicultural Backgrounds and Barriers That Affect Learning by Spanish-Speaking Children," 125–35; Armando M. Rodriguez, "Speak Up, Chicano: The Mexican American Fights for Educational Equality," 135–43; and Marcos de León, "Statement of Philosophy and Policy as They Pertain to the Acculturation and Education of the Mexican-American," 95–99. All of these articles can be found in John H. Burma, ed., *Mexican-Americans in the United States: A Reader* (Cambridge, MA: Schenkman Publishing, 1970).

50. One of the first books highlighting the emergence of these new educational activists was published in the early 1970s. See Alfredo Castañeda, Manuel Ramírez III, Carlos E. Cortés, and Mario Barrera, eds., *Mexican Americans and Educational Change* (New York: Arno Press, 1974).

Orfield acknowledged and publicly recognized the emergence of Latinas/os as researchers and practitioners by the mid-1980s. See Gary Orfield, "Hispanic Education: Challenges, Research, and Policies," *American Journal of Education* 95, no. 1 (1986): 1–25.

51. The histories of these organizations and the roles they played in school reform over the decades have not yet been written. For brief histories of two of these new organizations, see Karen O'Connor and Lee Epstein, "A Legal Voice for the Chicano Community: The Activities of the Mexican American Legal Defense and Educational Fund, 1968–1982," *Social Science Quarterly* 65 (June 1984): 245–56, and "Intercultural Development Research Association," *Handbook of Texas Online*, www.tsha.utexas.edu/handbook/online/articles/II/kai2.html (accessed June 8, 2007). Organizations dedicated to improving the education of Puerto Ricans also emerged, including Aspira of New York, Inc. and the Puerto Rican Legal Defense and Education Fund (PRLDEF). For a history of Aspira, see *The ASPIRA Story: 1961–1991* (Washington, DC: ASPIRA Association, 1991).

52. Mr. Rodriguez was appointed to the Office of Education in 1968 and officially given the title of "Chief of the Mexican American Affairs Unit" in that office. For a list of the fifteen Mexican Americans employed in a professional capacity in the US Office of Education in 1969, see *Mexican-American Affairs Information Bulletin* (Washington, DC: US Office of Education, March 1969). For a list of the members of the National Advisory Committee on Mexican American Education in the Office of Education, see *National Conference on Educational Opportunities for Mexican Americans, April 24–26, 1968, Austin, Texas: Program* (Austin: US Office of Education in association with the Southwest Educational Development Laboratory, 1968). Eight of fifteen members were Latinos.

53. On the support for exemplary programs in bilingual, migrant, and urban education, see *National Conference on Educational Opportunities for Mexican Americans, 1968*. On early childhood education programs, see Charles B. Brussell, *Disadvantaged Mexican American Children and Early Educational Experience* (Austin: Southwest Educational Development Corporation, 1968).

54. For an example of the collaboration between the Southwest Educational Development Corporation and the National Advisory Committee on Mexican American Education of the US Department of Education and their support of innovative reforms benefiting Latino students, see *National Conference on Educational Opportunities for Mexican Americans*, 1968.

55. For further elaboration of Mexican American support for bilingual education, see the next chapter. See also San Miguel, *Contested Policy*.

56. *Beyond Language: Social and Cultural Factors in the Schooling of Language Minority Children* (Los Angeles: Evaluation, Dissemination, and Assessment Center, California State University, Los Angeles, 1986). See also M. Beatriz Arias, "The Context of Education for Hispanic Students: An Overview," *American Journal of Education* 95, no. 1 (1986): 26–57; and Gary Orfield, "Hispanic Education: Challenges, Research, and Policies," *American Journal of Education* 95, no. 1 (1986): 1–25.

57. Hispanic Policy Development Project, *"Make Something Happen": Hispanics and Urban High School Reform*, vol. 2 (Washington, DC: National Commission on Secondary Education for Hispanics, 1984). See also Orfield, "Hispanic Education," 1–25.

58. Indeed, as the excellence in education movement gained ground, political opposition to bilingual education, affirmative action in the schools, and desegregation increased throughout the country. On opposition to bilingual education, see San Miguel, *Contested Policy*. On opposition to desegregation and affirmative action, see Gary Orfield, Susan E. Eaton, and the Harvard Project on School Desegregation, eds., *Dismantling Desegregation: The Quiet Reversal of Brown v. Board of Education* (New York: New Press, 1996).

59. National Commission on Excellence in Education, *A Nation at Risk* (Washington, DC: USGPO, 1983).

60. Peter D. Roos, "Equity and Excellence," in Hispanic Policy Development Project, "*Make Something Happen": Hispanics and Urban High School Reform*, vol. 2 (Washington, DC: National Commission on Secondary Education for Hispanics, 1984), 75–78.

61. Latina/o activists joined other educators to push the quality agenda of the 1980s within the Latina/o schools. For efforts in California, see *Unfinished Business: Fulfilling Our Children's Promise* (Los Angeles: The Achievement Council, 1988). For a study making the case more broadly for quality in education for minorities and the poor in general, see *Barriers to Excellence: Our Children at Risk* (Boston: National Coalition of Advocates for Students, 1985).

62. One of the earliest articles focusing on quality in bilingual education was written by the then director of the bilingual education program in Washington in the late 1970s. See Josué M. González, *Towards Quality in Bilingual Education / Bilingual Education in the Integrated School* (Rosslyn, VA: National Clearinghouse for Bilingual Education, 1979).

63. Valentina I. Kloosterman, E. I. Diaz, and others have been in the forefront of these struggles. On Latinas/os and gifted programs, see Valentina I. Kloosterman, "A Shameful Subject: The Condition of Latino Students in Gifted Education," in *Latino Students in American Schools: Historical and Contemporary Views*, ed. Valentina I. Kloosterman (Westport, CT: Praeger, 2003), 113–27. See also E. I. Diaz, "Framing a Contemporary Context for the Education of Culturally and Linguistically Diverse Students with Gifted Potential: 1990s to the Present," in *Reaching New Horizons: Gifted and Talented Education for Culturally and Linguistically Diverse Students*, ed. J. A. Castellano and E. I. Diaz (Boston: Allyn and Bacon, 2002), 29–46.

64. For an overview of activism in this area, see Alba A. Ortiz, "Addressing the Needs of Latinos in Special Education," in *Latino Students in American Schools: Historical and Contemporary views*, ed. Valentina I. Kloosterman (Westport, CT: Praeger, 2003); and Jim Cummins, "A Theoretical Framework for Bilingual Special Education," *Exceptional Children* 56 (1989): 111–19.

65. See Joseph A. Fernandez and John Underwood, *Tales Out of School* (Boston: Little, Brown, 1993); and http://biography.jrank.org/pages/3354/Fernandez-Joseph-1921 -Chancellor-Educator.html. His restructuring efforts were based on school-based management principles. For further information on this as well as other approaches to comprehensive school reform, see Charles Reavis and Harry Griffith, *Restructuring Schools: Theory and Practice* (Lancaster, PA: Technomic Publishing Company, 1992); and Joseph Murphy and Amanda Datnow,

eds., *Leadership Lessons from Comprehensive School Reforms* (Thousand Oaks, CA: Corwin Press, 2003).

66. On YISD, see "Press Release—2007 Preliminary TAKS Scores Released: Ysleta ISD Improves in All Areas," YISD News, May 8, 2007, http://www2.yisd.net/education/dept/dept .php?sectiondetailid=9180&sc_id=1185378769 (accessed July 25, 2007).

67. María "Cuca" Robledo Montecel, "A Quality Schools Action Framework: Framing Systems Change for Student Success," http://www.idra.org/IDRA_Newsletters/November_-_December _2005_Access_and_Success (accessed January 10, 2007).

68. For more information on IDRA's comprehensive school reform plan, see ibid.

69. *Toward Quality Education for Mexican Americans.* Report VI: Mexican American Education Study (Washington, DC: US Commission on Civil Rights, 1974), 8. In another study, John S. Gains noted that the "treatment of Mexican Americans in American history textbooks has been grossly inaccurate, subjective, and marred by the omission of important facts, the use of stereotypes, and elements of latent nativism." See John S. Gains, "Treatment of Mexican American History in High School Textbooks," *Civil Rights Digest* (October 1972): 35–40.

70. The Mexican American Education Commission was created by the Los Angeles Board of Education in response to community demands and student protests. Kay Gurule, "Truthful Textbooks and Mexican Americans," *Integrated Education* (March–April 1973): 35–36.

71. Gurule, "Truthful Textbooks and Mexican Americans," 35–42.

72. Among the twelve members of this ethnic task force were three Mexican Americans: Mr. Ignacio Aguilar, Dr. Carlos E. Cortés, and Dr. Porfirio Sanchez. For a list of all the members, see Gurule, "Truthful Textbooks and Mexican Americans," 41.

73. Ibid., 35–42.

74. Abraham Hoffman, "Where Are the Mexican Americans? A Textbook Omission Overdue for Revision," *History Teacher* 6, no. 1 (1972): 143–50. Quote is on page 145.

75. Castaneda is making reference to Jensen and Miller's seminal 1980 article titled "The Gentle Tamers Revised." Their new approach recognized and included the experiences of women from different races, ethnicities, cultures, and classes. See Joan M. Jensen and Darlis A. Miller, "The Gentle Tamers Revisited: New Approaches to the History of Women in the American West," *Pacific Historical Review* 40 (1980): 173–214.

76. Antonia I. Castaneda, "Women of Color and the Rewriting of Western History: The Discourse, Politics, and Decolonization of History," *Pacific Historical Review* (1992): 501–33.

77. Joseph A. Rodríguez and Vicki L. Ruiz, "At Loose Ends: Twentieth-Century Latinos in Current United States History Textbooks," *Journal of American History* 86, no. 4 (2000): 1689–700.

78. Michael B. Kane, *Minorities in Textbooks: A Study of Their Treatment in Social Studies Texts* (Chicago: Quadrangle Books, 1970); L. P. Carpenter and Dinah Rank, *The Treatment of Minorities: A Survey of Textbooks Used in Missouri High Schools* (Jefferson City: Missouri

Commission on Human Rights, 1968); and Task Force to Reevaluate Social Science Textbooks Grades Five through Eight, *Report and Recommendations* (Sacramento: California State Department of Education, 1971).

79. Carter Woodson, the well-noted African American historian, made similar arguments about the "mis-education" of African American children and the negative effects on self-esteem of these efforts in the 1930s. See Carter G. Woodson, *The Mis-Education of the Negro* (Washington, DC: Associated Publishers, 1933).

80. Joshua Fishman, "Childhood Indoctrination for Minority Group Membership," *Daedalus* 90, no. 2 (1961): 329–49; and Mildred V. Boyer, "Poverty and the Mother Tongue," *Educational Forum* 29, no. 3 (1965): 291–65. See also Theodore Andersson, "A New Focus on the Bilingual Child," paper presented at the Conference for the Teacher of the Bilingual Child, University of Texas, June 9, 1964 (in author's possession); A. Bruce Gaarder, "Teaching the Bilingual Child: Research, Development, and Policy," paper presented at the Conference for the Teacher of the Bilingual Child, University of Texas, June 10, 1964 (in author's possession). For one of the earliest studies to document the impact of discrimination on Mexican Americans in education, see Thomas P. Carter, *Mexican Americans in School* (New York: College Entrance Examination Board, 1970). See also Herschel T. Manuel, *Spanish-Speaking Children of the Southwest* (Austin: University of Texas Press, 1965).

81. Books written for the elementary grades include: John Tebbel and Ramón Eduardo Ruiz, *South by Southwest: The Mexican-American and His Heritage* (Garden City, NY: Doubleday, 1969); Charles J. Bustamante and Patricia L. Bustamante, *The Mexican-American in the United States* (Mountain View, CA: Patty-Lar Publications, 1969); Julian Nava, *Mexican Americans: Past, Present, and Future* (New York: American Book Company, 1973); and Gilbert Martínez and Jane Edwards, *The Mexican American: His Life across Four Centuries* (Boston: Houghton Mifflin, 1973).

82. Rodolfo Acuña, the most well known historian in Chicano Studies, wrote books for all grade levels, including postsecondary. For his precollege books, see Rodolfo Acuña: *The Story of the Mexican American: The Men and the Land* (New York: American Book Company, 1969) (lower elementary); *Cultures in Conflict* (with Peggy Shackelton) (Los Angeles: Charter School Books, 1970) (advanced elementary); and *A Mexican American Chronicle* (New York: American Book Company, 1971) (secondary).

83. Carlos E. Cortés, "Teaching the Chicano Experience," in *Teaching Ethnic Studies: Concepts and Strategies*, ed. J. A. Banks (Washington, DC: National Council for the Social Studies, 1973), 181–99, at 193.

84. The audiences that individuals wrote for also shifted from historians and scholars in general to educators and practitioners in particular. Cortés, "Teaching the Chicano Experience," 193. See also Jack D. Forbes, *Mexican Americans: A Handbook for Educators* (Berkeley: Far West Laboratory for Educational Research and Development, 1967); Carey McWilliams, *The Mexicans in America: A Students' Guide to Localized History* (New York: Teachers College Press, 1968); Feliciano Rivera, *A Mexican American Source Book with Study Guideline* (Menlo Park, CA: Educational Consulting Associates, 1970).

85. Cortés, "Teaching the Chicano Experience." See also Carlos E. Cortés, "Revising the 'All-American Soul Course': A Bicultural Avenue to Educational Reform," in *Mexican Americans and Educational Change*, ed. Alfredo Castañeda, Manuel Ramírez III, Carlos E. Cortés, and Mario Barrera (Riverside: Mexican-American Studies Program, University of California, 1971), 319–22.

86. See, for instance, Vicki L. Ruiz, "Teaching Chicano/American History: Goals and Methods," *History Teacher* 20, no. 2 (1987): 167–77. See also James A. Banks, ed., *Teaching Ethnic Studies: Concepts and Strategies* (Washington, DC: National Council for the Social Studies, 1973).

87. James A. Banks, *Multiethnic Education: Theory and Practice*, 3rd ed. (Boston: Allyn and Bacon, 1994), 64. Among the ethnic minority groups considered for incorporation during the 1970s other than Latinos were African Americans, Native Americans, and Asian Americans. Scholars and curriculum experts added women and individuals with disabilities in the 1980s. This became multicultural education.

88. James A. Banks, *Teaching Strategies for Ethnic Studies* (Boston: Allyn and Bacon, 1975), 18–19. For further development of this view of multiethnic education as a curriculum for empowerment, action, social change, and personal decision making, see Banks, *Multitethnic Education*, esp. 143–96.

89. Banks, *Multiethnic Education*, xviii.

90. For an example of his work on local history, see Carlos E. Cortés, "CHICOP: A Response to the Challenge of Local Chicano History," *Aztlán: Chicano Journal of the Social Sciences and the Arts* 1 (Fall 1970): 1–14.

91. Cortés, "Teaching the Chicano Experience."

92. Ibid.

93. James A. Banks, Carlos E. Cortés, Geneva Gay, Richard L. Garcia, and A. S. Ochoa, *Curriculum Guidelines for Multiethnic Education* (Washington, DC: National Council for the Social Studies, 1976). For an exciting look at his professional transformation from a Chicano to a multicultural scholar, see Carlos E. Cortés, *The Making, and Remaking, of a Multiculturalist* (New York: Teachers College Press, 2002)

94. For her ideas on multicultural education, see Sonia Nieto, *Affirming Diversity: The Sociopolitical Context of Multicultural Education* (New York: Longman, 1992). See also her other important works on the education of Puerto Ricans in the US mainland. See especially Sonia Nieto, ed., *Puerto Rican Students in US Schools* (Mahwah, NJ: Lawrence Erlbaum, 2000); Sonia Nieto, "A History of the Education of Puerto Rican Students in US Schools: 'Losers,' 'Outsiders,' or 'Leaders?,'" in *Handbook of Research on Multicultural Education*, ed., James A. Banks and Cherry Banks (New York: Macmillan, 1995), 388–411; and Sonia Nieto, "Fact and Fiction: Stories of Puerto Rican Students in US Schools," *Harvard Educational Review* 68 (Summer 1998): 133–63.

95. See the following written by Nieto: *The Light in Their Eyes: Creating Multicultural Learning Communities* (New York: Teachers College Press, 1999); *Diversity: The Sociopolitical Context of Multicultural Education* (New York: Allyn and Bacon, 1992); *Language, Culture, and Teaching:*

Critical Perspectives for a New Century (Mahwah, NJ: Lawrence Erlbaum, 2002); *What Keeps Teachers Going?* (New York: Teachers College Press, 2003); *Why We Teach* (New York: Teachers College Press, 2005).

96. Pedro A. Cabán, "Moving from the Margins to Where? Three Decades of Latino/a Studies," *Latino Studies* 1, no. 1 (2003): 5–35.

97. Puerto Ricans also developed their own knowledge base. This came to be known as Puerto Rican Studies. In the 1990s, a broader field of studies encompassing all Latinos emerged—Latino Studies. This field of study included those dealing with Mexican Americans and Puerto Ricans as well as the histories and cultures of Cubans, Dominicans, and all other groups who came from the Spanish-speaking countries of the Caribbean and South America. See Cabán, "Moving from the Margins to Where?, 5–35.

98. For an overview of the origins and development of ethnic studies, see ibid., 5–35; Evelyn Hu-DeHart, "Ethnic Studies in US Higher Education: History, Development, and Goals," in *Handbook of Research on Multicultural Education*, ed. James A. Banks and Cherry A. McGee Banks (San Francisco: Jossey-Bass, 2001), 696–707. See also Ramon A. Gutierrez, "Ethnic Studies: Its Evolution in American Colleges and Universities," in *Multiculturalism: A Critical Reader*, ed. David Theo Goldberg (Cambridge, MA: Blackwell, 1994), 157–67.

99. Ignacio M. García, "Chicano Studies since 'El Plan de Santa Bárbara,'" in *Chicanas/Chicanos at the Crossroads: Social, Economic, and Political Change*, ed. David R. Maciel and Isidro D. Ortiz (Tucson: University of Arizona Press, 1996), 181–203, at 182.

100. Carey McWilliams, *North from Mexico: The Spanish Speaking People of the United States* (New York: Greenwood, 1968; originally published in 1948); Manuel Gamio, *Mexican Immigration to the United States* (New York: Arno Press, 1969, originally published in 1930).

101. See, for instance, the following, all edited by Cortés: *Aspects of the Mexican-American Experience* (New York: Arno Press, 1976); *The Mexican Experience in Texas* (New York: Arno Press, 1976); *The Cuban Experience in the United States* (New York: Arno Press, 1980); *Cuban Exiles in the United States* (New York: Arno Press, 1980); *Regional Perspectives on the Puerto Rican Experience* (New York: Arno Press, 1980); and *Nineteenth-Century Latin Americans in the United States* (New York: Arno Press, 1980).

102. On Chicana/o Studies, see Carlos Muñoz Jr., "The Development of Chicano Studies, 1968–1981," in *Chicano Studies: A Multidisciplinary Approach*, ed. Eugene E. Garcia et al. (New York: Teachers College Press, 1984), 5–18. On ethnic studies more generally, see Hu-DeHart, "Ethnic Studies in US Higher Education"; Gutierrez, "Ethnic Studies. "

103. Cabán, "Moving from the Margins to Where?," 10. Hu-DeHart also makes the same point. See Hu-DeHart, "Ethnic Studies in US Higher Education."

104. Carlos Muñoz Jr., "The Quest for Paradigm: The Development of Chicano Studies and Intellectuals," in *History, Culture, and Society: Chicano Studies in the 1980s*, ed. Mario T. Garcia et al. (Ypsilanti, MI: Bilingual Press/Editorial Bilingue, 1983), 25.

105. See, for instance, Mario Barrera, Carlos Muñoz Jr., and Charles Ornelas, "The Barrio as Internal Colony," in *People and Politics in Urban Society*, ed. Harlan Hahn (Los Angeles: Sage Publications, 1972), 465–98; and Cabán, "Moving from the Margins to Where?," 14.

106. Fred A. Cervantes, "Chicanos as a Post-Colonial Minority: Some Questions concerning the Adequacy of the Paradigm of Internal Colonialism," in *Perspectivas en Chicano Studies*, ed. Reynaldo Flores Macías, Proceedings of the Third Annual Meeting of the National Association of Chicano Social Scientists (Los Angeles: NACS, 1977); and Gilbert G. González, "A Critique of the Internal Colonial Model," *Latin American Perspectives* (Spring 1974): 154–61. See also History Task Force, Centro de Estudios Puertorriqueños, *Labor Migration under Capitalism: The Puerto Rican Experience* (New York: Monthly Review, 1979).

107. María E. Montoya, "Beyond Internal Colonialism: Class, Gender, and Culture as Challenges to Chicano Identity," in *Voices of New Chicana/o History*, ed. Refugio I. Rochín and Dennis N. Valdés (East Lansing: Michigan State University Press, 2000), 183–96.

108. In the 1980s, conservative politicians and educators attacked the goals and objectives of Chicano Studies research, decreased funding for Latino Studies programs, and reduced its potential faculty by failing to give them tenure at major universities. For the case of Chicano Studies see García, "Chicano Studies since 'El Plan de Santa Bárbara,'" 185–87.

109. The campaign for ethnic studies on campus usually was broad in nature and entailed not only requiring students to take ethnic studies or multicultural education courses. It also included efforts to recruit minority students, hire minority faculty, promote racial sensitivity and tolerance through workshops or orientation sessions, and implement some type of antiharassment policies. For one university's effort to promote ethnic studies requirements, see Denise K. Magner, "Cultural-Diversity Requirement Adopted at U. of Cincinnati," *Chronicle of Higher Education*, January 19, 1990, http://chronicle.com.ezproxy.lib.uh.edu/che-data/articles.dir/articles-36.dir/issue-18.dir/18a . . . (accessed May 19, 2009).

110. Denise K. Magner, "Racial Tensions Continue to Erupt on Campuses Despite Efforts to Promote Cultural Diversity," *Chronicle of Higher Education*, June 6, 1990, http://chronicle.com/ezproxy.lib.uh.edu/che-data/articles.dir/articles-36.dir/issue-38.dir/38a . . . (accessed May 19, 2009).

111. William J. Bennett, *Our Children and Our Country: Improving America's Schools and Affirming the Common Culture* (New York: Simon and Schuster, 1988); Alan Bloom, *The Closing of the American Mind: How Higher Education Has Failed Democracy and Impoverished the Souls of Today's Students* (New York: Simon and Schuster, 1987); E. D. Hirsch Jr., *Cultural Literacy: What Every American Needs to Know* (Boston: Houghton Mifflin, 1987).

112. Floyd W. Hayes III, "Politics and Education in America's Multicultural Society: An African-American Studies' Response to Allan Bloom," *Journal of Ethnic Studies* 17 (Summer 1989): 73–74; Michael Soldatenko-Gutierrez, "Socrates, Curriculum, and the Chicano/Chicana: Allan Bloom and the Myth of US Higher Education," *Cultural Studies* 4 (October 1990): 304–19.

113. One of the most well known institutions to adopt a non-Western requirement in 1988 was Stanford University. For criticism of this decision, see "Bennett Calls Stanford's Curriculum Revision 'Capitulation' to Pressure," *Chronicle of Higher Education*, April 27, 1988, A2.

114. "Legislative History of Hispanic Heritage Month: Public Law 90–498, Approved September 17, 1968, 90th Congress." http://www.clnet.ucla.edu/heritage/hhhispan.htm.

115. Public Law 90–498, September 17, 1968, in "Legislative History of Hispanic Heritage Month," http://latino.sscnet.ucla.edu/heritage/hhhispan.html (accessed July 31, 2007).

116. See also the following websites on Hispanic Heritage Month: http://www.educationworld .com/a_lesson/lesson/lesson023.shtml. "Celebrate Hispanic Heritage Month!"; http://www .factmonster.com/spot/hhm1.html; http://teacher.scholastic.com/activities/hispanic/; http:// www.mcps.k12.md.us/curriculum/socialStd/Hispanic.html; http://www.history.com/ classroom/hhm/.

117. Public Law 100–402, August 17, 1988, in "Legislative History of Hispanic Heritage Month," http://latino.sscnet.ucla.edu/heritage/hhhispan.html (accessed July 31, 2007).

Chapter 4

1. In this chapter I will use various terms to designate those children bilingual education policies targeted. Although initially aimed at Mexican American children, federal policy labeled these and all others who spoke a language other than English differently over the decades. In the 1960s, the term used to identify them was *non-English-speaking* (NES). In the 1970s and 1980s it changed to *limited English speaking* (LES) and to *limited English proficient* (LEP), respectively. In the late 1990s and early twenty-first century, these children were referred to as English language learners (ELLS). Scholars and activists also used other terms such as *linguistically and culturally different* or *language minority group* to make reference to these children. I will use all of these terms in analyzing the evolution of bilingual education policy from the 1960s to the present.

2. Gaarder argues that bilingualism, despite problems, was not a matter of intelligence but of adequate teaching methods. See A. Bruce Gaarder, "Conserving Our Linguistic Resources," *Publications of the Modern Language Association* 80 (May 1965): 19–23.

3. Two important articles that helped to shift the emphasis of the impact of bilingualism on intelligence were Elizabeth Peal and Wallace Lambert, "The Relation of Bilingualism to Intelligence," *Psychological Monographs, General and Applied* 76 (1962): 1–23; and Joshua Fishman, "Bilingualism, Intelligence, and Language Learning," *Modern Language Journal* 49 (March 1965): 227–37.

4. Theodore Andersson, "A New Focus on the Bilingual Child," paper presented at the Conference for the Teacher of the Bilingual Child, University of Texas, June 9, 1964 (in author's possession); A. Bruce Gaarder, "Teaching the Bilingual Child: Research, Development, and Policy," paper presented at the Conference for the Teacher of the Bilingual Child, University of Texas, June 10, 1964 (in author's possession). See also Wallace E. Lambert and G. Richard Tucker, *Bilingual Education of Children: The St. Lambert Experiment* (Rowley, MA: Newbury House Publishers, 1972).

5. Annie Stemmler, "An Experimental Approach to the Teaching of Oral Language and Reading," *Harvard Educational Review* 36 (Summer 1966): 45.

6. For a summary of research studies on bilingualism and language learning, see A. Cohen, *A Sociolinguistic Approach to Bilingual Education* (Rowley, MA: Newbury House Publishers, 1976).

7. See, for instance, Joshua Fishman, "The Status and Prospects of Bilingualism in the US," *Modern Language Journal* 49 (March 1965): 143–55; Chester C. Christian Jr., "The Acculturation of the Bilingual Child," *Modern Language Journal* 69 (March 1965): 160–65; and Joshua Fishman, *Language Loyalty in the United States* (The Hague: Mouton, 1966).

8. Fishman, *Language Loyalty in the United States.*

9. The melting pot, in other words, was a myth. See Nathan Glazer and Daniel Moynihan, *Beyond the Melting Pot: The Negroes, Puerto Ricans, Jews, Italians, and Irish of New York City* (Cambridge, MA: MIT Press, 1963).

10. For an overview of this period, see the following sources: Harvard Sitkoff, *The Struggle for Black Equality, 1954–1992* (New York: Hill and Wang, 1993); Joel Spring, "Civil Rights," in *The Sorting Machine Revisited* (New York: Longman, 1989), 111–16; and Diane Ravitch, "Race and Education," in *The Troubled Crusade* (New York: Basic Books, 1983), 114–44. For a broader view of this period encompassing other groups besides blacks, see Leonard Dinnerstein, Roger L. Nichols, and David M. Reimers, *Natives and Strangers: Blacks, Indians and Immigrants in America*, 2nd ed. (New York: Oxford University Press, 1990), 293–333.

11. Andersson, "A New Focus on the Bilingual Child"; Gaarder, "Teaching the Bilingual Child." For one of the earliest studies to document the impact of this type of discrimination on Mexican Americans in education, see Thomas P. Carter, *Mexican Americans in School* (New York: College Entrance Examination Board, 1970). See also Herschel T. Manuel, *Spanish-Speaking Children of the Southwest* (Austin: University of Texas Press, 1965).

12. Andersson, "A New Focus on the Bilingual Child"; Gaarder, "Teaching the Bilingual Child"; Carter, *Mexican Americans in School.*

13. For a discussion of the importance of the War on Poverty and the role played by the Elementary and Secondary Education Act of 1965, see Joel Spring, "War on Poverty," in *The Sorting Machine Revisited* (New York: Longman, 1989), 111–16.

14. Julie Leininger Pycior, *LBJ and Mexican Americans: The Paradox of Power* (Austin: University of Texas Press, 1997); Craig A. Kaplowitz, *LULAC: Mexican Americans and National Policy* (College Station: Texas A&M University Press, 2005).

15. For examples of some of these studies, see Joshua Fishman, "Childhood Indoctrination for Minority Group Membership," *Daedalus* 90, no. 2 (1961): 329–49; and Mildred V. Boyer, "Poverty and the Mother Tongue," *Educational Forum* 29, no. 3 (1965): 291–65.

16. Mildred V. Boyer, "Texas Squanders Non-English Resources," *Texas Foreign Language Association Bulletin* 5, no. 3 (1963): 1–8; Gaarder, "Conserving Our Linguistic Resources," 19–23.

17. For an overview of their ideals, see Ignacio M. Garcia, *Chicanismo: The Forging of a Militant Ethos among Mexican Americans* (Tucson: University of Arizona Press, 1997).

18. NEA, *Pero No Invencibles—The Invisible Minority* (Washington, DC: NEA, Department of Rural Supervision, 1966); Armando Navarro, *The Cristal Experiment: A Chicano Struggle for Community Control* (Madison: University of Wisconsin Press, 1998); Carlos Muñoz Jr., *Youth, Identity, Power: The Chicano Movement* (New York: Verso, 1990).

19. Manuel Ramirez III, "Bilingual Education as a Vehicle for Institutional Change," in *Mexican Americans and Educational Change*, ed. Alfredo Castañeda et al. (New York: Arno Press, 1974), 387–407. See also Atilano A. Valencia, "Bilingual-Bicultural Education: A Quest for Institutional Reform," *Spring Bulletin* (Riverside: Western Regional Desegregation Projects, University of California, Riverside, April 1971), 11.

20. During these years a few Mexican American activists were distrustful of bilingual education and viewed it as an instrument of assimilation, not cultural pluralism. Luci Jaramillo, 1973, for instance, referred to bilingual education as a "por mientras" (in the meantime). Her statement implied cautious support for this untried reform. Parents in Crystal City also voiced doubts about the development of a bilingual education program in that city in 1970. See John Staples Shockley, *Chicano Revolt in a Texas Town* (Notre Dame, IN: University of Notre Dame Press, 1974), 163, 203. See also Muñoz, *Youth, Identity, Power*.

21. Carlos E. Cortés, "Revising the 'All-American Soul Course': A Bicultural Avenue to Educational Reform," in *Mexican Americans and Educational Change*, ed. Alfredo Castañeda et al. (New York: Arno Press, 1974), 314–39.

22. Ramirez, "Bilingual Education as a Vehicle for Institutional Change," 390–91. See more generally Guadalupe San Miguel Jr., "Actors Not Victims: Chicanas/Chicanos and the Struggle for Educational Equality," in *Chicanas/Chicanos at the Crossroads*, ed. David R. Maciel and Isidro D. Ortiz (Tucson: University of Arizona Press, 1996), 159–80.

23. Atilano A. Valencia, "Bilingual Education: A Quest for Bilingual Survival," in *Mexican Americans and Educational Change*, ed. Alfredo Castañeda et al. (New York: Arno Press, 1974), 345–62. See as well Rubén Donato, *The Other Struggle for Equal Schools: Mexican Americans during the Civil Rights Era* (Albany: State University of New York Press, 1997); and Shockley, *Chicano Revolt in a Texas Town*.

24. NEA, *Pero No Invencibles—The Invisible Minority*.

25. The belief that preservation of the linguistic and cultural heritage of Mexican American and other language minority children could overcome cultural degradation and low school performance was quite common during this period. See, for instance, Gaarder, "Conserving Our Linguistic Resources," 19–23; Southwest Council of Foreign Language Teachers, "A Resolution concerning the Education of Bilingual Children," in *Bilingual Education in the United States*, ed. Theodore Andersson and Mildred Boyer (Austin: Southwest Educational Development Laboratory, 1970), 284–86; Sister D. C. Noreen, "A Bilingual Curriculum for Spanish-Americans: A Regional Problem with Nation-Wide Implications," *Catholic School Journal* 66, no. 1 (1966): 25–26; California Department of Education, *Bilingual Education for Mexican American Children*

(Sacramento: Department of Education, 1967); Francesco M. Cordasco, "The Challenge of the Non-English Speaking Child in American Schools," *School and Society* 96 (March 30, 1968): 198–201.

26. NEA, *Pero No Invencibles—The Invisible Minority.*

27. For an overview of the dominance of cultural interpretations of low academic performance among Mexican Americans, see Nick C. Vaca, "The Mexican-American in the Social Sciences, 1912–1970, Part I: 1912–1935," *El Grito* (Fall 1970): 3–16, 21–24; Nick C. Vaca, "The Mexican-American in the Social Sciences, 1912–1970, Part II: 1936–1970," *El Grito* (Fall 1971): 17–51; Carter, *Mexican Americans in Schools;* and Thomas P. Carter and R. D. Segura, *Mexican Americans in School: A Decade of Change* (New York: College Entrance Examination Board, 1979).

28. NEA, *Pero No Invencibles—The Invisible Minority.*

29. Ibid. Other scholars also made similar arguments. See, for instance, Alfredo Castañeda, "Melting Potters vs. Cultural Pluralists: Implications for Education," *Mexican Americans and Educational Change, Symposium at the University of California, Riverside, May 21–22, 1971,* ed. Alfredo Castañeda, Manuel Ramírez III, Carlos E. Cortés, and Mario Barrera (New York: Arno Press, 1974), 22–40.

30. NEA, *Pero No Invencibles—The Invisible Minority.*

31. *Las voces nuevas del sudoeste: A Symposium on the Spanish-Speaking Child in the Schools of the Southwest, Tucson, Arizona, October 30–31, 1966* (Tucson: National Education Association, Committee on Civil and Human Rights of Educators of the Commission on Professional Rights and Responsibilities, 1966).

32. Many of these individuals, noted Armando Rodriguez, the highest-ranking Mexican American in a federal position in 1970, were veterans who had taken advantage of the GI Bill in the 1940s and 1950s and received their college education. In the early 1960s they realized "having been both student and teacher" that the public schools were not designed to provide equal educational opportunity. As these educators moved into positions of authority they began to raise the question of the failure of the school. See Armando Rodriguez, "Education for the Spanish-Speaking: Mañana in Motion," *National Elementary Principal* 49 (February 1970): 52–56. Also published in Earl J. Ogletree and David Garcia, eds., *Education of the Spanish Speaking Urban Child: A Book of Readings* (Springfield, IL: Charles C. Thomas, 1975), 259–68, at 260.

33. Gilbert Sanchez, "An Analysis of the Bilingual Education Act, 1967–1968" (PhD diss., University of Massachusetts, 1973).

34. Ralph Yarborough, "Two Proposals for a Better Way of Life for Mexican Americans in the Southwest," *Congressional Record* (January 17, 1967): 599–600.

35. Ibid., 600.

36. Sanchez, "An Analysis of the Bilingual Education Act, 1967–1968," 54–56.

37. For an overview of these conferences, see ibid.

38. Ibid., 72–80.

39. For the variety of reasons given in support of bilingual education legislation, see the following congressional hearings: US Sen., *Bilingual Education, Hearings before the Special Subcommittee on Bilingual Education of the Committee on Labor and Public Welfare on S. 428* (2 vols.) (90th Cong., 1st Sess.); and House of Rep., *Bilingual Education Programs, Hearings before the General Subcommittee on Education of the Committee on Education and Labor on H.R. 9840 and H.R. 10224* (90th Cong., 1st Sess.).

40. *Public Law 90–247* (January 2, 1968), 81 *Stat.* 816, 20 USC.A. 880 (b).

41. *Public Law 90–247* (January 2, 1968), 81 *Stat.* 816, 20 USC.A. 880 (b). For the authorization and uses of funds, see Sec. 703 and Sec. 704, respectively. For the section on the establishment of the advisory committee see Sec. 707.

42. One scholar noted that the bill, in essence, was an afterthought of the War on Poverty social legislation. See Colman Brez Stein Jr., *Sink or Swim: The Politics of Bilingual Education* (Westport, CT: Praeger, 1986), 10–19.

43. The capacity-building emphasis of the bill was reflected in the different parts of the bill. Part A focused on financial assistance for bilingual education programs, Part B emphasized administrative aspects, and Part C focused on supportive services and activities such as research and demonstration projects as well as data collection on the size and nature of the non-English-speaking student population. *PL 93–380*, Aug. 21, 1974, Parts A, B, C.

44. *Public Law 93–380*, Aug. 21, 1974, Parts A, B, C.

45. See *Public Law 95–562*, 1978, Parts A, B, C, and D.

46. Comptroller General Office, *Bilingual Education: An Unmet Need* (Washington, DC: GPO, May 19, 1976); *The Condition of Bilingual Education in the Nation-First Report by the US Commissioner of Education to the Congress and the President* (Fall River, MA: National Assessment and Dissemination Center, November, 1976); *Strengthening Bilingual Education: A Report from the Commissioner of Education to the Congress and the President* (Washington, DC: United States Office of Education, Department of Health, Education, and Welfare, June 1979).

47. James Crawford, *Bilingual Education: History, Politics, Theory* (Trenton, NJ: Crane Publishers, 1989), 33.

48. Joshua Fishman, "The Politics of Bilingual Education," in *Bilingual Schooling in the US*, ed. Francesco Cordasco (New York: McGraw-Hill, 1976), 141–49. For a similar analysis, see Herman Badillo, "The Politics and Realities of Bilingual Education," *Foreign Language Annals* 5, no. 3 (1972): 297–301.

49. Fishman, "The Politics of Bilingual Education," 141–49.

50. Comptroller General Office, *Bilingual Education: An Unmet Need* (Washington, DC: GPO, May 19, 1976); *The Condition of Bilingual Education in the Nation-First Report by the US Commissioner of Education to the Congress and the President* (Fall River, MA: National Assessment and Dissemination Center, November, 1976).

51. Richard R. Valencia, ed., *The Evolution of Deficit Thinking: Educational Thought and Practice* (Washington, DC: Falmer Press, 1997).

52. *Public Law 90–247*, January 2, 1968, 81 *Stat.* 817, Sec. 701.

53. The regulations issued in 1969 stated: "Children with limited English-speaking ability are eligible to participate (in bilingual programs) even though they are not from families with incomes below $3,000 per year, or from families receiving payments under a program of aid to families with dependent children under a State plan approved under Title IV of the Social Security Act." See the draft guidelines to the Bilingual Education program found in "Financial Assistance for Bilingual Education Programs," *Federal Register* 34, no. 4 (January 7, 1969): 201–205.

54. *Public Law 93–380*, Aug. 21, 1974, Sec. 702 (a.) and Sec. 703 (a)(4)(B).

55. *Public Law 95–561*, Nov. 1, 1978 Sec. 703 (a)(4)(A). The section stipulating the percent of English speakers in the program is found in *Public Law 95–561*, Nov. 1, 1978 Sec. 703 (a)(4)(B).

56. *Public Law 93–380*, Aug. 21, 1974, Sec. 722 (a)(5); *Public Law 95–561*, Nov. 1, 1978 Sec. 722 (a).

57. For a history of what Valencia refers to as "deficit thinking" in education, see Valencia, *The Evolution of Deficit Thinking*.

58. The label used for the targeted population was changed to limited English proficiency in 1978. See *Public Law 95–561*, Nov. 1, 1978, 92 *Stat.* 2269, Sec. 703 (a)(1).

59. *Public Law 90–247*, January 2, 1968, 81 *Stat.* 817, Sec. 701.

60. *Public Law 90–247*, January 2, 1968, 81 *Stat.* 817, Sec. 704 (c.) [1–8].

61. Garland Cannon, "Bilingual Problems and Developments in the United States," *Publications of the Modern Language Association* 86 (May 1971): 452–58; Theodore Andersson, "Bilingual Education: The American Experience," *Modern Language Journal* 55 (November 1971): 427–40; Maria M. Swanson, "Bilingual Education: The National Perspective," in *The ACTFL Review of Foreign Language Education*, vol. 5, ed. Gilbert A. Jarvis (Skokie, IL: National Textbook, 1974), 75–127; Lawrence Wright, "Bilingual Education Movement at the Crossroads," in *Education of the Spanish Speaking Child*, ed. Earl J. Ogletree and David Garcia (Springfield, IL: Charles C. Thomas, 1975), 335–45.

62. *Public Law 93–380*, Aug. 21, 1974, Sec. 702 (a)(5).

63. The law stated that "a program of bilingual education may make provision for the voluntary enrollment to a limited degree therein, on a regular basis, of children whose language is English, in order that they may acquire an understanding of the cultural heritage of the children of limited English-speaking ability for whom the particular program of bilingual education is designed." *Public Law 93–380*, Aug. 21, 1974, Sec. 703 a4B.

64. George Blanco, "The Education Perspective," in *Bilingual Education: Current Perspectives*, vol. 4 (Arlington, VA: Center for Applied Linguistics, 1977), 21–52.

65. See, for instance, Cordasco, "The Challenge of the Non-English-Speaking Child in American Schools," 198–201; Fishman, *Language Loyalty in the United States;* Gaarder, "Con-

serving Our Linguistic Resources," 19–23; Enrique T. Trueba, "Issues and Problems in Bilingual Bicultural Education Today," *Journal of the National Association for Bilingual Education* 1 (December 1976): 11–19; Lourdes Travieso, "Puerto Ricans and Education," *Journal of Teacher Education* 26 (Summer 1975): 128–30; and Muñoz, *Youth, Identity, Power.*

66. Several scholars argued that the inclusion of native language instruction in the definition of bilingual education was influenced by bilingual programs in Dade County, Florida, which were founded to address the needs of the first wave of middle-class Cuban immigrants. These immigrants saw themselves as temporary residents of the United States who would soon return to their country and therefore wanted to preserve their culture and language. The success of these programs gave encouragement to the idea of bilingual education as a method of instruction for students from disadvantaged backgrounds. See U. Casanova, "Bilingual Education: Politics or Pedagogy," in *Bilingual Education*, vol. 1, ed. O. Garcia (Amsterdam: John Benjamins, 1991), 167–82; Kenji Hakuta, *Mirror of Language* (New York: Basic Books, 1986).

67. *Public Law 93–380*, Aug. 21, 1974, Sec. 702 (a)(5).

68. "Memorandum of Frank Carlucci, Under Secretary of Education, to the Assistant Secretary for Education, December 2, 1974," in *Bilingual Education: An Unmet Need—Report to the Congress by the Comptroller General of the United States* (Washington, DC: Comptroller General of the United States, May 1976), 55–59.

69. This argument was made by Wiese and García in 1998. See Ann-Marie Wiese and Eugene E. García, "The Bilingual Education Act: Language Minority Students and Equal Educational Opportunity," *Bilingual Research Journal* 22, no. 1 (1998): 1–13.

70. *Public Law 95–561*, Nov. 1, 1978 Sec. 703 a4A & B.

71. For several examples of research studies documenting the primacy of learning English in bilingual education, see Rolf Kjolseth, "Bilingual Education Programs in the United States: Assimilation or Pluralism?," in *The Language Education of Minority Children*, ed. Bernard Spolsky (Rowley, MA: Newbury House Publishers, 1972), 94–121; A. Bruce Gaarder, "The First Seventy-Six Bilingual Education Projects," in *Bilingualism and Language Contact*, ed. James E. Alatis (Washington, DC: Georgetown University Press, 1970), 163–78; Jose Cardenas, in Noel Epstein, *Language, Ethnicity, and the Schools* (Washington, DC: Institute for Educational Leadership, 1977), 73.

72. In 1974, Congress also passed the Equal Educational Opportunity Act, a piece of congressional legislation that, among other things, mandated local school districts to take affirmative steps to deal with the language needs of minority group children. This also served as another legal mandate. The section dealing with language was Title II of this act. See Equal Educational Opportunity Act of 1974, *Public Law 93–380*, sec. 204 f.

73. In the first several years of the bill's enactment only a small proportion of school districts with large numbers of limited English speaking individuals applied for federal funds. The indifference and unwillingness of local school officials to participate in bilingual education led to litigation efforts by Asian, Mexican American, and Puerto Rican groups who charged them with discrimination for failing to address the linguistic concerns of their children. The first court case to reach the US Supreme Court was filed by Asian American activists in San Francisco. For an overview of these cases, see Peter D. Roos, "Bilingual Education: Hispanic Response to Unequal Education,"

Law and Contemporary Problems 42 (1978): 111–40; and Herbert Teitelbaum and Richard J. Hiller, "Bilingual Education: The Legal Mandate," *Harvard Educational Review* 47 (May 1977): 138–70.

74. *Lau v. Nichols*, 414 US 563 (1974).

75. J. Stanley Pottinger, *Memorandum of May 25, 1970 to School Districts with More Than Five Percent National Origin–Minority Group Children* (Washington, DC: Department of Health, Education, and Welfare, Office for Civil Rights, 1970). For a history of the making of this memo, see Martin H. Gerry, "Cultural Freedom in the Schools: The Right of Mexican-American Children to Succeed," in *Mexican Americans and Educational Change*, ed. Alfredo Castañeda et al. (New York: Arno Press, 1974), 226–55.

76. Pottinger, *Memorandum of May 25, 1970 to School Districts with More Than Five Percent National Origin-Minority Group Children*.

77. Teitelbaum and Hiller argue that it also had a significant impact on state legislation and on several additional lawsuits. See Herbert Teitelbaum and Richard J. Hiller, "The Legal Perspective," in *Bilingual Education: Current Perspectives—Law*, vol. 3 (Arlington, VA: Center for Applied Linguistics, 1977), 1–66, at 9.

78. Ibid., quote is on page 9. The section dealing with language was Title II of this act. See *Equal Educational Opportunity Act of 1974. Public Law 93–380*, sec. 204 f.

79. An English as a Second Language (ESL) program, noted the Lau Remedies, was not an appropriate approach for elementary school children because it did not "consider the affective nor cognitive development of students in this category and time and maturation variables are different here than for students at the secondary level." Office for Civil Rights, *Task Force Findings Specifying Remedies Available for Eliminating Past Educational Practices Ruled Unlawful under Lau v. Nichols* (Washington, DC: Department of Health, Education, and Welfare, Office for Civil Rights, 1975).

80. Office for Civil Rights, *Task Force Findings Specifying Remedies Available*.

81. For information on the status of bilingual education legislation, implementation, and compliance with the Lau Remedies during the latter part of the 1970s and early 1980s, see *Strengthening Bilingual Education: A Report from the Commissioner of Education to the Congress and the President* (Washington, DC: USOE, DHEW, June 1979); and *The Condition of Bilingual Education in the Nation, 1984: A Report from the Secretary of Education to the President and the Congress* (Washington, DC: USDOE, 1984).

82. Rolf Kjolseth, "Bilingual Education Programs in the United States: Assimilation or Pluralism?," in *The Language Education of Minority Children*, ed. Bernard Spolsky (Rowley, MA: Newbury House Publishers, 1972), 94–121.

83. *Brown v. Board of Education*, 347 US 483 (1954); *Lau v. Nichols*, 414 US 563 (1974).

84. González, for instance, makes this point. See Josué M. González, *Towards Quality in Bilingual Education / Bilingual Education in the Integrated School: Two Papers* (Rosslyn, VA: National Clearinghouse for Bilingual Education, 1979).

85. *Keyes v. School District Number One*, Denver, Colorado, 380 F. Supp. 673 (D. Colo. 1973), 521 F. 2d 465 (10th Cir. 1975).

86. For an overview of these arguments, see Keith A. Baker and Adriana A. de Kanter, *Effectiveness of Bilingual Education: A Review of the Literature* (Washington, DC: OPBE, 1981). See also Stephen D. Krashen, *Condemned without a Trial: Bogus Arguments against Bilingual Education* (Westport, CT: Heinemann, 1999).

87. See, for instance, Malcolm N. Danoff, *Evaluation of the Impact of ESEA Title VII Spanish/English Bilingual Education Programs* (Palo Alto, CA: AIR, 1978). For a critique of the AIR reports, see Jose Cardenas, "Response I," in Noel E. Epstein, *Language, Ethnicity, and the Schools* (Washington, DC: Institute for Educational Leadership, 1977), 71–84; Tracy C. Gray and M. Beatriz Arias, *Challenge to the AIR Report* (Arlington, VA: Center for Applied Linguistics, 1978); Joan S. Bissell, *A Review of the Impact Study of ESEA Title VII Spanish/English Bilingual Education Programs* (Sacramento, CA: Office of the Auditor General, State Legislature, 1979); and Robert A. Cervantes, *An Exemplary Consafic Chingatropic Assessment: The AIR Report* (Los Angeles: National Dissemination and Assessment Center, 1978).

88. Baker and de Kanter, *Effectiveness of Bilingual Education*. See also C. Rossell and K. Baker, "The Educational Effectiveness of Bilingual Education," *Research in the Teaching of English* 30, no. 1 (1996): 7–74.

89. See, for instance, Max Rafferty, "Bilingual Education: Hoax of the 1980s," *American Legion*, March 1981, 4, 15–16, 39–40; and William Raspberry, "No Sense—In Any Language," *Washington Post*, October 22, 1980, 23A.

90. Rafferty, "Bilingual Education: Hoax of the 1980s," 4, 15–16, 39–40; and Raspberry, "No Sense—In Any Language," 23A. Other popular arguments were made, including that most immigrants succeeded without bilingual education, and that the United States was the only country that promotes bilingual education. For a summary of these arguments, see Krashen, *Condemned without a Trial*, and James Crawford, "Ten Common Fallacies about Bilingual Education," *ERIC Digest*, November 1998 (EDO-FL-98–10).

91. Eduardo Hernandez-Chavez, Jose Llanes, Roberto Alvarez, and Steve Arvizu, *The Federal Policy toward Language and Education: Pendulum or Progress?* Monograph no. 12 (Sacramento: Cross Cultural Resource Center, California State University, 1981). They argue that this report invites the federal government to abrogate its responsibility for providing equal educational opportunity. Stanley S. Seidner, *Political Expediency or Educational Research: An Analysis of Baker and de Kanter's Review of the Literature of Bilingual Education* (Rosslyn, VA: National Clearinghouse for Bilingual Education, 1981).

92. US General Accounting Office, *Bilingual Education: A New Look at the Research Evidence* (Washington, DC: GPO, March 1987); James Crawford, *At War with Diversity: US Language Policy in an Age of Anxiety* (Buffalo, NY: Multilingual Matters, 2000); James Crawford, "Ten Common Fallacies"; Jay Greene, *A Meta-Analysis of the Effectiveness of Bilingual Education* (Claremont, CA: Tomás Rivera Center, 1998).

93. US General Accounting Office, *Bilingual Education: A New Look at the Research Evidence;* James Crawford, *At War with Diversity: US Language Policy in an Age of Anxiety* (Buffalo, NY:

Multilingual Matters, 2000); James Crawford, "Ten Common Fallacies"; Greene, *A Meta-Analysis of the Effectiveness of Bilingual Education.*

94. Stephen D. Krashen, *Under Attack: The Case against Bilingual Education* (Culver City, CA: Language Education Associates, 1996); Crawford, "Ten Common Fallacies"; and Krashen, *Condemned without a Trial.*

95. See Allan C. Ornstein, "The Changing Federal Role in Education," *American Education* 20 (December 1984): 4–7. See also Jack H. Shuster, "Out of the Frying Pan: The Politics of Education in a New Era," *Phi Delta Kappan* (May 1982): 583–91. A primary objective of his administration was to limit the role of the federal government. In keeping with this philosophy, Reagan and his congressional allies mounted an attack against bilingual education. See Ira Shor, *Culture Wars: School and Society in the Conservative Restoration, 1969–1984* (New York: Routledge and Kegan Paul, 1986).

96. This data can be gleaned from the following reports: *Strengthening Bilingual Education: A Report from the Commissioner of Education to the Congress and the President* (Washington, DC: USOE, DHEW, June 1979), and *The Condition of Bilingual Education in the Nation, 1984: A Report from the Secretary of Education to the President and the Congress* (Washington, DC: USDOE, 1984).

97. National Advisory and Coordinating Council on Bilingual Education, *Tenth Annual Report* (Washington, DC: US Department of Education, March 1986); James L. Lyons, "The View from Washington," *NABE News* 10 (Fall 1986): 11, 15.

98. His intention was to redirect the program toward more English instruction. See *Address by William J. Bennett, US Secretary of Education to the Association for a Better New York*, New York, New York, September 26, 1985 (in author's possession).

99. For a copy of these new regulations, see "Notice of Proposed Rulemaking," *Federal Register* 50, no. 226 (November 22, 1985): 48352–70.

100. For a detailed view of these and other actions illustrating "a declining federal leadership in promoting equal educational opportunity" between 1980 and 1982, see "US Commission on Civil Rights Addresses Educational Inequities," *IDRA Newsletter* (April 1982): 1–8. A general interpretation of the changing nature of the federal role in education under the Reagan administration is provided by Shuster, "Out of the Frying Pan," 583–91, and by Ornstein, "The Changing Federal Role," 4–7.

101. James Crawford, "Bilingual Program Grantees Told to Cut Travel, Salary Expenses," *Education Week*, June 11, 1986, 10; and "'Mainstreaming' Is Factor in Bilingual Grant Awards, Official Says," *Education Week*, October 22, 1986, 6. A copy of this action is found in "Text of Civil Rights Office Letters to Regional Heads, School Districts," *Education Week*, November 27, 1985, 16. See also James Hertling, "Flexibility Stressed in New Rules for Bilingual Classes," *Education Week*, November 27, 1985, 1, 16.

102. James Crawford, "Bennett's Plan for Bilingual Overhaul Heats Up Debate," *Education Week*, February 12, 1986, 1, 22; Lee May, "Latinos Assail Bilingual Education Plans," *Los Angeles Times*, January 25, 1986, part I, 3; Office of Research Advocacy and Legislation, *Secretary Bennett's Bilingual Education Initiative: Historical Perspectives and Implications* (Washington,

DC: National Council of La Raza, October 31, 1985); James L. Lyons, "Education Secretary Bennett on Bilingual Education: Mixed Up or Malicious?," *CABE Newsletter* 8, no. 2 (1985): 1, 15.

103. For changes in the provisions of these bills, see Bilingual Education Act, *Public Law 100–297* (April 28, 1988) and *Public Law 103–382* (September 28, 1994).

104. Officially, there were five fundable programs. Three of these were instructional programs for ELLs–Transitional Bilingual Education (TBE), Developmental Bilingual Education (DBE), and Special Alternative Instructional Programs (SAIP). The first two allowed for native language instruction, the latter one did not. See Bilingual Education Act, *Public Law 98–511* (October 19, 1984).

105. Bilingual Education Act, *Public Law 100–297* (April 28, 1988).

106. For an example of one author who continued making these charges, see Rosalie Pedalino Porter, *Forked Tongue: the Politics of Bilingual Education* (New York: Basic Books, 1990). For more general studies attacking bilingualism and diversity in American life, see Arthur M. Schlesinger Jr., *The Disuniting of America* (New York: W. W. Norton, 1992); and William J. Bennett, *The Devaluing of America: The Fight for Our Culture and Our Children* (New York: Touchstone, 1992).

107. The No Child Left Behind Act, *Public Law 107–110*, August 3, 2001.

108. See "House OKs School Reform Bill," *Houston Chronicle*, December 14, 2001, 10A.

109. Jeffrey J. Kuenzi, *Education of Limited English Proficient and Recent Immigrant Students: Provisions in the No Child Left Behind Act of 2001* (Washington, DC: Congressional Research Service, the Library of Congress, March 1, 2002), 1.

110. For two different responses to the Elementary and Secondary Education Act in general and the bilingual education bill in particular by supporters of this program, see National Council of La Raza, "Statement of Raul Yzaguirre on the Elementary and Secondary Education Act," December 14, 2001, 1–2 (in author's possession); and James Crawford, "Obituary: The Bilingual Education Act, 1968–2002," n.d., http://www.ourworld.compuserve.com/homepages/ JWCRAWFORD/new.htm. The former praises the bipartisan approach to the enactment of this bill and does not critique the new bill but cautions that the changes need to be more effectively monitored by the federal government; the latter argues that the new bill dismantles the federal Title VII program and turns most funding decisions over to the states.

111. See US Congress, House of Representatives, *No Child Left Behind Act of 2001*, 107th Congress, 1st Session, Report 107–334, December 13, 2001, Sec. 3001.

112. Kuenzi, *Education of Limited English Proficient and Recent Immigrant Students: Provisions in the No Child Left Behind Act of 2001, March 1, 2002*, 1.

113. James Crawford, *Obituary: The Bilingual Education Act, 1968–2002,"* 1, http://ourworld .compuserve.com/homepages/jwcrawford/T7obit.htm.

114. Crawford, *Obituary: The Bilingual Education Act, 1968–2002,"* 1, http://ourworld .compuserve.com/homepages/jwcrawford/T7obit.htm.

115. Ibid., 1–2. Much of his assessment has turned out to be correct. See "No Child Left Behind: Misguided Approach to School Accountability for English Language Learners, by James Crawford, Executive Director, National Association for Bilingual Education, September 14, 2004. Found at the James Crawford website (accessed December 23, 2009).

116. *Statement of Raul Yzaguirre on the Elementary and Secondary Education Act*, December 14, 2001, 1. NCLR website (in author's possession).

117. Ibid.

118. Josué M. Gonzalez, "Editor's Introduction: Bilingual Education and the Federal Role, If Any," *Bilingual Research Journal* 26, no. 2 (2002), v–ix. This quote is from page ix.

119. For a history of how the bilingual tradition has been kept alive in Texas despite opposition to it, see Carlos Kevin Blanton, *The Strange Career of Bilingual Education in Texas, 1836–1981* (College Station: Texas A&M University Press, 2004).

Chapter 5

1. Guadalupe San Miguel Jr., *Let All of Them Take Heed* (Austin: University of Texas Press, 1987), 8–10; Guadalupe San Miguel Jr., "The Schooling of Mexicanos in the Southwest, 1848–1891," in *The Elusive Quest for Equality: 150 Years of Chicano/Chicana Education*, ed. José F. Moreno (Cambridge, MA: Harvard Educational Review, 1999), 31–51.

2. F. Campbell, "Missiology in New Mexico, 1850–1900: The Success and Failure of Catholic Education," In in *Religion and Society in the American West*, ed. C. Guerneri and D. Alvarez (Lanham, MD: University Press of America, 1987): 59–78; Victoria-María MacDonald and Teresa García, "Historical Perspectives on Latino Access to Higher Education, 1848–1990," in *The Majority in the Minority: Expanding the Representation of Latina/o Faculty, Administrators and Students in Higher Education*, ed. Jeanette Castellanos and Lee Jones (Sterling, VA: Stylus Publishing, 2003); Gerald McKevitt, "Hispanic Californians and Catholic Higher Education: The Diary of Jesús María Estudillo, 1857–1864," *California History* 69, no. 4 (1990): 322.

3. Edith J. Agnew and Ruth K. Barber, "The Unique Presbyterian School System of New Mexico," *Journal of Presbyterian History* 49, no. 3 (1971): 197–221; Susan M. Yohn, *A Contest of Faiths: Missionary Women and Pluralism in the American Southwest* (Ithaca, NY: Cornell University Press, 1995), 167–211; Carolyn Atkins, "Menaul School: 1881–1930 . . . Not Leaders, Merely, but Christian Leaders," *Journal of Presbyterian History* 58, no. 4 (1980): 279–98.

4. For a history of this school, see *Spanish American Institute: 1913–1971 Service to Boys* (Gardena, CA: Spanish American Institute, 1971). The quote is from page 3.

5. On Menaul, see James Darryl Stevens, "The Menaul School: A Study of Cultural Convergence" (PhD diss., University of Houston, 1999); *Menaul School Centennial, 1881–1981* (Albuquerque, NM: Menaul Historical Library, 1981), and *Menaul School History*, www.menaulschool.com/frmContent.aspx?PageName=History (accessed April 28, 2009). On Lydia Patterson, see *About Us*, www.lydiapattersoninstitute.org/aboutus.php (accessed April 28, 2009), and Our Mission, www.lydiapattersoninstitute.org/ourmission.php (accessed April 28, 2009). On the Kingsville school, see *Presbyterian Pan American School* (Kingsville, TX: Presbyterian Pan American School, 1959).

6. For an overview of how the Archdiocese of Chicago celebrated the annual Feast of Our Lady of Guadalupe, see "Catholic Schools Celebrate Feast of Our Lady of Guadalupe," *Office of Catholic Schools: News Releases,* http://schools.archdiocese-chgo.org/news_releases/news_ . . . (accessed November 29, 2004).

7. See Committee on Education of the United States Conference of Catholic Bishops, *Renewing Our Commitment to Catholic Elementary and Secondary Schools in the Third Millennium* (Washington, DC: USCCB, 2005); Paul Vitello and Winnie Hu, "For Catholic Schools, Crisis and Catharsis," *New York Times,* January 18, 2009, www.nytimes.com/2009/01/18/education/18catholic.html?_r=2&ref=nyregion&page . . . (accessed April 27, 2009); Sarah Carr and Leonard Sykes Jr., "Big 'C' or Little 'c' Catholic?," *Milwaukee Journal Sentinel,* June 16, 2005, www.asu.edu/educ/epsl/EPRU/articles/EPRU-0506-129-OWI.pdf (accessed April 28, 2009).

8. Manya A. Brachear and Margaret Ramirez, "Catholic School Closings: Latino, Black Parishes Hit Hardest by Decision," www.chicagotribune. Com/news/nationworld/chi-0502250210feb25,1,3270027,print.story (accessed February 28, 2005).

9. Paul Vitello and Winnie Hu, "For Catholic Schools, Crisis and Catharsis," *New York Times,* January 18, 2009, www.nytimes.com/2009/01/18/education/18catholic.html?_r=2 &ref=nyregion&page . . . (accessed April 27, 2009).

10. For a brief overview of private schools found in the Mexican community in the Southwest during the nineteenth and twentieth century, see Francisco Hernandez, "Mexican Schools in the Southwest," unpublished paper, n.d., 1–25 (in author's possession).

11. San Miguel, *Let All of Them Take Heed;* Jovita Gonzalez, "Social Life in Cameron, Starr, and Zapata Counties" (master's thesis, University of Texas, Austin, 1930), 75; Hernandez, "Mexican Schools in the Southwest"; James W. Cameron, "Schools for Mexicans," in "The History of Mexican Public Education in Los Angeles, 1910–1930" (PhD diss., University of Southern California, 1976), 169–83.

12. Carlos S. Maldonado, *Colegio Cesar Chavez, 1973–1983: A Chicano Struggle for Educational Self-Determination* (New York: Garland Publishing, 2000), 9–25.

13. Ernesto B. Vigil, *The Crusade for Justice: Chicano Militancy and the Government's War on Dissent* (Madison: University of Wisconsin Press, 1982), 81–84.

14. Puerto Ricans founded several important schools, such as Pedro Albizu Campos in Chicago and both Boricua College and Hostos Community College in New York. These schools, similar to Chicano alternative ones, promoted nationalism, self-determination, and political praxis. See Ana Y. Ramos-Zayas, "Nationalist Ideologies, Neighborhood-Based Activism, and Educational Spaces in Puerto Rican Chicago," *Harvard Educational Review* 68, no. 2 (1998): 164–92; "Boricua College: General Information," www.boricuacollege.edu (accessed July 2, 2008); "History of Hostos Community College," www.hostos.cuny.edu/about/history.html (accessed July 2, 2008).

15. Juan Jose Sanchez, "A Study of Chicano Alternative Grade Schools in the Southwest, 1978–1980" (PhD diss., Harvard University, 1982); Joan Kalvelage, "Cinco Exemplos," *Edcen-*

tric, October–November, n.d., 5–7, 28–42; see also *Chicano Alternative Education* (Hayward, CA: Southwest Network, 1973); Clementina Almaguer, Francisco Hernandez, and Anais Mock, "Casa de la Raza," in *Parameters of Institutional Change: Chicano Experiences in Education* (Hayward, CA: Southwest Network of the Study Commission on Undergraduate Education, 1974), 69–77; *Casa de la Raza: Separatism or Segregation, Chicanos in Public Education* (Hayward, CA: Southwest Network, 1973); Elena Aragon de McKissack, *Chicano Educational Achievement: Comparing Escuela Tlatelolco, a Chicanocentric School, and a Public High School* (New York: Garland Publishing, 1999).

16. *Chicano Alternative Education;* Kalvelage, "Cinco Exemplos," 5–7, 28–42; Maldonado, *Colegio Cesar Chavez;* "Colegio Jacinto Trevino," Handbook of Texas online, www.tshaonline .org/handbook/online/articles/CC/kbc51.html; Leonard J. Mestas, "A Brief History of the Juárez-Lincoln University," *Hojas* (Austin: Juárez-Lincoln University, 1976): 52; Andres Guerrero, "Chicanismo in the Rio Grande Valley," *Hojas* (Austin: Juárez-Lincoln University, 1976): 22–24.

17. See Arnoldo De Léon, *Ethnicity in the Sunbelt: A History of Mexican Americans in Houston* (Houston: Center for Mexican American Studies, 1989), 227.

18. See Luis Rey Cano, "A Case Study of a Private Community-Based Alternative School Program for Dropouts and Potential Dropouts" (PhD diss., University of Houston, 1981). See also Marjorie Evans, "From Success Comes Growth at Sanchez," *Houston Chronicle*, September 20, 2001, 1A.

19. See, for instance, US Commission on Civil Rights, *Mexican American Education Study, Report 1: Ethnic Isolation of Mexican Americans in the Public Schools of the Southwest* (Washington, DC, 1971); US Commission on Civil Rights, *Mexican American Education Study, Report 3: The Excluded Student: Educational Practices Affecting Mexican Americans in the Southwest* (Washington, DC, 1972); US Commission on Civil Rights, *Mexican American Education Study, Report 6: Toward Quality Education for Mexican Americans* (Washington, DC, 1974).

20. Similar types of concerns led to the emergence of schools for Puerto Ricans. Boricua College, for instance, was established in New York City in 1973 because of the failure of postsecondary institutions in that city and state to solve the educational crisis that lay "at the root of many of the problems facing Puerto Ricans in the United States." Hostos Community College, in the South Bronx, was created in 1968 as a result of the Puerto Rican community's demands for access to institutions of higher learning and for a higher education to meet the diverse needs of the South Bronx community. On Hostos, see, for instance, "History of Hostos Community College," www.hostos.cuny.edu/about/history.html (accessed July 2, 2008).

21. Almaguer, Hernandez, and Mock, "Casa de la Raza," 70.

22. Quoted in Vigil, *Crusade for Justice*, 162.

23. Sanchez, "A Study of Chicano Alternative," 45.

24. Ibid., 54.

25. "Colegio Jacinto Trevino," Handbook of Texas online, www.tshaonline.org/handbook/online/articles/CC/kbc51.html; Daniel García Ordaz, "Once upon a Chicano College: Hispanics United to Create the First School of Its Kind in the US," *Valley Morning Star,* October 4, 2005, www.valleystar.com/articles/2005/10/04/rio_living/rio_living3.txt (1 of 5) (accessed October 4, 2005).

26. For Puerto Ricans, the idea of controlling the schools also emerged out of the nationalist struggle for independence for Puerto Rico and for equality and pluralism on the US mainland. Activists who established one of the few Puerto Rican high schools in the country, the Pedro Albuzu Campos High School in Chicago, acknowledged that independence and an education based on the principles of Puerto Rican self-determination was the only option for them. "La Escuelita," as it was affectionately known by the community, was created by a group of teachers and eleven Puerto Rican students who had been expelled from Murphy Tulley High School (this school was later renamed Roberto Clemente High School) for organizing protests demanding Puerto Rican independence in general and a more culturally sensitive curriculum for the predominantly Puerto Rican student body, among other things. The failure by the public schools to change and to promote pride in Puerto Rican history encouraged these activists to establish a school under their control aimed at accomplishing these goals. Ana Y. Ramos-Zayas, "Nationalist Ideologies, Neighborhood-Based Activism, and Educational Spaces in Puerto Rican Chicago," *Harvard Educational Review* 68, no. 2 (1998): 164–92.

27. Corky Gonzalez, "Chicano Nationalism: The Key to Unity for La Raza," in *A Documentary History of the Mexican Americans,* ed. Wayne Moquin and Charles Van Doren (New York: Bantam Books, 1971), 492–93.

28. Sanchez, "A Study of Chicano Alternative," 75.

29. For the impact of political infighting within the board of directors of two universities—Colegios Cesar Chavez and Jacinto Trevino—see Maldonado, *Colegio Cesar Chavez;* and "Colegio Jacinto Trevino," *Handbook of Texas Online,* respectively.

30. Isidro Ramon Macias, "The Chicano Movement," in *A Documentary History of the Mexican Americans,* ed. Wayne Moquin with Charles Van Doren (New York: Bantam Books, 1971), 499–506.

31. The two schools Puerto Ricans established in New York City—Hostos Community College and Boricua College—also utilized Spanish and Puerto Rican culture. In an effort to fulfill its mission of serving the predominantly Puerto Rican community located in the South Bronx, one of the poorest congressional districts in New York, Hostos Community College, for instance, offered Spanish/English bilingual education offerings to "foster a multicultural environment for all students." The college became nationally known for its bilingual approach to education and for "allowing Spanish-dominant students to begin courses in their native language while learning English." Boricua College also promoted language and culture throughout the school. From its beginning in the early 1970s, Puerto Rican activists and educators demanded that the college serving Puerto Ricans and other Latinos must "not only employ a bilingual faculty and staff and offer courses in Puerto Rican and Latino culture and history, but must employ in all its activities, an educational philosophy and method consistent with the basic principles of Latino Culture." See "ACRL Excellence in Academic Libraries Award: Eugenio Maria de Hostos Community College/City University of New York Library Application," www.ala.org/ala/acrlbucket/excellenceaward/hostosap.cfm (accessed July 2, 2008); and "Boricua College: General Information," www.boricuacollege.edu (accessed July 2, 2008).

32. Sanchez, "A Study of Chicano Alternative," 244.

33. Vigil, *Crusade for Justice*, 161.

34. Sanchez, "A Study of Chicano Alternative," 233.

35. Ibid., 241, 237, 245.

36. Ibid., 248.

37. Maldonado, *Colegio Cesar Chavez*, 37.

38. Almaguer, Hernandez, and Monk, "Casa de la Raza."

39. Maldonado, *Colegio Cesar Chavez*, 37.

40. *Chicano Alternative Education* (Hayward, CA: Southwest Network, 1973), 98.

41. Quoted in Vigil, *Crusade for Justice*, 162.

42. *Chicano Alternative Education*, 82.

43. Kalvelage, "Cinco Exemplos," 5–7, 28–42.

44. Ibid., 31–32.

45. Ibid., 29–30. The school continued to operate as a nationalist one into the early twenty-first century. For information on the school, see http://escuelatlatelolco.org/website/fundraising/fund.html (accessed May 13, 2008).

46. Kalvelage, "Cinco Exemplos," 29.

47. Ibid., 36–37.

48. Ibid., 37, 40. For a more recent history of *el colegio*, see Carlos Cantu, "Colegio Jacinto Trevino: The Rise and Fall of the First Chicano College," *South Texas Studies* (2009).

49. Kalvelage, "Cinco Exemplos," 41

50. Ibid., 42.

51. During the 1980s, the National Center for Neighborhood Enterprise, a research project in Washington, DC, reported that over thirty Latino/a independent schools served over 3,500 Latina/o students. Many more were believed to exist. Joan Davis Ratteray, "Hispanics Pursue Alternatives to Unresponsive Public Schools," *Caminos* (November 1984): 32–33; "Schooling Ourselves," *Minority Trendsletter* 2, no. 1(1989): 3–5. This latter article describes the origins of the Pedro Albizu Campos Puerto Rican High School in Chicago founded in 1972 by students involved in organizing a student boycott over bilingual education.

52. In 2008, the board of trustees included seven Latinos/as and six non-Latinos/as. Most of these individuals were part of the social and economic elites of American society and included several CEOs, a lawyer, a president of a US bank, a medical doctor, and a junior college chancellor. The members of the board of advisors, although dominated by Latinos/as, were mostly from corporations such as the Coca Cola Company, NBC/Universal Telemundo, Univision Music Group, Lockheed Martin Aeronautics, Anheuser Busch, and Office of the Secretary of

Defense. See www.nhu.edu/about_nhu/advisors.htm and www.nhu.edu/about_nhu/history
.htm (accessed July 3, 2008).

53. www.nhu.edu/about_nhu/goals.htm (accessed July 3, 2008).

54. www.nhu.edu/about_nhu/history (accessed July 3, 2008).

55. Language and culture played little if any role in these efforts. The charter school movement, however, did provide an opportunity for some Chicana/o activists to promote their
language and culture in the curriculum. And many of those involved in the charter school movement took advantage of this opportunity.

56. For an overview of the role that conservatism in general and the religious right and Republicans in particular have played in shaping educational policies and practices from the 1960s
to the early twenty-first century, see Joel Spring, *The American School: A Global Context from the
Puritans to the Obama Era*, 8th ed. (New York: McGraw-Hill, 2011), 425–59.

57. [1] US Charter Schools, "History," www.uschartershcools.org/pub/uscs_docs/o/history
.htm; see also the variety of reports on the status of charter schools in 2009 found in US Charter
Schools, "New Research and Reports," www.uscharterschools.org/cs/r/query/q/1558?x-title
=New+Non-Federal+Research+an . . . (accessed May 1, 2009).

58. US Department of Education, "Charter Schools Progress Report," *Office of Educational
Research and Improvement Bulletin* (Summer 1997): 5; *Charter School*, ERIC Digest, Number 118,
1998, www.ericdigests.org/1999–2/charter.htm (accessed April 27, 2009).

59. For supporting charter schools as a response to the neglect of Latinos in the public
schools, see Richard Farias, "Charter Schools Triumphing as Public Ones Fail," *Houston
Chronicle*, March 20, 2000, 23A.

60. For a brief overview of private schools found in the Mexican community in the Southwest during the nineteenth and twentieth century, see Hernandez, "Mexican Schools in the
Southwest," unpublished paper, n.d., 1–25 (in author's possession).

61. On KIPP, see "KIPP: Houston," www.kipphouston.org/kipp/Default_EN.asp (accessed May 6, 2009). KIPP, unlike YES Prep, grew into a nationwide movement of more than
sixty-six schools. KIPP Houston also served children at all grade levels—early childhood/
elementary, middle school, and high school. On YES Prep, see "The History of YES PREP,"
www.yesprep.org/about/history.htm (accessed May 2, 2009); "YES Prep Public Schools
(Formerly YES College Preparatory Schools): Honing the Pathways of Growth," February 1, 2006, www.bridgespan.org/LearningCenter/ResrouceDetail.aspx?id=418 (accessed
May 4, 2009).

62. "Teach for America, 2008, www.teachforamerica.org/about/index.htm (accessed
December 12, 2008). See also "YES Prep Public Schools (Formerly YES College Preparatory
Schools): Honing the Pathways of Growth."

63. "The History of YES PREP," www.yesprep.org/about/history.htm (accessed May 2,
2009); "YES Prep Public Schools (Formerly YES College Preparatory Schools): Honing the
Pathways of Growth."

64. "Results," www.yesprep.org/about/results.htm (accessed May 2, 2009).

65. "Results," in *YES College Preparatory School*, information sheet passed out at YES Prep parent night, fall 2003 (in author's possession), 2.

66. "Results," www.yesprep.org/about/results.htm (accessed May 2, 2009).

67. For a list of the members of the board of directors, advisory board, and leadership team, see "YES Leadership," www.yesprep.org/about/board.htm (accessed May 2, 2009).

68. For an overview of the origins, development, and success of the Little Schools, see San Miguel, *Let All of Them Take Heed*, 138–63.

69. Claudia Kilker, "New Ideas in Education/HISD's First Charter Schools Ready for Debut," *Houston Chronicle*, August 4, 1996, A1.

70. See, for instance, Melanie Markley, "Sanchez School Lifts Self-Esteem, Teachers Help Students Grow," *Houston Chronicle*, January 20, 1991, 1C.

71. "Charter School Development Initiative (CSDI)," www.nclr.org/section/charte_school (accessed April 27, 2009).

72. Hernandez, "Mexican Schools in the Southwest," 63.

73. Ibid.

74. This school was founded and directed by Alfredo Sanchez, a former chairperson of Mecha at San Jose State College. See Al Sanchez, "Chicano Student Movement at San Jose State," in *Parameters of Institutional Change*, 22–32. See also Hernandez, "Mexican Schools in the Southwest," 60.

75. Both the Centro Infantil de la Raza and La Escuelita are mentioned in Hernandez, "Mexican Schools in the Southwest," 62; Sanchez, "A Study of Chicano Alternative," 24.

76. Quoted in Hernandez, "Mexican Schools in the Southwest," 61.

77. Ibid., 63; Sanchez, "A Study of Chicano Alternative," 45.

78. Sanchez, "A Study of Chicano Alternative," 25.

79. Hernandez, "Mexican Schools in the Southwest," 65.

80. For brief history, see Cantu, "Colegio Jacinto Trevino." The school was moved to Mercedes in 1971. See Hernandez, "Mexican Schools in the Southwest," 65.

81. Hernandez states that it began during the summer of 1968 after members of the Chicano community unsuccessfully protested conditions in the public schools. Hernandez, "Mexican Schools in the Southwest," 59.

Conclusion

1. See, for instance, Rubén Donato, *The Other Struggle for Equal Schools* (Albany: State University of New York Press, 1997); Richard R. Valencia, *Chicano Students and the Courts: The Mexican American Legal Struggle for Educational Equality* (New York: New York University

Press, 2008); and Guadalupe San Miguel Jr., *Let All of Them Take Heed: Mexican Americans and the Campaign for Educational Equality* (College Station: Texas A&M University Press, 2001).

2. In late April 2011, high school students took over the local school board meeting in Tucson, Arizona, to protest the dismantling of the district's highly successful Mexican American Studies program. In the same month, university students at the Berkeley campus conducted several hunger strikes in opposition to the cutbacks in the Chicano Studies program on that campus. Neither of these actions got any major media attention. On the high school students, see "Students Take Over TUSD Boardroom in Faceoff over Ethnic Studies," http://www.kgun9 .com/story/14520347/students-take-over-tusd-board-meeting-over-ethnic-studies (accessed April 27, 2011). On the hunger strikes by students at the University of California, see "Ethnic Studies: Support the Strike and Stand in Solidarity," April 27, 2011, http://us.mg201.mail.yahoo .com/dc/launch?.gx=0&.rand=cq2ugtq6bdkvj (accessed April 27, 2011).

Bibliography

Government Sources

Act of April 11, 1991, ch. 20, Secs. 16.001–21930, 1991 Tex. Sess. Law Serv. 20 (Vernon).

Act of June 7, 1990, 71st Leg., 6th C.S., ch. 1, 1990 Tex. Gen. Laws 1.

Aspira of New York, Inc. v. Board of Education of the City of New York, 72 Civ. 4002 (S.D.N.Y., August 29, 1974) (Unreported consent decree).

Bilingual Education Act, *P. L. 90–247* (January 2, 1968).

Bilingual Education Act, *P. L. 93–380* (August 21, 1974).

Bilingual Education Act, *P. L. 95–561* (November 1, 1978).

Bilingual Education Act, *P. L. 98–511* (October 19, 1984).

Bilingual Education Act, *P. L. 100–297* (April 28, 1988).

Bilingual Education Act, *P. L. 103–382* (September 28, 1994).

Brown v. Board of Education of Topeka, 347 US 483 (1954).

Brown v. Board of Education, 347 US 483 (1954).

Castaneda v. Pickard, 648 F.2d 989 (5th Cir. 1981).

Chapa v. Odem Ind. School Dist., Civil Action No. 66-C-92 (S.D. Tex, July 28, 1967) (unreported).

Cintron v. Brentwood Union Free School District Board of Education, no. 75–8746 (Sup. Ct. August 14, 1975).

Cisneros v. Corpus Christi Independent School District, 324 F. Supp. 599 (S.D. Tex. 1970), No. 71–2397 (5th Cir., July 16, 1971).

Comptroller General Office, *Bilingual Education: An Unmet Need* (Washington, DC: GPO, May 19, 1976).

The Condition of Bilingual Education in the Nation-First Report by the US Commissioner of Education to the Congress and the President. Fall River, MA: National Assessment and Dissemination Center, November 1976.

The Condition of Bilingual Education in the Nation, 1984: A Report from the Secretary of Education to the President and the Congress. Washington, DC: USDOE, 1984.

Diana v. California State Board of Education, Complaint filed by Plaintiffs, C.A. No. c-70 37 RFP (N.D. Cal., Feb. 3, 1970), In *Student Classification Materials.* Cambridge, MA: Center for Law and Education, 1973, 218–22.

Diana v. California State Board of Education, No. c-70–37-FRP (N.D. Cal., May 24, 1974). In *Student Classification Materials.* Supplement. Cambridge, MA: Center for Law and Education, 1976, 4.

Doe v. Plyler, 458 F. Supp. 569 (E.D. Tex. 1978).

Edgewood Indep. School Dist. V. Kirby, No. 362, 516 (250th Dist. Ct., Travis Cty., Tex. June 1, 1987), rev'd, 761 S.W.2d 859 (Tex. Ct. App. 1988), rev'd, 777 S.W.2d 391 (Tex. 1989).

Equal Educational Opportunity Act of 1974, *Public Law 93–380,* sec. 204 f.

"Financial Assistance for Bilingual Education Programs," *Fed. Reg.* 34, no. 4 (Tuesday, January 7, 1969): 201–205.

G.I. Forum et al v. Texas Education Agency et al, 87 F. Supp.2d 667 (W.D. Tex. 2000).

Guadalupe v. Tempe Elementary School District, No. 3, Civ. No. 71–435 (D. Ariz., 1972).

Hernandez v. Houston Independent School District, 558 S.W.2d 123 (Tex. Civ. App. 1977), *application for writ of error refused*, id.

Hernandez v. Stockton Unified Sch. Dist., No. 101016 (Superior Ct. of San Joaquin County, 10/1/75) (Clearinghouse Review #7805), In *Student Classification Materials.* Cambridge, MA: Center for Law and Education, 1973, 85.

In re Alien Children Educ. Litigation, 501 F. Supp. 544 (S.D. Tex 1980).

Keyes v. School District No. 1, 313 F. Supp. 61 (D. Colo. 1970), rev'd, 445 F.2d 990 (10th Cir. June 11, 1971), cert. granted, 40 USL.W. 3335 (US Jan. 18, 1972); 380 F. Supp. 673 (D. Col. 1973), 521 F. 2d 465 (10th Cir. 1975).

Lau v. Nichols, 488 f.2d 791 (9th Cir. 1973), 414 US 563 (1974).

Lora v. Board of Education of the City of New York, Complaint (E.D. N. Y, no date). In *Student Classification Materials.* Cambridge, MA: Center for Law and Education, 1973, 85.

"Memorandum of Frank Carlucci, Under Secretary of Education, to the Assistant Secretary for Education, December 2, 1974." In *Bilingual Education: An Unmet Need- Report to the Congress by the Comptroller General of the United States.* Washington, DC: Comptroller General of the United States, May 1976, 55–59.

Morales v. Shannon, 516 F.2d 411 (C.A. 5, 1975).

National Advisory and Coordinating Council on Bilingual Education, *Tenth Annual Report* (Washington, DC: US Dept of Education, March 1986).

No Child Left Behind Act, *P. L. 107–110* (August 3, 2001).

"Notice of Proposed Rulemaking," *Fed. Reg.* 50, no. 226 (Friday, November 22, 1985): 48352–48370.

Office for Civil Rights, *Task Force Findings Specifying Remedies Available for Eliminating Past Educational Practices Ruled Unlawful under Lau v. Nichols.* Washington, DC: Department of Health, Education, and Welfare, Office for Civil Rights, 1975.

Otero v. Mesa County Valley School District No. 51, 408 F. Supp. 162 (D. Colo, 1975).

Perez v. Sonora Ind School District, Civil Action No. 6–224 (N.D Tex., November 5, 1970).

Plyler v. Doe, 458 F. Supp. 573–574 (1978); 457 US 202 (June 15, 1982).

Pottinger, J. Stanley. *Memorandum of May 25, 1970 to School Districts with More Than Five Percent National Origin-Minority Group Children.* Washington, DC: Department of Health, Education, and Welfare, Office for Civil Rights, 1970.

P. L. 100–402, August 17, 1988. In Legislative History of Hispanic Heritage Month, http://latino .sscnet.ucla.edu/heritage/hhhispan.html (accessed July 31, 2007).

Regents of the University of California v. Bakke, 438 US 265 (1978).

Rios v. Read, 73 F.R.D. 589 (E.D.N.Y. 1977).

Rodriguez v. San Antonio Independent School District, C.A. No. 68–175–5A (W.D. Tex 1971).

Rodriguez v. San Antonio, ISD 337 F. Supp. 280 (W.D. Tex. 1971).

Romero v. Weakly, 131 F. Supp. 818 (S.D. Cal.), rev'd 226 F.2d 399 (9th Cir. 1955).

Ross v. Eckels, 434 F.2d 1140 (5th Cir. 1970).

San Antonio ISD v. Rodriguez, 411 US 1 (1973).

Serna v. Portales Municipal Schools, 351 F. Supp. 1279 (N.D. Mex. 1972), aff'd, 499 F.2d 1147 (10th Cir. 1974).

Serrano v. Priest, 5 Cal.3d 584, 96 Cal. Reptr. 601, 487 Pac.2d 1241 (1971).

Serrano v. Priest, Gen. Civil No. 938254 (Superior Court for L.A. County, Cal, January 8, 1969).

Serrano v. Priest, App., 89 Cal. Rptr 345 (September 1, 1970).

Serrano v. Priest, Sup., 96 Cal. Rptr. 601 (August 30, 1971).

Serrano v. Priest, Civil No. 938, 254 (Cal. Super.Ct., April 10, 1974).

Serrano v. Priest, 557 P.2d 929. (December 30, 1976).

Soria v. Oxnard School District Board of Trustees, 328 F. Supp. 155 (1971).

Strengthening Bilingual Education: A Report from the Commissioner of Education to the Congress and the President. Washington, DC: United States Office of Education, Dept. of Health, Education, and Welfare, June 1979.

Texas Education Code, Annotated Title 1, Section 21.031.

US Commission on Civil Rights, *Mexican American Education Study, Report 1: Ethnic Isolation of Mexican Americans in the Public Schools of the Southwest.* Washington, DC, 1971.

US Commission on Civil Rights, *Mexican American Education Study, Report 3: The Excluded Student: Educational Practices Affecting Mexican Americans in the Southwest.* Washington, DC, 1972.

US Commission on Civil Rights, *Mexican American Education Study, Report 6: Toward Quality Education for Mexican Americans.* Washington, DC, 1974.

US Congress, House of Representatives, *No Child Left Behind Act of 2001*, 107th Congress, 1st Session, Report 107–334, December 13, 2001, Sec. 3001.

US Department of Education, "Charter Schools Progress Report," *Office of Educational Research and Improvement Bulletin* (Summer 1997).

US General Accounting Office, *Bilingual Education: A New Look at the Research Evidence*. Washington, DC: GPO, March 1987.

US Sen., *Bilingual Education, Hearings before the Special Subcommittee on Bilingual Education of the Committee on Labor and Public Welfare on S. 428* (2 vols.) (90th Cong., 1st Sess.), and House of Rep., *Bilingual Education Programs, Hearings before the General Subcommittee on Education of the Committee on Education and Labor on H.R. 9840 and H.R. 10224* (90th Cong., 1st Sess.).

Williams v. State of California, http://www.decentschools.com/ (accessed September 11, 2010).

Secondary Sources

About Us. www.lydiapattersoninstitute.org/aboutus.php (accessed April 28, 2009).

"ACRL Excellence in Academic Libraries Award: Eugenio Maria de Hostos Community College / City University of New York Library Application." www.ala.org/ala/acrlbucket/ excellenceaward/hostosap.cfm (accessed July 2, 2008).

Acuña, Rodolfo. *Cultures in Conflict* (with Peggy Shackelton). Los Angeles: Charter School Books, 1970.

———. *A Mexican American Chronicle*. New York: American Book Company, 1971.

———. *Occupied America: A History of Chicanos*. 6th ed. New York: Pearson Longman, 2007.

———. *Sometimes There Is No Other Side: Chicanos and the Myth of Equality*. Notre Dame, IN: University of Notre Dame Press, 1998.

———. *The Story of the Mexican American: The Men and the Land*. New York: American Book Company, 1969.

Address by William J. Bennett, US Secretary of Education to the Association for a Better New York. New York, September 26, 1985 (in author's possession).

Agnew, Edith J., and Ruth K. Barber. "The Unique Presbyterian School System of New Mexico." *Journal of Presbyterian History* 49, no. 3 (1971): 197–221.

Aguirre, Adalberto, Jr., and Ruben O. Martinez, *Chicanos in Higher Education: Issues and Dilemmas for the 21st Century*. ASHE-ERIC Higher Education Report no. 3. Washington, DC: George Washington University, School of Education and Human Development, 1993.

Al Día Newspaper. "Congress Kills the American DREAM." *Al Día Newspaper*, November 3, 2007. www.pontealdia.com/press.php?article=26026&section=53&edition=390 (accessed November 3, 2007).

Allsup, Carl. "Education Is Our Freedom: The American GI Forum and the Mexican American School Segregation in Texas, 1948–1957." *Aztlán* 8 (Spring 1977): 27–50.

Almaguer, Clementina, Francisco Hernandez, and Anais Mock. "Casa de la Raza." In *Parameters of Institutional Change: Chicano Experiences in Education*, 69–77. Hayward, CA: Southwest Network of the Study Commission on Undergraduate Education, 1974.

Alna M. Zambone, and Margarita Alicea-Sáez. "Latino Students in Pursuit of Higher Education: What Helps or Hinders Their Success? In *Latino Students in American Schools: Histori-*

cal and Contemporary Views, edited by Valentina I. Kloosterman, 63–78. Westport, CT: Praeger, 2003.

Alvarez, Roberto, Jr. "The Lemon Grove Incident: The Nation's First Successful Desegregation Court Case." *Journal of San Diego History* 32 (Spring 1986): 116–35.

Analysis of the Seals Decision In Re: Alien Children Decision and Its Implications for US Immigration Law and Policy, A Report Prepared by Mario Cantú and Francisco X. Garza for the National Council of La Raza. Washington, DC: National Council of La Raza, February 3, 1981, 7.

Andersson, Theodore. "Bilingual Education: The American Experience," *Modern Language Journal* 55 (November 1971): 427–40.

———. "A New Focus on the Bilingual Child." Paper presented at the Conference for the Teacher of the Bilingual Child, University of Texas, June 9, 1964 (in author's possession).

Angel, Frank. "Program Content to Meet the Educational Needs of Mexican Americans." In the National Conference on Educational Opportunities for Mexican-Americans, April 25–26, 1968, Austin, Texas. Las Cruces, NM: The ERIC Clearinghouse on Rural Education and Small Schools, New Mexico State University, 1968.

Apodaca, Ed C. *Crisis in the Ranks: The Under-Representation of Hispanic Faculty and Administrators in Texas Public Institutions of Higher Education*. Report prepared by Ed C. Apodaca to the Texas Association of Chicanos in Higher Education, 1974 (in author's possession).

Arce, Carlos. "Chicano Participation in Academe: A Case of Academic Colonialism." *Grito del Sol: A Chicano Quarterly* 3 (1978): 75–104.

Arciniega, Tomás A. "The Myth of the Compensatory Education Model Education of Chicanos." In *Chicanos and Native Americans: The Territorial Minorities*, edited by Rudolph O. de la Garza, Z. Anthony Druszewski, and Tomás A. Arciniega, 173–83. Englewood Cliffs, NJ: Prentice-Hall, 1971.

Arias, M. Beatriz. "The Context of Education for Hispanic Students: An Overview." *American Journal of Education* 95, no. 1 (1986): 26–57.

———. "Desegregation and the Rights of Hispanic Students: The Los Angeles Case." *Center for the Study of Evaluation*, UCLA, vol. 6, no. 1 (1979): 14–18.

Arriola, Christopher. "Knocking on the Schoolhouse Door: *Mendez v. Westminster*—Equal Protection, Public Education, and Mexican Americans in the 1940s." *La Raza Law Journal* 8 (1995): 166–207.

Aspira of New York, Inc. v. Board of Education of the City of New York. See *New York Times*, May 2, 1963, 37, col. 1. "Statement of Policy of Board of Education of New York City," adopted April 18, 1965, issued April 28, 1965.

Associated Press. "Judge Kills California Immigration Law." *Austin American-Statesman*, March 19, 1998, A3.

Atkins, Carolyn. "Menaul School: 1881–1930 . . . Not Leaders, Merely, but Christian Leaders." *Journal of Presbyterian History* 58, no. 4 (1980): 279–98.

Bachelor, David. *Educational Reform in New Mexico: Tireman, San José, and Nambé*. Albuquerque: University of New Mexico Press, 1991.

Badillo, Herman. "The Politics and Realities of Bilingual Education." *Foreign Language Annals* 5, no. 3 (1972): 297–301.

Baker, Keith A., and Adriana A. de Kanter. *Effectiveness of Bilingual Education: A Review of the Literature.* Washington, DC: OPBE, 1981.

Balderrama, Francisco E. "The Battle against School Segregation." In *The Los Angeles Mexican Consulate and the Mexican Community in Los Angeles, 1929–1936,* 55–72. Tucson: University of Arizona Press, 1982.

Banks, James A. *Multiethnic Education: Theory and Practice.* 3rd ed. Boston: Allyn and Bacon, 1994.

————. *Teaching Strategies for Ethnic Studies.* Boston: Allyn and Bacon, 1975.

Banks, James A., Carlos E. Cortés, Geneva Gay, Richard L. Garcia, and A. S. Ochoa. *Curriculum Guidelines for Multiethnic Education.* Washington, DC: National Council for the Social Studies, 1976.

Barr, Rita. "Should Texas Change the Top 10 Percent Law?" *Focus Report,* February 25, 2005. Austin: House Research Organization, Texas House of Representatives, 2005.

Barrera, Baldemar James. "Edcouch Elsa High School Walkout: Chicano Student Activism in a South Texas Community." Master's thesis, University of Texas, El Paso, May 2001.

Barrera, Mario, Carlos Muñoz Jr., and Charles Ornelas. "The Barrio as Internal Colony." In *People and Politics in Urban Society,* edited by Harlan Hahn, 465–98. Los Angeles: Sage Publications, 1972.

Barriers to Excellence: Our Children at Risk. Boston: National Coalition of Advocates for Students, 1985.

"Bennett Calls Stanford's Curriculum Revision 'Capitulation' to Pressure." *Chronicle of Higher Education,* April 27, 1988, A2.

Bennett, Christine I. "Research on Racial Issues in American Higher Education." In *Handbook of Research on Multicultural Education,* edited by James Banks and Cherry McGee Banks. San Francisco: Jossey-Bass, 2004.

Bennett, William J. *The Devaluing of America: The Fight for Our Culture and Our Children.* New York: Touchstone, 1992.

————. *Our Children and Our Country: Improving America's Schools and Affirming the Common Culture.* New York: Simon and Schuster, 1988.

Bernal, Dolores Delgado. "Chicana School Resistance and Grassroots Leadership: Providing an Alternative History of the 1968 East Los Angeles Blowouts." PhD diss., University of California, Los Angeles, 1997.

Bernstein, Robert. "Hispanics Become More Prevalent on College Campuses." www.census.gov/population/www/socdemo/school.html (accessed March 4, 2009).

Betances, Samuel. "Puerto Ricans and Mexican Americans in Higher Education." *The Rican* 1, no. 4 (1974): 27–36.

Beyond Language: Social and Cultural Factors in the Schooling of Language Minority Children. Los Angeles: Evaluation, Dissemination, and Assessment Center, California State University, 1986.

Bissell, Joan S. *A Review of the Impact Study of ESEA Title VII Spanish/English Bilingual Education Programs.* Sacramento, CA: Office of the Auditor General, State Legislature, 1979.

Blanco, George. "The Education Perspective." In *Bilingual Education: Current Perspectives, Volume 4,* 21–52. Arlington, VA: Center for Applied Linguistics, 1977.

Blanton, Carlos Kevin. *The Strange Career of Bilingual Education in Texas, 1836–1981.* College Station: Texas A&M University Press, 2004.

Bloom, Alan. *The Closing of the American Mind: How Higher Education Has Failed Democracy and Impoverished the Souls of Today's Students.* New York: Simon and Schuster, 1987.

Board of Trustees. www.nhu.edu/about_nhu/advisors.htm (accessed July 3, 2008).

Board of Trustees. www.nhu.edu/about_nhu/goals.htm (accessed July 3, 2008).

Board of Trustees. www.nhu.edu/about_nhu/history.htm (accessed July 3, 2008).

"Boricua College: General Information." www.boricuacollege.edu (accessed July 2, 2008).

Bowles, Samuel, and Herbert Gintis. *Schooling in Capitalist America.* New York: Basic Books, 1976.

"Boycott Cripples City Schools; Absences 360,000 above Normal; Negroes and Puerto Ricans Unite." *New York Times,* February 4, 1964; ProQuest Historical Newspapers The New York Times (1851–2005), 1.

Boyer, Mildred V. "Poverty and the Mother Tongue." *Educational Forum* 29, no. 3 (1965): 291–65.

———. "Texas Squanders Non-English Resources." *Texas Foreign Language Association Bulletin* 5, no. 3 (1963): 1–8.

Brace, Clayton. *Federal Programs to Improve Mexican-American Education.* Washington, DC: US Office of Education, Mexican-American Affairs Unit, 1967, ERIC Document No. ED014338.

Brachear, Manya A., and Margaret Ramirez. "Catholic School Closings: Latino, Black Parishes Hit Hardest by Decision." www.chicagotribune. Com/news/nationworld/chi-0502250210 feb25,1,3270027,print.story (accessed February 28, 2005).

Briegel, Kaye. "Chicano Student Militancy: The Los Angeles High School Strike of 1968." In *An Awakened Minority: The Mexican Americans,* edited by Manuel P. Servin, 215–25. New York: Macmillan, 1974.

Brookover, W. Ed. *School Social Systems and Student Achievement: Schools Can Make a Difference.* Brooklyn, NY: F. F. Bergin, 1979.

Brussell, Charles B. *Disadvantaged Mexican American Children and Early Educational Experience.* Austin: Southwest Educational Development Corporation, 1968.

Bustamante, Charles J., and Patricia L. Bustamante. *The Mexican-American in the United States.* Mountain View, CA: Patty-Lar Publications, 1969.

Cabán, Pedro A. "Moving from the Margins to Where? Three Decades of Latino/a Studies." *Latino Studies* 1, no. 1 (2003): 5–35.

California Department of Education. *Bilingual Education for Mexican American Children.* Sacramento: Department of Education, 1967.

Cameron, James William. "The History of Mexican Public Education in Los Angeles, 1910–1930." PhD diss., University of Southern California, 1976.

Campbell, Frances. "Missiology in New Mexico, 1850–1900: The Success and Failure of Catholic Education." In *Religion and Society in the American West,* edited by Carl Guerneri and David Alvarez, 59–78. Lanham, MD: University Press of America, 1987.

Cannon, Garland. "Bilingual Problems and Developments in the United States." *Publications of the Modern Language Association* 86 (May 1971): 452–58.

Cano, Luis Rey. "A Case Study of a Private Community-Based Alternative School Program for Dropouts and Potential Dropouts." PhD diss., University of Houston, 1981.

Cantu, Carlos. "Colegio Jacinto Trevino: The Rise and Fall of the First Chicano College." *South Texas Studies* (2009): 33–51.

Cárdenas, Blandina. "Defining Equal Access to Educational Opportunity for Mexican American Children: A Study of Three Civil Rights Actions Affecting Mexican American Students and the Development of a Conceptual Framework for Effecting Institutional Responsiveness to the Educational Needs of Mexican American Children." EdD diss., University of Massachusetts, 1974.

Cardenas, Jose A. "Response I." In *Language, Ethnicity and the Schools,* edited by Noel E. Epstein, 71–84. Washington, DC: Institute for Educational Leadership, 1977.

Carpenter, L. P., and Dinah Rank. *The Treatment of Minorities: A Survey of Textbooks Used in Missouri High Schools.* Jefferson City: Missouri Commission on Human Rights, 1968.

Carr, Sarah, and Leonard Sykes Jr. "Big 'C' or little 'c' Catholic?" *Milwaukee Journal Sentinel,* June 16, 2005. www.asu.edu/educ/epsl/EPRU/articles/EPRU-0506-129-OWI.pdf (accessed April 28, 2009).

Carter, Thomas P., and Roberto D. Segura. *Mexican Americans in School: A Decade of Change.* New York: College Entrance Exam Board, 1979.

Carter, Thomas P. *Mexican Americans in School: A History of Educational Neglect.* Princeton, NJ: College Entrance Examination Board, 1970.

Casa de la Raza: Separatism or Segregation, Chicanos in Public Education. Hayward, CA: Southwest Network, 1973.

Casanova, U. "Bilingual Education: Politics or Pedagogy." In *Bilingual Education,* vol. 1, edited by O. Garcia, 167–182. Amsterdam: John Benjamins, 1991.

Casso, Henry J. "A Descriptive Study of Three Legal Challenges for Disproportionate Placement of Mexican American and Other Linguistically and Culturally Different Children into Educably Mentally Retarded Classes." EdD diss., University of Massachusetts, March 1973.

Castañeda, Alfredo. "Melting Potters vs. Cultural Pluralists: Implications for Education. In *Mexican Americans and Educational Change, Symposium at the University of California, Riverside, May 21–22, 1971,* edited by Alfredo Castañeda, Manuel Ramírez III, Carlos E. Cortés, and Mario Barrera, 22–40. New York: Arno Press, 1974.

Castañeda, Alfredo, Manuel Ramírez III, Carlos E. Cortés, and Mario Barrera, eds. *Mexican Americans and Educational Change.* New York: Arno Press, 1974.

Castaneda, Antonia I. "Women of Color and the Rewriting of Western History: The Discourse, Politics, and Decolonization of History." *Pacific Historical Review* (1992): 501–33.

Castellanos, Jeanett, Alberta M. Gloria, and Mark Kamimura, eds. *The Latina/o Pathway to the Ph.D.: Abriendo Caminos.* Sterling, VA: Stylus Publishing, 2006.

"Catholic Schools Celebrate Feast of Our Lady of Guadalupe." *Office of Catholic Schools: News Releases.* http://schools.archdiocese-chgo.org/news_releases/news_ . . . (accessed November 29, 2004).

"Celebrate Hispanic Heritage Month!" http://www.factmonster.com/spot/hhm1.html.

Cervantes, Fred A. "Chicanos as a Post-Colonial Minority: Some Questions concerning the Adequacy of the Paradigm of Internal Colonialism." In *Perspectivas en Chicano Studies,* edited by Reynaldo Flores Macías. Proceedings of the Third Annual Meeting of the National Association of Chicano Social Scientists. Los Angeles: NACS, 1977.

Cervantes, Robert A. *An Exemplary Consafic Chingatropic Assessment: The AIR Report.* Los Angeles: National Dissemination and Assessment Center, 1978.

Chapa, Sergio. "Late-Night Fire Damages Sanctuary, but Officials Pledge to Rebuild." *Dallas Morning News,* August 19, 2007. . www.dallasnews.com/sharedcontent/dws/pt/ slideshows/2007/08/stceciliafire081807 (accessed August 22, 2007).

Charter School. ERIC Digest, Number 118, 1998, www.ericdigests.org/1999–2/charter.htm (accessed April 27, 2009).

Christian, Chester C., Jr. "The Acculturation of the Bilingual Child." *Modern Language Journal* 69 (March 1965): 160–65.

Cohen, A. *A Sociolinguistic Approach to Bilingual Education.* Rowley, MA: Newbury House Publishers, 1976.

Cohen, Linda M. "Meeting the Needs of Gifted and Talented Minority Language Students: Issues and Practices." FOCUS: The National Clearinghouse for Bilingual Education." www .ncela.gwu.edu/pubs/classics/focus/08gifted.htm (accessed June 14, 2007).

"Colegio Jacinto Trevino." Handbook of Texas online. www.tshaonline.org/handbook/online/articles/CC/kbc51.html.

"College Expels Fraternity." *Houston Chronicle,* October 30, 1997, 10.

Committee on Education of the United States Conference of Catholic Bishops. *Renewing Our Commitment to Catholic Elementary and Secondary Schools in the Third Millennium.* Washington, DC: USCCB, 2005.

Condon, E. C., J. Y. Peters, and C. Suiero-Ross. "Educational Testing and Spanish-Speaking Exceptional Children." In *Special Education and the Hispanic Child: Cultural Perspectives,* 16–32. Reston, VA: Council for Exceptional Children, 1979.

Coon, Arthur F. "Separate and Unequal: Serrano Played an Important Role in Development of School District Policy." library.findlaw.com/199/Dec/1/129939.

Coons, John, William H. Clune III, and Stephen D. Sugarman. *Private Wealth and Public Education.* Cambridge, MA: Harvard University Press, 1971.

Cordasco, Francesco. "The Challenge of the Non-English Speaking Child in American Schools." *School and Society* 106 (March 30, 1968): 198–201.

Cortés, Carlos E. *Aspects of the Mexican American Experience.* New York: Arno Press, 1976.

———. "A Bicultural Process for Developing Mexican American Heritage Curriculum." *Multilingual Assessment Project: Riverside Component, 1971–1972 Annual Report,* edited by Alfredo Castañeda, Manuel Ramirez, and Leslie Herold. Riverside, CA: Systems and Evaluations in Education, 1972.

———. "CHICOP: A Response to the Challenge of Local Chicano History." *Aztlán: Chicano Journal of the Social Sciences and the Arts* 1 (Fall 1970): 1–14.

———. *Cuban Exiles in the United States.* New York: Arno Press, 1980.

———. *The Cuban Experience in the United States.* New York: Arno Press, 1980.

———. *The Making, and Remaking, of a Multiculturalist.* New York: Teachers College Press, 2002.

———. *The Mexican Experience in Texas.* New York: Arno Press, 1976.

———. *Nineteenth-Century Latin Americans in the United States.* New York: Arno Press, 1980.

———. *Regional Perspectives on the Puerto Rican Experience.* New York: Arno Press, 1980.

———. "Revising the 'All-American Soul Course': A Bicultural Avenue to Educational Reform." In *Mexican Americans and Educational Change*, edited by Alfredo Castañeda, Manuel Ramírez III, Carlos E. Cortés, and Mario Barrera, 314–39. New York: Arno Press, 1974.

———. "Teaching the Chicano Experience." In *Teaching Ethnic Studies: Concepts and Strategies*, edited by J. A. Banks, 181–99. Washington, DC: National Council for the Social Studies, 1973.

Crawford, James. *At War with Diversity: US Language Policy in an Age of Anxiety*. Buffalo, NY: Multilingual Matters, 2000.

———. "Bennett's Plan for Bilingual Overhaul Heats Up Debate." *Education Week*, February 12, 1986, 1, 22.

———. *Bilingual Education: History, Politics, Theory*. Trenton, NJ: Crane Publishers, 1989.

———. "Bilingual Program Grantees Told to Cut Travel, Salary Expenses." *Education Week*, June 11, 1986, 10.

———. "'Mainstreaming' Is Factor in Bilingual Grant Awards, Official Says." *Education Week*, October 22, 1986, 6.

———. "No Child Left Behind: Misguided Approach to School Accountability for English Language Learners," by James Crawford, Executive Director, National Association for Bilingual Education, September 14, 2004. Found at James Crawford website http://www.languagepolicy.net/articles.html (accessed June 15, 2012).

———. "Obituary: The Bilingual Education Act, 1968–2002." Spring 2002, 1. http://www.languagepolicy.net/articles.html.

———. "Ten Common Fallacies about Bilingual Education." *ERIC Digest*, November 1998 (EDO-FL-98-10).

Cummins, Jim. "A Theoretical Framework for Bilingual Special Education." *Exceptional Children* 56 (1989): 111–19.

Dannenberg, Arlene C. *Meeting the Needs of Gifted and Talented Bilingual Students: An Introduction to Issues and Practices*. Quincy: Massachusetts Department of Education, Office for Gifted and Talented, 1984, reprint.

Danoff, Malcolm N. *Evaluation of the Impact of ESEA Title VII Spanish/English Bilingual Education Programs*. Palo Alto, CA: AIR, 1978.

Davis, Matthew D. *Exposing a Culture of Neglect: Herschel T. Manuel and Mexican American Schooling*. Greenwich, CT: Information Age Publishing, 2005.

De León, Arnoldo. "Blowout 1910 Style: A Chicano School Boycott in West Texas." *Texana* 12 (1974): 124–40.

———. *Ethnicity in the Sunbelt: A History of Mexican Americans in Houston*. Houston: Center for Mexican American Studies, 1989.

de León, Marcos. "Statement of Philosophy and Policy as They Pertain to the Acculturation and Education of the Mexican-American." In *Mexican-Americans in the United States: A Reader*, edited by John H. Burma, 95–99. Cambridge, MA: Schenkman Publishing, 1970.

Delgado Bernal, Dolores. "Chicana/o Education from the Civil Rights Era to the Present." In *The Elusive Quest for Equality: 150 Years of Chicana/o Education*, edited by José F. Moreno, 77–11. Cambridge, MA: Harvard Educational Review, 1999.

Delgado-Gaitan, Concha. "Consejos: The Power of Cultural Narratives." *Anthropology and Education Quarterly* 25, no. 3 (1994): 298–316.

———. "Involving Parents in the Schools: A Process of Empowerment." *American Journal of Education* 100, no. 1 (1991): 20–46.

———. "School Matters in the Mexican American Home: Socializing Children to Education." *American Educational Research Journal* 29, no. 3 (1992): 495–513.

Diaz, E. I. "Framing a Contemporary Context for the Education of Culturally and Linguistically Diverse Students with Gifted Potential: 1990s to the Present," In *Reaching New Horizons: Gifted and Talented Education for Culturally and Linguistically Diverse Students*, edited by J. A. Castellano and E. I. Diaz, 29–46. Boston: Allyn and Bacon, 2002.

Dinnerstein, Leonard, Roger L. Nichols, and David M. Reimers. *Natives and Strangers: Blacks, Indians, and Immigrants in America*. 2nd ed. New York: Oxford University Press, 1990.

District and School Profiles. Houston: Houston Independent School District, 2002.

Donato, Rubén. "Hispano Education and the Implications of Autonomy: Four School Systems in Southern Colorado, 1920–1963." *Harvard Educational Review* 69 (Summer 1999): 117–49.

———. *The Other Struggle for Equal Schools: Mexican Americans during the Civil Rights Era*. Albany: State University of New York Press, 1997.

Ebel, Clara Peterson. "Developing an Experience Curriculum in a Mexican First Grade." Master's thesis, Arizona State Teachers College, Tempe, 1940.

Edson, E. H. "Risking the Nation: Historical Dimensions on Survival and Educational Reform." *Issues in Education* 1, nos. 2 and 3 (1983): 171–84.

Epstein, Noel. *Language, Ethnicity, and the Schools*. Washington, DC: Institute for Educational Leadership, 1977.

Erickson, Frederick. "Transformation and School Success: The Politics and Culture of Educational Achievement." *Anthropology and Education Quarterly* 18, no. 4 (1987): 335–56.

Ernst, Gisela, and Elsa L. Statzner. "Alternative Visions of Schooling: An Introduction." *Anthropology and Education Quarterly* 25, no. 3 (1994): 200–207.

Espinoza-Herold, Mariella. *Issues in Latino Education: Race, School Culture, and the Politics of Academic Success*. Boston: Pearson Education Group, 2003.

Evans, Marjorie. "From Success Comes Growth at Sanchez." *Houston Chronicle*, September 20, 2001, 1A.

Farias, Richard. "Charter Schools Triumphing as Public Ones Fail." *Houston Chronicle* March 20, 2000, 23A.

Fernandez, Joseph A., and John Underwood. *Tales Out of School*. Boston: Little, Brown, 1993.

Ferrín, Richard I., Richard W. Jonsen, and Cesar M. Trimble. *Access to College for Mexican Americans in the Southwest*. Higher Education Surveys Report no. 6. Princeton, NJ: College Entrance Examination Board, July 1972.

Fine, Michelle. *Framing Dropouts: Notes on the Politics of an Urban High School*. Albany: State University of New York Press, 1991.

Fishman, Joshua. "Bilingualism, Intelligence, and Language Learning." *Modern Language Journal* 49 (March 1965): 227–37.

————. "Childhood Indoctrination for Minority Group Membership." *Daedalus* 90, no. 2 (1961): 329–49.

————. *Language Loyalty in the United States: The Maintenance and Perpetuation of Non-English Mother Tongues by American Ethnic and Religious Groups*. The Hague: Mouton, 1966.

————. "The Politics of Bilingual Education." In *Bilingual Schooling in the US*, edited by Francesco Cordasco, 141–49. New York: McGraw-Hill, 1976.

————. "The Status and Prospects of Bilingualism in the US" *Modern Language Journal* 49 (March 1965): 143–55.

Flores-González, Nilda. "Puerto Rican High Achievers: An Example of Ethnic and Academic Identity Compatibility." *Anthropology and Education Quarterly* 30, no. 3 (1999): 343–62.

Flores, Susana, and Enrique G. Murillo Jr. "Power, Language, and Ideology: Historical and Contemporary Notes on the Dismantling of Bilingual Education." *Urban Review* 33, no. 3 (2001): 183–206.

Foley, Douglas E. "Reconsidering Anthropological Explanations of Ethnic School Failure." *Anthropology and Education Quarterly* 22, no. 1 (1991): 60–94.

Forbes, Jack D. *Mexican Americans: A Handbook for Educators*. Berkeley: Far West Laboratory for Educational Research and Development, 1967.

From Risk to Opportunity: Fulfilling the Educational Needs of Hispanic Americans in the 21st Century. Washington, DC: The President's Advisory Commission on Educational Excellence for Hispanic Americans, 2003.

Gaarder, A. Bruce. "Conserving Our Linguistic Resources." *Publications of the Modern Language Association* 80 (May 1965): 19–23.

————. "The First Seventy-Six Bilingual Education Projects." In *Bilingualism and Language Contact*, edited by James E. Alatis, 163–78. Washington, DC: Georgetown University Press, 1970.

————. "Teaching the Bilingual Child: Research, Development, and Policy." Paper presented at the Conference for the Teacher of the Bilingual Child, University of Texas, June 10, 1964 (in author's possession).

Gains, John S. "Treatment of Mexican American History in High School Textbooks." *Civil Rights Digest* (October 1972): 35–40.

Galicia, H. Homero, and Clementina Almaguer. *Chicano Alternative Education*. Hayward, CA: Southwest Network, 1973.

Gamio, Manuel. *Mexican Immigration to the United States*. New York: Arno Press, 1969; originally published in 1930.

Gándara, Patricia. *Over the Ivy Walls: The Educational Mobility of Low-Income Chicanos*. Albany: State University of New York Press, 1995.

————. "Passing through the Eye of the Needle: High-Achieving Chicanas." *Hispanic Journal of Behavioral Sciences* 4, no. 2 (1982): 167–79.

García, Ignacio M. *Chicanismo: The Forging of a Militant Ethos among Mexican Americans*. Tucson: University of Arizona Press, 1997.

————. "Chicano Studies since 'El Plan de Santa Bárbara.'" In *Chicanas/Chicanos at the Crossroads: Social, Economic, and Political Change*, edited by David R. Maciel and Isidro D. Ortiz, 181–203. Tucson: University of Arizona Press, 1996.

García, Mario T. "Education and the Mexican American: Eleuterio Escobar and the School Improvement League of San Antonio." In *Mexican Americans*, 62–83. New Haven, CT: Yale University Press, 1989.

———. *Mexican Americans: Leadership, Ideology, and Identity, 1930–1960*. New Haven, CT: Yale University Press, 1989.

Garms, Walter I., James W. Guthrie, and Lawrence C. Pierce, eds. *School Finance: The Economic and Politics of Public Education*. Englewood Cliffs, NJ: Prentice-Hall, 1978.

Gerry, Martin H. "Cultural Freedom in the Schools: The Right of Mexican-American Children to Succeed." In *Mexican Americans and Educational Change*, edited by Alfredo Castañeda and others, 226–55. New York: Arno Press, 1974.

Getz, Lynne Marie. *Schools of Their Own: The Education of Hispanos in New Mexico, 1850–1940*. Albuquerque: University of New Mexico Press, 1997.

Glazer, Nathan, and Daniel Moynihan. *Beyond the Melting Pot: The Negroes, Puerto Ricans, Jews, Italians, and Irish of New York City*. Cambridge, MA: MIT Press, 1963.

Glickstein, Howard A. *Inequality in School Financing: The Role of the Law*. Washington, DC: US Commission on Civil Rights, 1972.

Goldman, R. D., and B. N. Hewitt. "An Investigation of Test Bias for Mexican American College Students." *Journal of Educational Measurement* 12 (1975): 187–96.

Gonzales-Berry, Erlinda. "Which Language Will Our Children Speak? The Spanish Language and Public Education Policy in New Mexico, 1890–1930." In *The Contested Homeland: A Chicano History of New Mexico*, edited by Erlinda Gonzales-Berry and David R. Maciel, 169–90. Albuquerque: University of New Mexico Press, 2000.

González, Corky. "Chicano Nationalism: The Key to Unity for La Raza." In *A Documentary History of the Mexican Americans*, edited by Wayne Moquin and Charles Van Doren, 488–94. New York: Bantam Books, 1971.

González, Gilbert G. *Chicano Education in the Era of Segregation*. Philadelphia: Balch Institute Press, 1990.

———. "A Critique of the Internal Colonial Model." *Latin American Perspectives* (Spring 1974): 154–61.

———. "Culture, Language, and the Americanization of Mexican Children." In *Chicano Education in the Era of Segregation*, 30–45. Philadelphia: Balch Institute Press, 1990.

———. "Racism, Education, and the Mexican Community in Los Angeles, 1920–1930." *Societas* 4 (1974): 287–301.

———. "The System of Public Education and Its Function within the Chicano Communities, 1910–1930." PhD diss., University of California, Los Angeles, 1974.

González, Josué M. "Editor's Introduction: Bilingual Education and the Federal Role, If Any." *Bilingual Research Journal* 26, no. 2 (2002): v–ix.

———. *Towards Quality in Bilingual Education / Bilingual Education in the Integrated School*. Rosslyn, VA: National Clearinghouse for Bilingual Education, 1979.

González, Jovita. "Social Life in Cameron, Starr, and Zapata Counties." Master's thesis, University of Texas, Austin, 1930, 75.

Gray, Tracy C., and M. Beatriz Arias. *Challenge to the AIR Report*. Arlington, VA: Center for Applied Linguistics, 1978.

Greene, Jay. *A Meta-Analysis of the Effectiveness of Bilingual Education*. Claremont, CA: Tomás Rivera Center, 1998.

Guajardo, Miguel A., and Francisco J. Guajardo. "The Impact of Brown on the Brown of South Texas: A Micropolitical Perspective on the Education of Mexican Americans in a South Texas Community." *American Educational Research Journal* 41, no. 3 (2004): 501–26.

Guerrero, Andres. "Chicanismo in the Rio Grande Valley." *Hojas* (Austin: Juárez-Lincoln University, 1976): 22–24.

Gurule, Kay. "Truthful Textbooks and Mexican Americans." *Integrated Education* (March–April, 1973): 35–36.

Gutierrez, Ramon A. "Ethnic Studies: Its Evolution in American Colleges and Universities." In *Multiculturalism: A Critical Reader*, edited by David Theo Goldberg, 157–67. Cambridge, MA: Blackwell, 1994.

Hakuta, Kenji. *Mirror of Language*. New York: Basic Books, 1986.

Hanif S. Hirji. "Inequalities in California's Public School System." *Loyola of Los Angeles Law Review* 32, no. 583 (1999). llr.lls.edu/volumes/v32-isssue2/hirjipdf (accessed September 28, 2007).

Haro, Carlos. *Mexican/Chicano Concerns and School Desegregation in Los Angeles.* Monograph no. 9. Los Angeles: Chicano Studies Center Publications, UCLA, 1977.

Haro, Carlos Manuel, ed. *The Bakke Decision: The Question of Chicano Access to Higher Education*. Chicano Studies Center Document no. 4. Los Angeles: University of California at Los Angeles, 1976.

Haro, Roberto. "Choosing Trustees Who Care about Things That Matter." *Chronicle of Higher Education,* December 8, 1995, B1–B2.

———. "The Dearth of Latinos in Campus Administration." *Chronicle of Higher Education,* December 11, 2001. http://chronicle.com.ezproxy.lib.uh.edu/article/The-Dearth-of -Latinos . . . (accessed June 3, 2011).

———. "Latinos and Academic Leadership in American Higher Education." In *Latinos in Higher Education*, edited by David J. León, 155–91. New York: JAI, 2003.

Hart, Elinor, ed. *Las voces nuevas del sudoeste: A Symposium on the Spanish-Speaking Child in the Schools of the Southwest, Tucson, Arizona, October 30–31, 1966.* Tucson: National Education Association, Committee on Civil and Human Rights of Educators of the Commission on Professional Rights and Responsibilities, 1966.

Harvey, William B., and Eugene L. Anderson. *Minorities in Higher Education: Twenty-First Annual Status Report*. Washington, DC: American Council on Education, 2005.

Haycock, Kati, and Susana M. Navarro. *Unfinished Business: Fulfilling Our Children's Promise.* Los Angeles: The Achievement Council, 1988.

Hayes, Floyd W., III. "Politics and Education in America's Multicultural Society: An African-American Studies' Response to Allan Bloom." *Journal of Ethnic Studies* 17 (Summer 1989): 73–74.

Henderson, R. W., and R. R. Valencia. "Nondiscriminatory School Psychological Services: Beyond Nonbiased Assessments." In *School Psychology in Contemporary Society*, edited by J. R. Bergan, 340–77. Columbus, OH: Charles E. Merrill, 1985.

Hernandez-Chavez, Eduardo, Jose Llanes, Roberto Alvarez, and Steve Arvizu. *The Federal Policy toward Language and Education: Pendulum or Progress?* Monograph no. 12. Sacramento: Cross Cultural Resource Center, California State University, 1981.

Hernandez, Francisco. "Mexican Schools in the Southwest." Unpublished paper. N.d. (in author's possession).

Hernandez, Jessica. "More Hispanics Are Needed on HISD Board." *Houston Chronicle*, April 12, 1991, 15.

Hertling, James. "Flexibility Stressed in New Rules for Bilingual Classes." *Education Week*, November 27, 1985, 1, 16.

Hess, Fredrick M. *School Boards at the Dawn of the 21st Century*. Alexandria, VA: National School Boards Association, 2002.

Hirsch, E. D., Jr. *Cultural Literacy: What Every American Needs to Know*. Boston: Houghton Mifflin, 1987.

Hispanic Heritage Month. http://www.educationworld.com/a_lesson/lesson/lesson023.shtml.

Hispanic Policy Development Project. *"Make Something Happen": Hispanics and Urban High School Reform,*. Vol. 2. Washington, DC: National Commission on Secondary Education for Hispanics, 1984.

"Hispanics Upset by Sorority Garb: Baylor Students at Party Dressed as Gangsters, Pregnant Women." *Houston Chronicle*, April 29, 1998, 19A.

"History of Hostos Community College." www.hostos.cuny.edu/about/history.html (accessed July 2, 2008).

History Task Force, Centro de Estudios Puertorriqueños. *Labor Migration under Capitalism: The Puerto Rican Experience*. New York: Monthly Review, 1979.

Hobby, William P., Jr., and Billy D. Walker. "Legislative Reforms of the Texas Public School Finance System, 1973–1991." *Harvard Journal on Legislation* 28, (1991): 379–94.

Hoffman, Abraham. "Where Are the Mexican Americans? A Textbook Omission Overdue for Revision." *History Teacher* 6, no. 1 (1972): 143–50.

"House OKs School Reform Bill." *Houston Chronicle*, December 14, 2001, 10A.

Hu-DeHart, Evelyn. "Ethnic Studies in US Higher Education: History, Development, and Goals." In *Handbook of Research on Multicultural Education*, edited by James A. Banks and Cherry A. McGee Banks, 696–707. San Francisco: Jossey-Bass, 2001.

Hurtado, Sylvia, Alma R. Clayton-Pedersen, Walter Recharde Allen, and Jeffrey F. Milem, "Enhancing Campus Climates for Racial/Ethnic Diversity: Educational Policy and Practice," *Review of Higher Education* 21, no. 3 (1998): 279–302.

"Intercultural Development Research Association." *The Handbook of Texas Online*. www.tsha.utexas.edu/handbook/online/articles/II/kai2.html (accessed June 8, 2007).

Jensen, Joan M., and Darlis A. Miller. "The Gentle Tamers Revisited: New Approaches to the History of Women in the American West." *Pacific Historical Review* 40 (1980): 173–214.

Kalvelage, Joan. "Cinco Exemplos." *Edcentric*, October–November, n.d., 5–7, 28–42.

Kane, Michael B. *Minorities in Textbooks: A Study of Their Treatment in Social Studies Textbooks*. Chicago: Quadrangle Books, 1970.

Kaplowitz, Craig A. *LULAC: Mexican Americans and National Policy*. College Station: Texas A&M University Press, 2005.

Kihss, Peter. "Puerto Ricans Gain." *New York Times*, February 6, 1964; ProQuest Historical Newspapers The New York Times (1851–2005), 1.

Kilker, Claudia. "New Ideas in Education/HISD's First Charter Schools Ready for Debut."
    Houston Chronicle, August 4, 1996, A1.

Kirp, D. "Schools as Sorters: The Constitutional and Policy Implications of Student Classifica-
    tion." *University of Pennsylvania Law Review* 121, no. 705 (1973).

Kjolseth, Rolf. "Bilingual Education Programs in the United States: Assimilation or Pluralism?"
    In *The Language Education of Minority Children,* edited by Bernard Spolsky, 94–121.
    Rowley, MA: Newbury House Publishers, 1972.

Kloosterman, Valentina I. "A Shameful Subject: The Condition of Latino Students in Gifted
    Education." In *Latino Students in American Schools: Historical and Contemporary Views,*
    edited by Valentina I. Kloosterman, 113–27. Westport, CT: Praeger, 2003.

Knowledge Is Power Program (KIPP). "KIPP: Houston." www.kipphouston.org/kipp/
    Default_EN.asp (accessed May 6, 2009).

Krashen, Stephen D. *Condemned without a Trial: Bogus Arguments against Bilingual Education.*
    Westport, CT: Heinemann, 1999.

Krashen, Stephen D. *Under Attack: The Case against Bilingual Education.* Culver City, CA: Lan-
    guage Education Associates, 1996.

Kuenzi, Jeffrey J. *Education of Limited English Proficient and Recent Immigrant Students: Provi-
    sions in the No Child Left Behind Act of 2001.* Washington, DC: Congressional Research
    Service, the Library of Congress, March 1, 2002.

Kurlaender, Michal, and Stella M. Flores. "The Racial Transformation of Higher Education." In
    Higher Education and the Color Line: College Access, Racial Equity, and Social Change, ed-
    ited by Gary Orfield, Patricia Marin, and Catherine L. Horn. Cambridge, MA: Harvard
    Education Press, 2005.

Lambert, Wallace E., and G. Richard Tucker. *Bilingual Education of Children: The St. Lambert
    Experiment.* Rowley, MA: Newbury House Publishers, 1972.

"Language Legislation in the USA." James Crawford Language Policy Web Site and Emporium.
    http://www.languagepolicy.net/articles.html.

Leibowitz, Arnold. *Educational Policy and Political Acceptance: The Imposition of English as
    the Language of Instruction in American Schools.* Washington, DC: Center for Applied
    Linguistics, 1971.

León, David J., ed. *Latinos in Higher Education.* New York: JAI, 2003).

Levin, Betsy. "Recent Developments in the Law of Equal Educational Opportunity," *Journal of
    Law and Education* 4, no. 3 (July 1975): 411–47.

López, Ronald W., Arturo Madrid-Barela, and Reynaldo Flores Macías. *Chicanos in Higher
    Education: Status and Issues.* Monograph no. 7. Los Angeles: Chicano Studies Center
    Publications, UCLA, 1976.

Lyons, James L. "Education Secretary Bennett on Bilingual Education: Mixed Up or Malicious?"
    CABE Newsletter 8, no. 2 (1985): 1, 15.

Lyons, James L. "The View from Washington." *NABE News* 10 (Fall 1986): 11, 15.

Mabin, Connie. "Property-Rich Districts Claim Funding System Is Illegal Tax." *Houston
    Chronicle,* March 28, 2003, 1A, 43A.

Macdonald, Victoria-María, J. M. Botti, and L. H. Clark. "From Visibility to Autonomy: Latinos and Higher Education in the US, 1965–2005." *Harvard Educational Review* 77, no. 4 (2007): 474–504.

MacDonald, Victoria-María. "Hispanic, Latino, Chicano, or 'Other'?: Deconstructing the Relationship between Historians and Hispanic American Educational History." *History of Education Quarterly* 41, no. 3 (2001): 365–413.

MacDonald, Victoria-María. *Latino Education*. New York: Palgrave Macmillan, 2004.

MacDonald, Victoria-María, and Teresa García. "Historical Perspectives on Latino Access to Higher Education, 1848–1990." In *The Majority in the Minority: Expanding the Representation of Latina/o Faculty, Administrators and Students in Higher Education*, edited by Jeanette Castellanos and Lee Jones. Sterling, VA: Stylus Publishing, 2003.

Machado, M. "Gifted Hispanics Underidentified in Classrooms." *Hispanic Link Weekly Report*, February 1987, 1.

Macias, Isidro Ramon. "The Chicano Movement." In *A Documentary History of the Mexican Americans*, edited by Wayne Moquin with Charles Van Doren, 499–506. New York: Bantam Books, 1971.

Magner, Denise K. "Cultural-Diversity Requirement Adopted at U. of Cincinnati." *Chronicle of Higher Education*, January 19, 1990. http://chronicle.com.ezproxy.lib.uh.edu/che-data/articles.dir/articles-36.dir/issue-18.dir/18a . . . (accessed May 19, 2009).

———. "Racial Tensions Continue to Erupt on Campuses Despite Efforts to Promote Cultural Diversity." *Chronicle of Higher Education*, June 6, 1990. http://chronicle.com/ezproxy.lib.uh.edu/che-data/articles.dir/articles-36.dir/issue-38.dir/38a . . . (accessed May 19, 2009).

Make Something Happen: Hispanics and Urban High School Reform. Vols. 1 and 2. Washington, DC: Hispanic Policy Development Project, 1984.

MALDEF. "School Opening Alert." Flyer, n.d. Distributed by MALDEF.

Maldonado, Carlos S. *Colegio Cesar Chavez, 1973–1983: A Chicano Struggle for Educational Self-Determination*. New York: Garland Publishing, 2000.

Manougian, Nancy. "*Plyler v. Doe:* Equal Protection for Illegal Aliens." *Capital University Law Review* 12, no. 1 (1982–83).

Manuel, Herschel T. *Spanish-Speaking Children of the Southwest*. Austin: University of Texas Press, 1965.

Marcus, Lloyd. *The Treatment of Minorities in Secondary School Textbooks*. New York: Anti-Defamation League of B'nai B'rith, 1961.

Mariscal, George. *Brown-Eyed Children of the Sun: Lessons from the Chicano Movement, 1965–1975*. Albuquerque: University of New Mexico Press, 2005.

Martinez, Elizabeth. *500 Years of Chicano History*. Albuquerque, NM: SouthWest Organizing Project, 1991.

Martinez, George A. "Legal Indeterminacy, Judicial Discretion, and the Mexican American Litigation Experience: 1930–1980." *University of California at Davis Law Review* 27 (1994): 557–618.

Martínez, Gilbert, and Jane Edwards. *The Mexican American: His Life across Four Centuries*. Boston: Houghton Mifflin, 1973.

Matute-Bianchi, Maria Eugenia. "Ethnic Identities and Patterns of School Success and Failure among Mexican-Descent and Japanese-American Students in a California High School: An Ethnographic Analysis." *American Journal of Education* 95, no. 1 (1986): 233–55.

May, Lee. "Latinos Assail Bilingual Education Plans." *Los Angeles Times*, January 25, 1986, part I, 3.

McAdams, Donald R. *Fighting to Save Our Urban Schools—And Winning: Lessons from Houston*. New York: Teachers College Press, 2000.

McBay, S. *The Racial Climate on the MIT Campus: A Report of the Minority Student Issues Group*. Boston: MIT, Office of the Dean for Student Affairs, 1986.

McCormick, Jennifer, and César Ayala. "Felícita 'La Prieta' Méndez and the End of Latino Segregation in California." *Centro: Journal of the Center for Puerto Rican Studies* 19 (2007): 13–35.

McDermott, John. "Serrano: What Does It Mean?" *Un Nuevo Dia* (newsletter published by the Chicano Education Project, Lakewood, Colorado) 3 (Spring 1977): 5, 18–19.

McKevitt, Gerald. "Hispanic Californians and Catholic Higher Education: The Diary of Jesus María Estudillo, 1857–1864." *California History* 69, no. 4 (1990): 322.

McKissack, Elena Aragon de. *Chicano Educational Achievement: Comparing Escuela Tlatelolco, a Chicanocentric School, and a Public High School*. New York: Garland Publishing, 1999.

McWilliams, Carey. *The Mexicans in America: A Students' Guide to Localized History*. New York: Teachers College Press, 1968.

———. *North from Mexico: The Spanish Speaking People of the United States*. New York: Greenwood, 1968; originally published in 1948.

Medina, Jose A. "Legal Overview." In *Conference on the Education of Undocumented Students: Status and Suggested Remedies*, 10–14. San Antonio, TX: Intercultural Development Research Association, May 11, 1979.

Mehan, Hugh, Lea Hubbard, and Irene Villanueva. "Forging Academic Identities: Accommodation without Assimilation among Involuntary Minorities." *Anthropology and Education Quarterly* 25, no. 2 (1994): 91–117.

Mehan, Hugh, Irene Villanueva, Lea Hubbard, and Angela Lintz. *Constructing School Success: The Consequences of Untracking Low-Achieving Students*. New York: Cambridge University Press, 1996.

Melcher, Mary. "'This Is Not Right': Rural Arizona Women Challenge Segregation and Ethnic Division, 1925–1950." *Frontiers* 20, no. 2 (1999): 190–214.

Menaul School History. www.menaulschool.com/frmContent.aspx?PageName=History (accessed April 28, 2009).

Mendoza, Louis, and Rodolfo Rosales, eds. *Bringing the University Home: The San Antonio Community's Struggle for Educational Access*. San Antonio, TX: Hispanic Research Center, 1999.

Mercer, J., and J. Lewis. *System of Multicultural and Pluralistic Assessment: Technical Manual*. New York: Psychological Corporation, 1979.

Mercer, J. R. "In Defense of Racially and Culturally Non-Discriminatory Assessment." *School Psychology Digest* 8 (1979): 89–115.

Mestas, Leonard J. "A Brief History of the Juárez-Lincoln University." *Hojas* (Austin: Juárez-Lincoln University, 1976).

Mexican-American Affairs Information Bulletin. Washington, DC: US Office of Education, March 1969.

Minority Report: Making HISD Educational Policies and Programs More Responsive and Responsible to Needs of Educationally Deprived Students. February 24, 1975 (in author's possession).

Montoya, María E. "Beyond Internal Colonialism: Class, Gender, and Culture as Challenges to Chicano Identity." In *Voices of New Chicana/o History,* edited by Refugio I. Rochín and Dennis N. Valdés, 183–96. East Lansing: Michigan State University Press, 2000.

Muñoz, Carlos, Jr. "The Development of Chicano Studies, 1968–1981." In *Chicano Studies: A Multidisciplinary Approach,* edited by Eugene E. García, Francisco A. Lomelí, and Isidro D. Ortiz, 5–18. New York: Teachers College Press, 1984.

———. "The Politics of Educational Change in East Los Angeles." In *Mexican Americans and Educational Change,* edited by Alfredo Castañeda, Manuel Ramírez III, Carlos E. Cortés, and Mario Barrera, 83–104. New York: Arno Press, 1974.

———. "The Politics of Protest and Chicano Liberation: A Case Study of Repression and Cooperation." *Aztlán* 5, nos. 1 and 2 (1974): 119–41.

———. "The Quest for Paradigm: The Development of Chicano Studies and Intellectuals." In *History, Culture, and Society: Chicano Studies in the 1980s,* edited by Mario T. García et al., 19–36. Ypsilanti, MI: Bilingual Press/Editorial Bilingue, 1983.

———. *Youth, Identity, Power: The Chicano Movement.* New York: Verso, 1990.

Muñoz, Laura K. "Separate but Equal? A Case Study of *Romo v. Laird* and Mexican American Education." *Organization of American Historians Magazine of History* 15, no. 2 (2001): 28–35.

Murphy, Joseph, and Amanda Datnow, eds. *Leadership Lessons from Comprehensive School Reforms.* Thousand Oaks, CA: Corwin Press, 2003.

National Commission on Excellence in Education. *A Nation at Risk.* Washington, DC: USGPO, 1983.

National Conference on Educational Opportunities for Mexican Americans, April 24–26, 1968, Austin, Texas. Austin: US Office of Education in association with the Southwest Educational Development Laboratory, 1968.

National Council of La Raza. "Statement of Raul Yzaguirre on the Elementary and Secondary Education Act." December 14, 2001, 1–2 (in author's possession).

National Lawyers Guild and the National Congress of Black Lawyers. *Affirmative Action in Crisis: A Handbook for Activists.* Detroit, 1977.

Nava, Julian. "Bicultural Backgrounds and Barriers That Affect Learning by Spanish-Speaking Children." In *Mexican-Americans in the United States: A Reader,* edited by John H. Burma, 125–35. Cambridge, MA: Schenkman Publishing, 1970.

———. *Mexican Americans: Past, Present, and Future.* New York: American Book Company, 1973.

Navarro, Armando. *The Cristal Experiment: A Chicano Struggle for Community Control.* Madison: University of Wisconsin Press, 1998.

———. "Educational Change through Political Action." In *Mexican Americans and Educational Change,* edited by Alfredo Castañeda, Manuel Ramírez III, Carlos E. Cortés, and Mario Barrera, 105–39. New York: Arno Press, 1974; originally printed in 1971.

———. *MAYO: Avante Garde of the Chicano Movement.* Austin: University of Texas Press, 1995.

NCLR. "Charter School Development Initiative (CSDI)." www.nclr.org/section/charte_school (accessed April 27, 2009).

———. *Statement of Raul Yzaguirre on the Elementary and Secondary Education Act.* December 14, 2001, 1. NCLR website (in author's possession).

NEA, *Pero No Invencibles—The Invisible Minority.* Washington, DC: NEA, Department of Rural Supervision, 1966.

Neal, Elma A. "Adapting the Curriculum to Non-English-Speaking Children." *Elementary English Review* 6–7 (September 1929): 183–85.

Nieto, Sonia. *Affirming Diversity: The Sociopolitical Context of Multicultural Education.* New York: Longman, 1992.

———. *Diversity: The Sociopolitical Context of Multicultural Education.* New York: Allyn and Bacon, 1992.

———. "Fact and Fiction: Stories of Puerto Rican Students in US Schools." *Harvard Educational Review* 68 (Summer 1998): 133–63.

———. "A History of the Education of Puerto Rican Students in US Schools: 'Losers,' 'Outsiders,' or 'Leaders?'" In *Handbook of Research on Multicultural Education,* edited by James A. Banks and Cherry Banks, 388–411. New York: Macmillan, 1995.

———. *Language, Culture, and Teaching: Critical Perspectives for a New Century.* Mahwah, NJ: Lawrence Erlbaum, 2002.

———. *The Light in Their Eyes: Creating Multicultural Learning Communities.* New York: Teachers College Press, 1999.

———. *What Keeps Teachers Going?* New York: Teachers College Press, 2003.

———. *Why We Teach.* New York: Teachers College Press, 2005.

Nieto, Sonia, ed. *Puerto Rican Students in US Schools.* Mahwah, NJ: Lawrence Erlbaum, 2000.

Noreen, Sister D. C. "A Bilingual Curriculum for Spanish-Americans: A Regional Problem with Nation-Wide Implications." *Catholic School Journal* 66, no. 1 (1966): 25–26.

O'Connor, Karen, and Lee Epstein. "A Legal Voice for the Chicano Community: The Activities of the Mexican American Legal Defense and Educational Fund, 1968–1982." *Social Science Quarterly* 65 (June 1984): 245–56.

Oclander, Jorge. "Hispanics Condemn Lack of School Jobs." *Chicago Sun-Times,* December 12, 1994, 6.

Office of Research Advocacy and Legislation. *Secretary Bennett's Bilingual Education Initiative: Historical Perspectives and Implications.* Washington, DC: National Council of La Raza, October 31, 1985.

"Office of the President: President Murano's Biography." www.tamu.edu/president/biography.html (accessed April 6, 2009).

Ogbu, John. *Minority Education and Caste: The American System in Cross-Cultural Perspective.* New York: Academic Press, 1978.

———. *The Next Generation: An Ethnography of Education in an Urban Neighborhood.* New York: Academic Press, 1974.

———. "Variability in Minority School Performance: A Problem in Search of an Explanation." *Anthropology and Education Quarterly* 18, no. 4 (1987): 312–34.

Olivas, Michael A. *The Dilemma of Access.* Washington, DC: Howard University Press, 1979.

———. "Hispanics in Higher Education: Status and Issues." *Educational Evaluation and Policy Analysis* 4 (1982): 301–10.

———. "IIRIRA, The DREAM Act, and Undocumented College Student Residency." *Journal of College and University Law* 30, no. 435 (2004).

———. "*Plyler v. Doe,* the Education of Undocumented Children, and the Polity." In *Immigration Stories,* edited by David Martin and Peter Schuck, 197–220. New York: Foundation Press, 2005.

———. "*Plyler v. Doe, Toll v. Moreno,* and Postsecondary Admissions: Undocumented Adults and 'Enduring Disability,'" *Journal of Law and Education* 15, no. 19 (1986).

———. "Storytelling Out of School: Undocumented College Residency, Race, and Reaction." *Hastings Constitutional Law Quarterly* 22, no. 1019 (1995).

Olivas, Michael A., ed. *Latino College Students.* New York: Teachers College Press, 1986.

Ordaz, Daniel García. "Once upon a Chicano College: Hispanics United to Create the First School of Its Kind in the US" *Valley Morning Star,* October 4, 2005. www.valleystar.com/articles/2005/10/04/rio_living/rio_living3.txt (1 of 5) (accessed October 4, 2005).

Orfield, Gary. "The Growth of Segregation: African Americans, Latinos, and Unequal Education." In *Dismantling Desegregation: The Quiet Reversal of Brown v. Board of Education,* edited by Gary Orfield, Susan E. Eaton, and the Harvard Project on School Desegregation, 53–72. New York: New Press, 1996.

———. "Hispanic Education: Challenges, Research, and Policies." *American Journal of Education* 95, no. 1 (1986): 1–25.

———. *Must We Bus? Separate Schools and National Policy.* Washington, DC: Brookings Institution, 1978.

———. "Schools More Separate: Consequences of a Decade of Resegregation." *Harvard Civil Rights Project.* Cambridge, MA, 2001.

Orfield, Gary, Susan E. Eaton, and the Harvard Project on School Desegregation. *Dismantling Desegregation: The Quiet Reversal of Brown v. Board of Education.* New York: New Press, 1996.

Ornstein, Allan C. "Recent Historical Perspectives for Educating the Disadvantaged." In *Educating the Disadvantaged,* edited by Russell C. Doll and Maxine Hawkins, 147–67. New York: AMS Press, 1971.

Ornstein, Allan C. "The Changing Federal Role in Education." *American Education* 20 (December 1984): 4–7.

Ortiz, Alba A. "Addressing the Needs of Latinos in Special Education." In *Latino Students in American Schools: Historical and Contemporary Views,* edited by Valentina I. Kloosterman, 95–112. Westport, CT: Praeger, 2003.

Our Mission. www.lydiapattersoninstitute.org/ourmission.php (accessed April 28, 2009).

Padrón, E. "Hispanics and Community Colleges." In *A Handbook on the Community College in America,* edited by George A Baker, 82–93. Westport, CT: Greenwood Press, 1994.

Pallasch, Abdon M. "Curie Principal Still Out: Hispanic Majority on LSC Refuses to Reverse Vote." *Chicago Sun-Times,* March 11, 2007. http://www.suntimes.com/news/education/292313,CST-NWS-curie11.article (accessed March 11, 2007).

Peal, Elizabeth, and Wallace Lambert. "The Relation of Bilingualism to Intelligence." *Psychological Monographs, General and Applied* 76 (1962): 1–23.

Pena, E. "Dynamic Assessment: The Model and Language Applications." In *Assessment of Communication and Language,* edited by K. Cole, P. Dales, and D. Thal, 281–307. Baltimore, MD: Brookes, 1996.

Pennock-Roman, Maria. "Fairness in the Use of Tests for Selective Admissions of Hispanics." In *Latino College Students,* edited by Michael A. Olivas. New York: Teachers College Press, 1986.

Phelan, Christine. "Youth Shut Out by Labor Market: Nearly 5.5 Million Youth Out-of-School and Jobless." http://www.clasp.org/CampaignForYouth/PolicyBrief/YouthShutOutBy LaborMarket.htm (accessed May 19, 2009).

Phillips, S. E., ed. "Defending a High School Graduation Test: *GI Forum v. Texas Education Agency." Applied Measurement in Education* 13, no. 4 (2000): 323–25.

"*Plyler v. Doe:* 25 Years Later." www.dallasnews.com/s/dws/photography/2007/plyler website (accessed September 11, 2007).

Porter, Rosalie Pedalino. *Forked Tongue: The Politics of Bilingual Education.* New York: Basic Books, 1990.

Potter, Will. "Texas Admissions Plan Has Not Increased Diversity at Flagship Campuses, Study Finds." *Chronicle of Higher Education.* http://chronicle.com/daily/2003/01/2030124001n .htm. January 24, 2003 (accessed October 30, 2007).

Powers, Jeanne M., and Lirio Patton. "Between *Mendez* and *Brown: Gonzales v. Sheely* (1951) and the Legal Campaign against Segregation." *Law and Social Inquiry* 33, no. 1 (2008): 127–71.

Presbyterian Pan American School. Kingsville, TX: Presbyterian Pan American School, 1959.

Pycior, Julie Leininger. *LBJ and Mexican Americans: The Paradox of Power.* Austin: University of Texas Press, 1997.

Rafferty, J. R. "Missing the Mark: Intelligence Testing in Los Angeles Public Schools." *History of Education Quarterly* 28 (1988): 73–93.

Rafferty, Max. "Bilingual Education: Hoax of the 1980s." *American Legion* (March 1981): 4, 15–16, 39–40.

Ramirez, Manuel, III. "Bilingual Education as a Vehicle for Institutional Change." In *Mexican Americans and Educational Change,* edited by Alfredo Castañeda et al., 387–407. New York: Arno Press, 1974.

Ramos-Zayas, Ana Y. "Nationalist Ideologies, Neighborhood-Based Activism, and Educational Spaces in Puerto Rican Chicago." *Harvard Educational Review* 68, no. 2 (1998): 164–92.

Rangel, Jorge C., and Carlos M. Alcala. "Project Report: De Jure Segregation of Chicanos in Texas Schools." *Harvard Civil Rights–Civil Liberties Law Review* 7 (1972): 331–49.

Raspberry, William. "No Sense-In Any Language." *Washington Post,* October 22, 1980, 23A.

Ratliff, Lt. Gov. Bill. "Finding a Way to Equitably Fund Texas Schools Hasn't Been Easy." *Houston Chronicle,* October 28, 2001, editorial.

Ratteray, Joan Davis. "Hispanics Pursue Alternatives to Unresponsive Public Schools." *Caminos* (November 1984): 32–33.

———. "Schooling Ourselves." *Minority Trendsletter* 2, no. 1 (1989): 3–5.

Ravitch, Diane. *The Troubled Crusade.* New York: Basic Books, 1983.

Reavis, Charles, and Harry Griffith. *Restructuring Schools: Theory and Practice.* Lancaster, PA: Technomic Publishing, 1992.

Rendón, Laura, and A. Nora. "Hispanic Students: Stopping the Leaks in the Pipeline." *Educational Record* 68, no. 4 (1988): 79–85.

Rendón, Laura, R. Jalomo, and K. Garcia. "The University and Community College Paradox: Why Latinos Do Not Transfer." In *The Educational Achievement of Latinos: Barriers and Success,* edited by A. Hurtado and E. Garcia, 227–58. Santa Cruz: Regents of the University of California, 1994.

Report by the National Advisory Committee on Mexican American Education. *The Mexican American: Quest for Equality.* Washington, DC: US Department of Health, Education and Welfare, 1968. ERIC No. ED049841.

Reyes, Pedro, Jay D. Scribner, and Alicia Paredes Scribner, eds. *Lessons from High-Performing Hispanic Schools: Creating Learning Communities.* New York: Teachers College Press, 1999.

Rice, Jill. *The ASPIRA Story: 1961–1991.* Washington, DC: ASPIRA Association, 1991.

Rivera, Feliciano. *A Mexican American Source Book with Study Guideline.* Menlo Park, CA: Educational Consulting Associates, 1970.

Robledo Montecel, María "Cuca." "A Quality Schools Action Framework: Framing Systems Change for Student Success." http://www.idra.org/IDRA_Newsletters/November_-_December _2005_Access_and_Success (accessed January 10, 2007).

Rocha, Gregory C., and Robert H. Webking. *Politics and Public Education: Edgewood v. Kirby and the Reform of Public School Financing in Texas.* Minneapolis: West Publishers, 1992.

Rodriguez, Armando. "Education for the Spanish-Speaking: Mañana in Motion." *National Elementary Principal* 49 (February 1970): 52–56. Also published in Earl J. Ogletree and David Garcia, eds. *Education of the Spanish Speaking Urban Child: A Book of Readings.* Springfield, IL: Charles C. Thomas, 1975.

Rodriguez, Armando M. "Education: 'A Futuristic Goal.'" In *Mexican Americans and Education Change: Symposium at the University of California,* Riverside, May 21–22, 1971, edited by Alfredo Castaneda, Manuel Ramírez III, Carlos E. Cortés, and Mario Barrera, 2–8. New York: Arno Press, 1974.

———. "Speak Up, Chicano: The Mexican American Fights for Educational Equality." In *Mexican-Americans in the United States: A Reader,* edited by John H. Burma, 135–43. Cambridge, MA: Schenkman Publishing, 1970.

Rodríguez, Javier. "Blackboard Bungle, Part I: How Houston Cheats Its Inner-City Students out of a Decent Education." *Houston Press,* April 19, 1990, 8–20.

———. "Blackboard Bungle, Part II: What Has HISD Learned from the Walkout at Austin High School?" *Houston Press,* April 26, 1990, 8–15.

Rodríguez, Joseph A., and Vicki L. Ruiz. "At Loose Ends: Twentieth-Century Latinos in Current United States History Textbooks." *Journal of American History* 86, no. 4 (2000): 1689.

Romo, Harriett D., and Toni Falbo. *Latino High School Graduation: Defying the Odds.* Austin: University of Texas Press, 1996.

Romo, Harriett, and Joanne Salas. "Successful Transition of Latino Students from High School to College." In *Latinos in Higher Education,* edited by David J. León, 107–30. Boston: Elsevier Science, 2003.

Roos, Peter D. "Bilingual Education: Hispanic Response to Unequal Education." *Law and Contemporary Problems* 42 (1978): 111–40.

———. "Equity and Excellence." In Hispanic Policy Development Project, *"Make Something Happen": Hispanics and Urban High School Reform*. Vol. 2. Washington, DC: National Commission on Secondary Education for Hispanics, 1984, 75–78.

Rosales, Francisco A. "The Fight for Educational Reform." In *Chicano: The History of the Mexican American Civil Rights Movement*, 175–195. Houston: Arte Público Press, 1997.

Rosales, Rodolfo. *The Illusion of Inclusion: The Untold Political Story of San Antonio*. Austin: University of Texas Press, 2000.

Rossell, C., and K. Baker. "The Educational Effectiveness of Bilingual Education." *Research in the Teaching of English* 30, no. 1 (1996): 7–74.

Ruiz, Vicki L. "South by Southwest: Mexican Americans and Segregated Schooling, 1900–1950." *OAH Magazine of History* 15, no. 2 (2001): 23–27.

———. "'We Always Tell Our Children They Are Americans': *Mendez v. Westminster* and the California Road to *Brown v. Board of Education*." *College Board Review* 200 (Fall 2003): 21–27.

Rumberger, Russell W. "Chicano Dropouts: A Review of Research and Policy Issues." In *Chicano School Failure and Success: Research and Policy Agendas for the 1990s*, edited by Richard R. Valencia, 64–90. New York: Falmer Press, 1991.

Salvucci, Linda K. "Mexico, Mexicans, and Mexican Americans in Secondary-School United States History Textbooks." *History Teacher* 24, no. 2 (1991): 203–22.

San Miguel, Guadalupe, Jr. "Actors Not Victims: Chicanas/os and the Struggle for Educational Equality." In *Chicanas/Chicanos at the Crossroads: Social, Economic, and Political Change*, edited by David R. Maciel and Isidro Ortiz. Tucson: University of Arizona Press, 1996.

———. *Brown, Not White: School Integration and the Chicano Movement*. College Station: Texas A&M University Press, 2001.

———. "The Community Is Beginning to Rumble: The Origins of Chicano Educational Protest in Houston, 1965–1970." *Houston Review* 13 (1991): 127–47.

———. *Contested Policy: The Rise and Fall of Federal Bilingual Education Policy in the United States, 1960–2001*. Denton: University of North Texas Press, 2004.

———. "Cycles of Concern: A Historical Perspective on the Dropout Problem." *California Public Schools Forum* 1 (Fall 1986): 20–31.

———. "Ignoring Ethnicity Is a Slap in the Face of All Colors by HISD." *Houston Chronicle*, September 28, 1997, C1, C5.

———. "The Impact of Brown on Mexican American Desegregation Litigation, 1950s to 1980s." *Journal of Latinos and Education* 4, no. 4 (2005): 221–36.

———. *Let All of Them Take Heed*. College Station: Texas A&M University Press, 2000; originally published in 1987.

———. "Mexican American Organizations and the Changing Politics of School Desegregation in Texas, 1945–1980." *Social Science Quarterly* 63 (December 1982): 701–15.

———. "Status of the Historiography of Mexican American Education: A Preliminary Analysis." *History of Education Quarterly* 26 (1986): 523–36.

———. "The Struggle against Separate and Unequal Schools: Middle Class Mexican Americans and the Desegregation Campaign in Texas, 1929–1957." *History of Education Quarterly* 23 (Fall 1983): 343–59.

San Miguel, Guadalupe, Jr., and Richard R. Valencia. "From the Treaty of Guadalupe Hidalgo to Hopwood: The Educational Plight and Struggle of Mexican Americans in the Southwest." *Harvard Educational Review* 68, no. 3 (1998): 363–77.

Sánchez, Alfredo. "Chicano Student Movement at San Jose State." In *Parameters of Institutional Change: Chicano Experiences in Education*, 22–32. Hayward, CA: Southwest Network of the Study Commission on Undergraduate Education, 1974.

Sánchez, Corinne. "Higher Education y La Chicana?" *Encuentro Femenil* 1, no. 1 (1973): 27–33.

Sánchez, Gilbert. "An Analysis of the Bilingual Education Act, 1967–1968." PhD diss., University of Massachusetts, 1973.

Sánchez, Juan Jose. "A Study of Chicano Alternative Grade Schools in the SW, 1978–1980." PhD diss., Harvard University, 1982.

Sánchez, Juan O. "Encina: The Uvalde School Walkout." Master's thesis, Sul Ross State University, 1992.

Sánchez, Juan O. "Walkout Cabrones: The Uvalde School Walkout of 1970." *West Texas Historical Association Year Book* 68 (1992): 122–33.

Santiago, Isaura Santiago. "*Aspira of New York, Inc. v. Board of Education* Revisited." *American Journal of Education* 95, no. 1 (1986): 149–99.

Scharrer, Gary "Critics Lambaste Education Board on English Curriculum." *Houston Chronicle*, March 27, 2008, B4.

———. "Hispanic Input Urged on Curriculum." *Houston Chronicle*, March 15, 2008, B4.

Scharrer, Gary, Jenny Caputo, Zeke MacCormack, and Jennifer Radcliffe. "Report Points to 'Dropout Factories' / Study Highlights 185 Texas Schools Losing Students Quickly, Including 42 in Houston Area." *Houston Chronicle*, October 31, 2007, 2. www.Houstonchronicle.com (accessed November 7, 2007).

Schlesinger, Arthur M., Jr. *The Disuniting of America*. New York: W. W. Norton, 1992.

Scott, H. H. "Desegregation in Nashville: Conflicts and Contradictions in Preserving Schools in Black Communities." *Education and Urban Society* 15 (1983): 235–44.

Seidner, Stanley S. *Political Expediency or Educational Research: An Analysis of Baker and de Kanter's Review of the Literature of Bilingual Education*. Rosslyn, VA: National Clearinghouse for Bilingual Education, 1981.

Shockley, John Staples. *Chicano Revolt in a Texas Town*. Notre Dame, IN: University of Notre Dame Press, 1974.

Shor, Ira. *Culture Wars: School and Society in the Conservative Restoration, 1969–1984*. New York: Routledge and Kegan Paul, 1986.

Shuster, Jack H. "Out of the Frying Pan: The Politics of Education in a New Era." *Phi Delta Kappan* (May 1982): 583–91.

Simmons, Timothy. "The Citizen Factories: The Americanization of Mexican Students in the Texas Public Schools, 1920–1945." PhD diss., Texas A&M University, College Station, 1976.

Sitkoff, Harvard. *The Struggle for Black Equality, 1954–1992*. New York: Hill and Wang, 1993.

Soldatenko-Gutierrez, Michael. "Socrates, Curriculum, and the Chicano/Chicana: Allan Bloom and the Myth of US Higher Education." *Cultural Studies* 4 (October 1990): 304–19.

Sorgen, M. "Testing and Tracking in Public Schools." *Hastings Law Journal* 24 no. 1129 (1973).

Soto, Lourdes D. "Success Stories." In *Research and Multicultural Education: From the Margins to the Mainstream*, edited by Carl A. Grant, 153–64. London: Falmer Press, 1992.

Soto, Lourdes Diaz. *Language, Culture, and Power: Bilingual Families and the Struggle for Quality Education*. Albany: State University of New York Press, 1997.

Southwest Council of Foreign Language Teachers. "A Resolution concerning the Education of Bilingual Children." In *Bilingual Education in the United States*, edited by Theodore Andersson and Mildred Boyer, 284–86. Austin: Southwest Educational Development Laboratory, 1970.

Spanish American Institute: 1913–1971 Service to Boys. Gardena, CA: Spanish American Institute, 1971.

Spring, Joel. *The Sorting Machine Revisited*. New York: Longman, 1989.

Stein, Colman Brez, Jr. *Sink or Swim: The Politics of Bilingual Education*. Westport, CT: Praeger, 1986.

Steinberg, Laurence, Patricia Lin Blinde, and Kenyon S. Chan. "Dropping Out among Language Minority Youth." *Review of Educational Research* 54, no. 1 (1984): 113–32.

Stemmler, Annie. "An Experimental Approach to the Teaching of Oral Language and Reading." *Harvard Educational Review* 36 (Summer 1966): 45.

Stevens, James Darryl. "The Menaul School: A Study of Cultural Convergence." PhD diss., University of Houston, 1999.

Straus, Emily E. "Unequal Pieces of a Shrinking Pie: The Struggle between African Americans and Latinos over Education, Employment, and Empowerment in Compton, California." *History of Education Quarterly* 49, no. 4 (2009): 507–29.

Stubbs, A. Thomas. "After Rodriguez: Recent Developments in School Finance Reform." *Tax Lawyer* 44, no. 1 (1991): 313–41.

Student Classification Materials. Cambridge, MA: Center for Law and Education, 1973.

Suárez-Orozco, Marcelo. "Immigrant Adaptation of Schooling: A Hispanic Case." *Minority Status and Schooling: A Comparative Study of Immigrant and Involuntary Minorities*, edited by Margaret A. Gibson and John U. Ogbu, 37–61. New York: Garland Publishing, 1991.

"Supreme Court Justice Orders That Undocumented Children in Texas May Attend Public School Free." *El Sol* (Houston, Texas), no. 36, vol. 15. September 10, 1982.

"Surge in Latino Activism." Insidehigheredcom news, April 10, 2006. www.insidehighered.com/ news/2006/04/10/latino (accessed December 26, 2008).

Suro, R., and D. Balz. "Proposition 187 Dominates, Divides California Races." *Austin American-Statesman*, November 3, 1994, A9.

Swanson, Maria M. "Bilingual Education: The National Perspective." In *The ACTFL Review of Foreign Language Education*, vol. 5, edited by Gilbert A. Jarvis, 75–127. Skokie, IL: National Textbook, 1974.

Task Force to Reevaluate Social Science Textbooks Grades Five through Eight. *Report and Recommendations*. Sacramento: California State Department of Education, 1971.

"Teach for America, 2008. www.teachforamerica.org/about/index.htm (accessed December 12, 2008).

Tebbel, John, and Ramón Eduardo Ruiz. *South by Southwest: the Mexican-American and His Heritage*. Garden City, NY: Doubleday, 1969.

Teitelbaum, Herbert, and Richard J. Hiller. "Bilingual Education: The Legal Mandate." *Harvard Educational Review* 47 (May 1977): 138–70. Also in Henry T. Trueba and Carol Barnett-Mizrahi, eds. *Bilingual Multicultural Education and the Professional: From Theory to Practice*, 20–53. Rowley, MA: Newbury House Publishers, 1979.

————. "The Legal Perspective." In *Bilingual Education: Current Perspectives—Law*, vol. 3, 1–66. Arlington, VA: Center for Applied Linguistics, 1977.

"Testimony Given by Dr. Bernard E. Donovan, Superintendent of Schools, New York City, before the House General Subcommittee on Education of the House Committee on Education and Labor on H.R. 9840 and H.R. 10224." Press release #451–6667. New York City Board of Education, July 7, 1967, 46. In Herbert Teitelbaum and Richard J. Hiller, "Bilingual Education: The Legal Mandate," 20–53. In Henry T. Trueba and Carol Barnett-Mizrahi, eds. *Bilingual Multicultural Education and the Professional: From Theory to Practice*. Rowley, MA: Newbury House Publishers, 1979.

"Text of Civil Rights Office Letters to Regional Heads, School Districts." *Education Week*, November 27, 1985, 16.

Ting, Siu-Man Raymond. "Predicating First-Year Grades and Academic Progress of College Students of First-Generation and Low-Income Families." *Journal of College Admissions* (Winter 1998): 15–23.

Travieso, Lourdes. "Puerto Ricans and Education." *Journal of Teacher Education* 26 (Summer 1975): 128–30.

Trombley, William. "Court Rejects College Plans for Minorities." *Los Angeles Times*, September 17, 1976, A1, A25.

Trueba, Enrique T. "Issues and Problems in Bilingual Bicultural Education Today." *Journal of the National Association for Bilingual Education* 1 (December 1976): 11–19.

Trueba, Henry T. *Success or Failure? Learning and Language Minority Students*. New York: Newbury House Publishers, 1987.

Trujillo, Armando L. *Chicano Empowerment and Bilingual Education: Movimiento Politics in Crystal City*. New York: Garland Publishing, 1998.

Tyack, David, ed. *Turning Points in American Educational History*. Lexington, MA: Xerox College Publishing, 1967.

Ulibarri, Horacio. "Educational Needs of the Mexican-American." In the National Conference on Educational Opportunities for Mexican-Americans, April 25–26, 1968, Austin, Texas. Las Cruces, NM: The ERIC Clearinghouse on Rural Education and Small Schools, New Mexico State University, 1968.

"US Commission on Civil Rights Addresses Educational Inequities." *IDRA Newsletter* (April 1982): 1–8.

US Charter Schools. "History." www.uschartershcools.org/pub/uscs_docs/o/history.htm.

US Charter Schools. "New Research and Reports." www.uscharterschools.org/cs/r/query/q/1558?x-title=New+Non-Federal+Research+an (accessed May 1, 2009).

Vaca, Nick C. "The Mexican-American in the Social Sciences, 1912–1970, Part I: 1912–1935." *El Grito* (Fall 1970): 3–16, 21–24.

————. "The Mexican-American in the Social Sciences, 1912–1970, Part II: 1936–1970," *El Grito* (Fall 1971): 17–51.

Valencia, Atilano A. "Bilingual-Bicultural Education: A Quest for Institutional Reform." *Spring Bulletin*. Riverside, CA: Western Regional Desegregation Projects, University of California, Riverside, April 1971.

———. "Bilingual Education: A Quest for Bilingual Survival." In *Mexican Americans and Educational Change*, edited by Alfredo Castañeda et al., 345–62. New York: Arno Press, 1974.

Valencia, Richard R. *Chicano Students and the Courts: The Mexican American Legal Struggle for Educational Equality*. New York: New York University Press, 2008.

———. "Educational Testing and Mexican American Students: Problems and Prospects." In *The Elusive Quest for Equality: 150 Years of Chicano/Chicana Education*, edited by J. F. Moreno, 123–40. Cambridge, MA: Harvard Educational Review, 1999.

———. "Explaining Cultural Bias in Educational Tests: How Important Is 'Opportunity to Learn?'" *Child Assessment News* 2 (1992): 8–11.

———. "The Mexican American Struggle for Equal Educational Opportunity in *Mendez v. Westminster:* Helping to Pave the Way for *Brown v. Board of Education*." *Teachers College Record* 107, no. 3 (2005): 389–423.

———. "The School Closure Issue and the Chicano Community." *Urban Review* 12 (1980): 5–21.

———. "The School Closure Issue and the Chicano Community: A Follow-Up Study of the Angeles Case." *Urban Review* 16 (1984): 145–63.

———. *School Closures and Policy Issues*. Policy Paper No. 84-C3. Stanford, CA: Stanford University, Institute for Research on Educational Finance and Governance, 1984.

———. *Understanding School Closures: Discriminatory Impact on Chicano and Black Students*. Policy Monograph Series, no. 1. Stanford, CA: Stanford University Stanford Center for Chicano Research, 1984.

Valencia, Richard R., ed. *Chicano School Failure and Success: Research and Policy Agendas for the 1990s*. New York: Falmer Press, 1991.

———. *The Evolution of Deficit Thinking: Educational Thought and Practice*. Washington, DC: Falmer Press, 1997.

Valencia Richard R., and S. Aburto. "The Uses and Abuses of Educational Testing: Chicanos as a Case in Point." In *Chicano School Failure and Success: Research and Policy Agendas for the 1990s*, edited by R. R. Valencia, 203–51. London: Falmer Press, 1991.

Valencia, Richard R., and Ernesto M. Bernal, eds. "The Texas Assessment of Academic Skills (TAAS) Case: Perspectives of Plaintiffs' Experts." *Hispanic Journal of Behavioral Sciences* 22, no. 4 (2000): 405–10.

Valencia, Richard R., Martha Menchaca, and Rubén Donato. "Segregation, Desegregation, and Integration of Chicano Students: Old and New Realities." In *Chicano School Failure and Success: Past, Present, and Future*, edited by Richard R. Valencia. London: Routledge Falmer, 2002.

Valencia, Richard R., and R. J. Rankin. "Evidence of Content Bias on the McCarthy Scales with Mexican American Children: Implications for Test Translation and Nonbiased Assessment." *Journal of Educational Psychology* 77 (1985): 197–207.

Valencia, Richard R., Bruno J. Villarreal, and Moises F. Salinas. "Educational Testing and Chicano Students: Issues, Consequences, and Prospects for Reform." In *Chicano School*

Failure and Success: Past, Present, and Future, edited by Richard R. Valencia, 289–92. London: Routledge Falmer, 2002.

Valenzuela, Angela. *Subtractive Schooling: US-Mexican Youth and the Politics of Caring.* Albany: State University of New York Press, 1999.

Vigil, Ernesto B. *The Crusade for Justice: Chicano Militancy and the Government's War on Dissent.* Madison: University of Wisconsin Press, 1982.

Vitello, Paul, and Winnie Hu. "For Catholic Schools, Crisis and Catharsis." *New York Times,* January 18, 2009. www.nytimes.com/2009/01/18/education/18catholic.html?_r=2 &ref=nyregion&page . . . (accessed April 27, 2009).

Walker, Constance. "Hispanic Underachievement: Old Views and New Perspectives." In *Success or Failure?: Learning and the Language Minority Student,* edited by Henry Trueba, 15–32. Cambridge, MA: Newbury House Publishers, 1987.

Watkins, Melissa. "The Top 10 Percent Plan." www.utexas.edu/depts/cms/anniversary/top-tenpercent.html (accessed October 30, 2007).

Weinberg, Meyer. *A Chance to Learn: The History of Race and Education in the United States.* Cambridge: Cambridge University Press, 1977.

Wiese, Ann-Marie, and Eugene E. García. "The Bilingual Education Act: Language Minority Students and Equal Educational Opportunity." *Bilingual Research Journal* 22, no. 1 (1998): 1–13.

Wilson, Steven H. "Brown over 'Other White': Mexican Americans' Legal Arguments and Litigation Strategy in School Desegregation Lawsuits." *Law and History Review* 21, no. 1 (2003): 145–94.

Wollenberg, Charles. *All Deliberate Speed: Segregation and Exclusion in California Schools, 1855–1975.* Berkeley: University of California Press, 1976.

———. "Mendez v. Westminster." *California History Quarterly* 55 (Winter 1974): 317–32.

Woodson, Carter G. *The Mis-Education of the Negro.* Washington, DC: Associated Publishers, 1933.

Wright, Lawrence. "Bilingual Education Movement at the Crossroads." In *Education of the Spanish Speaking Child,* edited by Earl J. Ogletree and David Garcia, 335–45. Springfield, IL.: Charles C. Thomas, 1975.

Yarborough, Ralph. "Two Proposals for a Better Way of Life for Mexican Americans in the Southwest." *Congressional Record* (January 17, 1967): 599–600.

Yasso, Tara J., and Daniel G. Solórzano. "Leaks in the Chicana and Chicano Educational Pipeline." *Latino Policy and Issues Brief* 13 (March 2006). UCLA Chicano Studies Research Center.

YES "Results." www.yesprep.org/about/results.htm (accessed May 2, 2009).

YES Board of Directors, Advisory Board, and Leadership team. "YES Leadership." www.yesprep .org/about/board.htm (accessed May 2, 2009).

YES PREP. "The History of YES PREP." www.yesprep.org/about/history.htm (accessed May 2, 2009).

"YES Prep Public Schools (Formerly YES College Preparatory Schools): Honing the Pathways of Growth." February 1, 2006. www.bridgespan.org/LearningCenter/ResrouceDetail .aspx?id=418 (accessed May 4, 2009).

YISD. "Press Release—2007 Preliminary TAKS Scores Released: Ysleta ISD Improves in All Areas." *YISD News,* May 8, 2007. http://www2.yisd.net/education/dept/dept.php ?sectiondetailid=9180&sc_id=1185378769 (accessed July 25, 2007).

Yohn, Susan M. *A Contest of Faiths: Missionary Women and Pluralism in the American Southwest.* Ithaca, NY: Cornell University Press, 1995.

Zambone, Alana M., and Margarita Alicea-Sáez. "Latino Students in Pursuit of Higher Education: What Helps or Hinders Their Success?" In *Latino Students in American Schools: Historical and Contemporary Views,* edited by Valentina I. Kloosterman, 63–78. Westport, CT: Praeger, 2003.

Index

Other Titles in the University of Houston Series in Mexican American Studies